Wasted Evangelism

Wasted Evangelism

Social Action and the Church's Task of Evangelism
A Journey in the Gospel of Mark

CHIP M. ANDERSON

RESOURCE *Publications* • Eugene, Oregon

WASTED EVANGELISM
Social Action and the Church's Task of Evangelism
A Journey in the Gospel of Mark

Copyright © 2013 Chip M. Anderson. All rights reserved. Except for brief quotations in critical publications or reviews, no part of this book may be reproduced in any manner without prior written permission from the publisher. Write: Permissions. Wipf and Stock Publishers, 199 W. 8th Ave., Suite 3, Eugene, OR 97401.

Unless otherwise indicated Scripture quotations are taken from the New American Standard Bible®, Copyright © 1960, 1962, 1963, 1968, 1971, 1972, 1973, 1975, 1977, 1995 by The Lockman Foundation. Used by permission. (www.Lockman.org)

Scripture quoted within the paragraphs of this book are typically indicated by *italicized* text by the author rather than with quotation marks. Indented texts of Scripture are not italicized.

The Old and New Testament as a whole are referred to as OT and NT throughout the studies in this book.

Resource Publications
An Imprint of Wipf and Stock Publishers
199 W. 8th Ave., Suite 3
Eugene, OR 97401

www.wipfandstock.com

ISBN 13: 978-1-62032-545-2

Manufactured in the U.S.A.

To my good friends and colleagues in social action who have taught me so very much about those affected by poverty, particularly

—Diane Stroman, Bonnie Bodak, Rich Knoll and all my colleagues at TEAM, Inc. who were the first to guide me as I cut my eye-teeth in community action

—David Yovaisis, Toni Hirst, Deidra Ierardi and all my fellow community action Planners (1997–2012) who were patient and supportive of this evangelical conservative as I learned to advocate for our economically vulnerable neighbors here in Connecticut

—Joe Carbone, President and Chief Executive Officer of the WorkPlace, Inc., mentor and friend who has supported me over the years as I learned how to express my Christian faith within the arena of workforce development and social action

—Henry Yordon (in memoriam, 1926–2005), pastor of the First Congregational Church on the Green in Norwalk, CT, my mentor and friend who found in me a like-minded advocate for the poor and who taught me that one can believe the Bible is the inspired Word of God and at the same time take the side of those living with the effects of poverty

He who oppresses the poor taunts his Maker,
But he who is gracious to the needy honors Him
(Proverbs 14:31).

Contents

Foreword by Drs. Aida and Bill Spencer • ix
Author's Preface: Some Personal Notes and Acknowledgments • xi

Introduction
Evangelism and Social Action: An Exegetical Argument • 1

1 **Widows in our Courts (Mark 12:38–44)**
The Public Advocacy Role of Local Congregations as Discipleship • 15

2 **Wasted Evangelism (Mark 4)**
Social Action Outcomes and The Church's Task of Evangelism • 46

Excursus
The Logic of Social Action as Evangelism • 78

3 **"You Will Appear as *Fishers*" (Mark 1:17)**
Disciples as Agents of Judgment • 80

4 **A Prelude to Judgment (Mark 3:20–35)**
The Beelzebul Episode and Its Significance for Evangelistic Social Action • 106

5 **Idolatry and Poverty**
Social Action as Christian Apologetics • 141

6 **Significance *Before* Application (Mark 3:14–15)**
The Mark 3 Commission and Its Implications for Social Action • 172

Bibliography • 201
Scripture Index • 211

Foreword

WE HAVE KNOWN CHIP Anderson for almost 30 years, first as a student and then as a colleague. For many years, he has been devoted to this project—to show how the good news of Jesus Christ includes both individual spiritual renewal and social justice. Is it sufficient for Jesus to be our Savior or must Jesus also be Lord of our lives, including our actions? With painstaking attention to detail, Chip clearly concludes that evangelistic outreach must have multi-dimensional implications. To enlist in the company of Jesus, the Messiah-King, is to become a faithful agent of God's kingdom to societies whose people and structures are often in rebellion against God. Who can disagree with such a view after hearing or reading the domestic and global news of even one day? But Chip looks deeply into the reasons for this conclusion. According to Chip, biblical evangelism includes both proclamation in word and proclamation in action, intentional demonstrations of God's reign in this world. Especially all students of Mark's Gospel need to study these thoughtful, well-researched, exegetical reflections on the narrative of Mark in light of its Old Testament background, as well as those interested in the relationship between the task of proclaiming and acting on Jesus' good news as recorded by his disciple, Mark. Chip, as our guide, brings to this study both academic preparation and business experience, being seminary trained and having served in a social work agency for many years. Thus, he is sensitive to both the individual and the corporate dimensions of a fully-orbed Christian life, and he lives out the individual salvific and corporate social dimensions of the gospel as completely as he can.

We have enjoyed knowing Chip through these years as a careful worker, a passionate and diligent scholar, and a dedicated, committed, and delightful Christian. We commit his thoughts to your consideration.

Wasted Evangelism

Aída Besançon Spencer, Professor of New Testament, Gordon-Conwell Theological Seminary/South Hamilton campus and William David Spencer, Ranked Adjunct Professor of Theology and the Arts, Gordon-Conwell Theological Seminary/Boston campus are co-authors and editors of the *Africanus Journal, Reaching for the New Jerusalem: A Biblical and Theological Framework for the City, The Global God: Multicultural Evangelical Views of God, Joy through the Night: Biblical Resources on Suffering, Global Voices on Biblical Equality: Women and Men Serving Together in the Church, Marriage at the Crossroads,* and their newest titles *Name in the Papers* (an urban adventure novel) and *1 Timothy* (a New Covenant Commentary).

Author's Preface
Some Personal Notes and Acknowledgments

"I have no idea what I'm supposed to do. I only know what I can do."

—Young Captain James T. Kirk, Star Trek, Into the Darkness, the movie

"Excellence is . . . caring more than others think is wise; risking more than others think is safe; dreaming more than others think is practical. Expecting more than others think is possible."

—Winston Churchill

Someone recently asked me, "Chip, what is your dream job?" I responded without hesitation. "A job where I connect non-poor churches to the issues of poverty and justice."

After a decade of church ministry and five years as a professor at Prairie Bible College, God's crooked lines led me to a new vocation. From 1997 through 2012 I worked as a community action grant writer and planner, a job that soon became a passion that formed my vocational concern for the poor and for the issues of poverty. The thousand plus community action agencies across the US offer a wide-range of services and programs to improve the quality of life for our economically vulnerable neighbors by providing necessary resources to promote self-sufficiency. At present, I am a grant writer, customer service skills instructor, curriculum developer, and program consultant for the Morrison Group, LLC, a training provider that helps low-income and at-risk populations gain the necessary skills and motivation to enter the workforce. Social action has been my vocational life for the past sixteen years.

For me, not only is social action my profession, it has been an important part of my spiritual journey as well. Over these years I have come to realize there is a wide gap, a very unbiblical breach, between the issues of poverty and my evangelical Christian community. For many years I lived out my faith at the far "right" end of that gap. For the last sixteen years on the other side of this gap I have had the privilege of working with people dedicated to moving our economically vulnerable neighbors, often trapped in poverty, toward self-sufficiency. As a result of experiencing both ends of this gap, I often find myself alone in most any room I am in. Among my peers and colleagues in social action I am extremely conservative as an evangelical Christian, sometimes even politically suspect; among my conservative Christian family I am often viewed as too liberal regarding social action and the gospel, sometimes even borderline heretical. During the summer of 2006 I began to seek out my own biblical rationale for my new vocation in community action—I wanted some personal justification from God's Word that my faith should be legitimately connected to my work in social action. This book is a reflection of that search.

Wasted Evangelism is the result of a seven year journey in Mark's Gospel, seeking to determine the relationship of the gospel to the wider biblical material regarding poverty and justice. This was no mere academic exercise alone, but a deeply spiritual one that made it clear to me that the church has a biblical responsibility to be intentionally involved in social action.

At my first *Wasted Evangelism* workshop I mentioned that I was writing this book and it should be available in about a year's time. I commented, rather light-heartedly, that I will hardly obtain the fame and fortunes like the Christian authors producing popular church growth and self-help Christian literature these days . . . the pastor interrupted me and said out loud in the midst of his congregation: "You are right. You will not get rich and famous from an academic book with the title *Wasted Evangelism*. But, you should. Everyone should read it—it's an urgent topic."[1] My goal is nei-

---

1. The pastor was a former student of mine from my days as a professor at Prairie Bible College in Three Hills, AB, Freddie Whaples. I very much appreciate his support

Author's Preface

ther fame nor riches, but to provoke the evangelical Christian community into a much needed conversation on the topic of the gospel, evangelism, and advocating for the poor. It is my hope that serious minded Christians, particularly evangelical church leaders, will take this journey with me through the Gospel of Mark and become better listeners to the gospel story, which I have discovered is directly and intimately linked to God's concern for those who live with the effects of poverty.

MY TARGET AUDIENCE AND READERS/LISTENERS

The reader will notice rather quickly that I have a target audience in mind. Though the subject matter in these studies is for all Christians to consider, it will be quite obvious that I am attempting to speak to my more conservative, non-poor, suburban and exurban evangelical church community. I make no apologies for this. Without hesitation, I consider myself an evangelical Christian and, believe it or not, a conservative one who takes very seriously the inspiration and infallibility of the Bible. Because of this, it is my burden to help the non-poor evangelical community to hear the biblical association that links together the gospel, the church's task of evangelism, and the issues of poverty and justice. Although the work of these studies is for the general Christian population, I do not hide that I am speaking to my evangelical family, particularly its leadership.

I frequently refer to *readers/listeners*. The term may seem a bit cumbersome, but the purpose is to stress that the Biblical text is for both *readers*—those who read, study, and struggle to interpret the inspired words that have been passed down to us in the Old and New Testaments; and *listeners*—those who listen to the text read aloud and then explained in sermons, Bible studies, Sunday school lessons, and college or seminary classes by those who have studied the texts of the Old Testament and the New Testament. Readers/listeners are those individuals and groups of people who stand in front of the texts of Scripture, today, and are called to hear, discern, and, then, seek to obey.

and his kind encouragement—and advertisement!

ACKNOWLEDGMENTS

I owe much more than mere words can convey to a number of people who have listened to me for a long time—for some, ad nauseam, I am afraid—on the subject of the gospel and the issues of poverty. My thoughts and struggles over exegetical decisions and interpretative conclusions would not have had a chance of any clarity on the written page if it were not for friends, family and mentors, patient colleagues, church family, and even some Facebook friends.

As for friends and mentors in the arena of social action, I had the privilege of learning from a number of people who deserve special acknowledgment: Diane Stroman, Bonnie Bodak, Rich Knoll, Joe Carbone, Rina Bakalar, Fran Freer, Scott Wilderman, Bobby and Mimi Burgess, Dina Kubelle, and, of course, the Reverend Henry Yordon (1926–2005) have all contributed beyond measure to my understanding of social action as a profession and as personal passion.

While much of these studies were being researched and crafted I had a vocational home with the Planners of Connecticut's community action agencies. These dedicated people were my family for nearly fifteen years, meeting monthly, along with CAFCA[2] staff, to discuss community action, legislation, the needs of the economically vulnerable, our various programs, funding and resources (and too often the lack of funding and resources), our systems of services, and, as well, our heart-felt, deep passion to see the end of poverty for individuals, families, and communities. This group of women and men, above all others, broke down the stereo-type of the social action professional that I had developed as a non-poor, politically conservative evangelical Christian—on that other side of the gap. They want no one poor. They work tirelessly, sometimes without the resources, on behalf of their agencies and Connecticut's economically vulnerable. I am indebted and thankful to David Yovaisis, Toni Hirst, Deidra Ierardi, Julie Ackerman, Bill Rybczyk, Marlo Greponne, Edith Karsky, David MacDonald, Elizabeth Hill Bohmier, Rhonda Evans, and all my fellow community action Planners (1997–2012) who provoked me to think deeply about the poor and the issues of poverty.

I would be remiss not to mention my gratitude to Connecticut community action Executive Directors and CEOs, who treated me as a peer

---

2. The Connecticut Association for Community Action, the convening association of community action agencies in the State of Connecticut, added support to its Planners as well.

Author's Preface

while I was among them: Bobby Burgess, Peter DeBiasi, Dr. James Gatling, Rich Knoll, Joe Mann, Phil McCain, Deborah Monahan, Thomas Morrow, Bobbie Poole, Paul Puzzo, Lena Rodriguez, Amos Smith, Charlie Tisdale, and Rocco Tricarico. Thank you for entrusting the likes of me to sit at your table to learn about leadership in social action.

To say I had help editing and proof-reading these chapters is an understatement. Without the editing support of Michael O'Brien, Ray Pennoyer, George Luft, Janette Araya, Drs. Aida and Bill Spencer, and my mother, Judy Hawley, I would be even more cautious to allow the general public to see these pages. Their proofing skills and grammatical insight are much appreciated. I even had some Facebook Friends who offered help on a number of grammar questions—and some rewrites of my twisted thoughts: in particular thank you to Robyn Yonemura, Sarah Cady Hall Thomas, Corrie Knight, Carla Eisberg, Julie Daube, Scott Davis, Dr. Michael Pahl, Dr. Martyn Smith, Jeffery Stiles, and my daughter, Amanda Anderson. Of course any typos, poor grammatical choices, or stylistic gaffes that remain are all mine.

The support and friendship of Drs. Aida and Bill Spencer have been invaluable to me. As my former Gordon-Conwell Theological Seminary professors and now colleagues and friends they have been my chief encouragers to keep studying and writing. Their invitation in 2006 to join the Other Voices in Interpretation study group of the Evangelical Theological Society was an incalculable gift that provided me with the means to present my studies on evangelism and social action to a wider audience. Thank you also to Gordon College professor Dr. Megan Shannon DeFranza; Dr. Mimi Haddad, President of Christians for Biblical Equality International; Dr. Woodrow Walton; and other members of the Other Voices study group for your encouragement.

Four of the chapters in this volume were originally presented as papers at the Other Voices in Interpretation section of annual meetings of the Evangelical Theological Society. They were subsequently and graciously published by the *Africanus Journal* and, with kind permission, are reprinted here with some minor changes:

> "'Wasted Evangelism' (Mark 4): The Task of Evangelism and Social Action Outcomes." *Africanus Journal* 1, no. 2 (November 2009) 39–58.

"Idolatry and Poverty: Social Action as Christian Apologetics." *Africanus Journal* 2, no. 2 (November 2010) 24–43.

"'You Will Appear as Fishers' (Mark 1:17): Disciples as Agents of Judgment." *Africanus Journal* 5, no. 1 (April 2013) 21–36.

"A Prelude to Judgment: The Beelzebul Episode (Mk 3:22–28) and Its Significance for Evangelistic Social Action." *Africanus Journal* 5, no. 2 (forthcoming).

I want to thank Gary Gavlan-Salinas, my former Customer Service Skills student, who graciously designed the graphic used in the excursus at the end of chapter 2, "Wasted Evangelism." Also, I appreciate Rich Phillips and his lovely wife, Lisa, who spent some time talking with me about the content of the book and my crazy ideas about kingdom-centered logic models; Rich will be helping in the future with the graphics that will visually explain some of my ideas and thoughts here in *Wasted Evangelism*. I am grateful to the Yale University Divinity School Library for providing space for research and writing; and, for its resourceful and helpful staff.

Some of my good friends deserve special acknowledgment for their more in-depth dialog and input on my exegetical decisions and interpretative conclusions: Dr. Ray Pennoyer and Dr. John Demassa, my colleagues at the New England School of Theology; Doran Wright, pastor of Grace City Church Bridgeport (CT); George Luft, Reverend Freddie Whaples, and Caleb Tromsness; my Facebook friend Julie Daube; and my friends from Trinity Baptist Church (Fairfield, CT), especially my persevering Greek students, Kent Miller and Rick Varrone.

Of course, thank you to my wife, Lisa, and my daughter Amanda, who both listened to my discoveries and thoughts, and in return often offered their own insight.

The conclusions I draw from my exegesis of Mark's Gospel are mine and I take full responsibility for them. In fact not all of the people acknowledged and thanked above agree with my conclusions, nor do all agree with my Christian assumptions about the Bible or my conclusions about evangelism and social action. Nonetheless, this material is better for their input and insight, and sometimes even their arguments with me. At the end of the day I received more encouragement to pursue this course of study than I can acknowledge.

Introduction

Evangelism and Social Action: An Exegetical Argument

"We have become famous for what we oppose, rather than who we are for."
—David Kinnaman, *Unchristian*

"The church's role in the global city may be to identify and nurture new possibilities within the fault lines, back alleys, and lower circuits."
— Andrew Davey, *Urban Christianity and Global Order*

Gandalf: You will have a tale or two to tell of your own when you come back.
Bilbo Baggins: Can you promise I will come back?
Gandalf: No. And if you do, you will not be the same.
—*The Hobbit: An Unexpected Journey*, the movie

Whenever someone attempts to redefine terms like "gospel" or "evangelism," one must tread carefully for hallowed ground is being disturbed and sacred pillars are being moved. I am fully aware that I have entered a debate on the subject of evangelism and social action that has a history of polarizing positions, in which relationships can become strained or, all too often, severed. I recognize that I have made conclusions in the following chapters that will make many within my conservative and evangelical Christian family uncomfortable. My hope is, nonetheless, that these studies will cause many to dig deeper into the text, specifically the Gospel of Mark, to hear what the Bible says about the relationship between the gospel, evangelism, and social action.

This book is not a typical review of Bible proof texts about the poor, poverty, and justice; nor is it an argument from my own experience in community action,[1] or for advancing a political position regarding social concern for the poor. The six studies contained in this volume are intensely exegetical in nature, seeking to hear Mark's presentation of *the gospel of Jesus Christ* (1:1)—and to consider, as well, how those of us on this side of Mark's Gospel can listen more effectively to the text. The studies do not promote a particular "how to evangelize" or "how to address the issues of poverty." They are, however, an encounter with the text of Mark's Gospel so we may wrestle with the *significance* of his understanding of the appearance of Jesus, God's Messiah-King, and the in-breaking of his kingdom. After a close study of Mark's Gospel, I find it impossible not to hear that God's concern for the poor and issues of justice are inescapably associated with *the gospel of God* (Mark 1:14c). As Christians, we must deal with this despite our own political leanings, our treasured church traditions, and our social location (our home address and with whom we associate); and, then, obey accordingly.

In *The Hole in Our Gospel*, Richard Stearns, President of World Vision US, admonishes the American Christian community:

> One of the disturbing things about Church history is the Church's appalling track record of being on the wrong side of the great social issues of the day. If the Church is indeed a revolutionary kind of institution called to foment a social revolution by promoting justice, lifting up the sanctity of human life, fighting for the underdog, and challenging the prevailing value systems in our world, then it seems we should be out in front on social justice issues rather than bringing up the rear.[2]

---

1. From 1997 through 2012 I worked as a grant writer and planner in two community action agencies that helped to form my vocational concern for the poor and issues of poverty.

2. Stearns, *The Hole in Our Gospel*, 190.

Introduction

In almost the same breath, Stearns sustains his reproof by turning to Martin Luther King Jr., who, from a Birmingham jail, wrote to the sleepy, indifferent church of his day:

> The contemporary church is a weak, ineffectual voice with an uncertain sound. So often it is an archdefender of the status quo. Far from being disturbed by the presence of the church, the power structure of the average community is consoled by the church's silent and often even vocal sanction of things as they are.[3]

The church community, Stearns admonishes, loses its relevance in the world when it loses its voice for justice. It is impossible to spend several years in a deeply intense study of Mark's Gospel narrative without hearing that the gospel of Jesus Christ is also an alarm set to awaken a slumbering church to its responsibilities as an advocate on behalf of those who live with the effects of poverty.

The Gospel of Mark is not so much about re-ordering the world as it is about reorienting the Christian community toward the full significance of what it actually means *to believe and obey the gospel of Jesus Christ*. Just as Mark wrote to a church that was marginalized in Roman society and was being blamed for many of the ills of the empire, the contemporary church in America, particularly the evangelical community, is losing its own place and power as a voice in political and cultural affairs. The Markan call is not to advocate for self-preservation, but to be truly *with* Jesus (3:14b) as he breaks his kingdom into a society whose people and structures are often in rebellion against God and who repeatedly disregard his creative design for living in the land. The relevance of the gospel according to Mark's narrative is not for our sustainability as church communities,[4] but for calling the church to reflect its role as faithful agents of God's kingdom, which has been inaugurated with the appearance of Jesus, his Messiah-King.[5]

A narrow, proclamation-centered definition of evangelism, based exclusively on word-studies and isolated proof-texts, does not match the narrative meaning of the gospel, particularly as Mark presents *the gospel of Jesus Christ, the Son of God* (1:1). These studies demonstrate that a mere verbal and cognitive-based understanding of evangelism solely related to

---

3. Ibid., 193; Stearns quotes King from his "Letter from Birmingham Jail" (April 16, 1963, www.mlkonline.net/jail.html).

4. Davey, *Urban Christianity*, 112.

5. See chapter 3, "You Will Appear as *Fishers*," for background on the church's role as agents of God's kingdom.

3

the etymology of the word "evangelize" is too narrow and is devoid of the rich biblical content that Mark gives his Gospel narrative. The following six chapters are an extensive, in-depth, and exegetically-based argument that seeks to demonstrate that the programmatic content of Mark's Gospel narrative links together the gospel, evangelism, and social action.

THE WASTED EVANGELISM THESIS—SOCIAL ACTION CAN BE EVANGELISM

Chapters 1 through 5 of *Wasted Evangelism* were originally presented as papers at annual meetings of the Evangelical Theological Society between 2006 and 2012.[6] On a very personal level I was attempting to formulate a biblical rationale for my own vocation and work in social action—and I wanted to do so publicly and before my own evangelical church community. These studies were as much a spiritual exercise as they were an academic journey through Mark's Gospel that led me to conclude that social action can, indeed, be evangelism.

Many within the Christian community from all political persuasions and church traditions advocate for ministry to the poor. This is nothing new. What is similar among the various Christian views, however, even at the opposite ends of the spectrum, is that evangelism and social action are considered two distinct activities. For some, social concern is "a fruit of spiritual conversion"; while others regard social action as a potential "means of evangelism,"[7] or as pre-evangelism. Even for such an advocate of evangelical social action as Ron Sider, the two are separate responsibilities for the Christian community: "Evangelism and social concern are equally important but distinct aspects of the total mission of the church."[8] The present set of studies gathered in this volume propose that social action should not be considered a separate, distinct responsibility for the church, but is rather a component of evangelism. Properly understood,

---

6. Four of the chapters were originally presented as papers for the Other Voices in Interpretation section of the Evangelical Theological Society and were subsequently and graciously published by the *Africanus Journal*: "'Wasted Evangelism' (Mark 4): The Task of Evangelism and Social Action Outcomes," 39–58; "Idolatry and Poverty: Social Action as Christian Apologetics," 24–43; "'You Will Appear as Fishers' (Mark 1:17): Disciples as Agents of Judgment," 21–36; "A Prelude to Judgment: The Beelzebul Episode (Mk 3:22–28) and Its Significance for Evangelistic Social Action," (forthcoming).

7. Ro, "Perspectives of Church History," 33.

8. Ibid., 12; also see Mott, "Evangelism and Social Action."

Introduction

biblical evangelism ought to be *both* proclamation in word *and* proclamation through action,[9] that is, actions that are intentional demonstrations of God's kingdom in this world.

For many, the definition of evangelism is self-evident: Evangelism is the activity of proclaiming *the evangel*, that is, *the good news*. It is as simple as that. Everyone knows what the "good news" is—Jesus died and rose again for your salvation and mine, the forgiveness of our sins, so we may have entrance by faith into heaven after death. This aspect of the gospel is true and is important to proclaim; it is, nonetheless, a selective reading of the NT. For when one turns to the Gospel accounts, the "good news" is intrinsically associated with the kingdom of God that has arrived in the appearance of Jesus Christ (Mark 1:1; 1:14–15). Any discussion on the topic of biblical evangelism must take into consideration how the "good news" relates to the "the kingdom of God." The reign of God is foundational for defining biblical evangelism and offers insight for implementing relevant evangelistic activities. As William Abraham points out, "Evangelism is at the very least a continuation of vital elements in the work of the early apostles, prophets, and martyrs who found themselves dramatically caught up in the reign of God in the world."[10] The following studies provide a model that seriously considers the role of the kingdom of God and, as well, the Gospel narrative in defining biblical evangelism. Based on this, we can determine what constitutes legitimate evangelistic activities and an appropriate range of potential outcomes that should be included in a church's evangelistic activities.

A WORKING DEFINITION OF SOCIAL ACTION

The basic dictionary definition of *social action* is "individual or group behavior that involves interaction with other individuals or groups, especially organized action toward social reform."[11] Within the discipline of sociology the concept is associated with the work of Max Weber, who understood social action in terms of the relationships people have between social structures and the individuals whose actions create them.[12] Acadia

---

9. See chapter 6, "Significance *Before* Application," for the concept of action as the content of proclamation.

10. Abraham, *Logic of Evangelism*, 39.

11. Social action. Dictionary.com. Dictionary.com Unabridged. Random House, Inc. http://dictionary.reference.com/browse/social action (accessed: May 27, 2013).

12. Weber, *Economy and Society*, 1:78; also see Weber's *Theory of Social and Economic*

University professor Peter Horvath defines social action as "participation in social issues to influence their outcome for the benefit of people and the community" and concludes that "[s]ocial action can, under favorable circumstances, produce actual empowerment, impact, or social change."[13] Horvath underscores the importance of seeking and implementing necessary change on behalf of others who do not have access to power for needed change. This can be seen within the social service and welfare arena in which the term "social action" is often used simply to mean efforts to improve social conditions or to address the needs of a particular group within a social setting or societal structure. Social action can be understood as attempts to improve human welfare and to develop commitment to each other, advocating for and/or making changes in social structures (whether at the individual, community, or legislative levels) for the betterment of all.

Social action, therefore, is principally the means by which one group offers alternative means to an end for another group, taking action or advocating for action to address social issues and community life. Within the context of poverty, social action is not merely charity, alms-giving, or the transfer of wealth. It is actions taken to address relationships between the poor and the non-poor and, as well, the relationship between the poor, the social structures that can cause or promote poverty, and individuals or groups whose actions create those social structures. Social action is, therefore, associated with actions taken by individuals or groups on behalf of others, in particular advocating on behalf of marginalized or powerless individuals or groups whose access to the systems of power are limited or nonexistent.[14]

Organization for an in-depth understanding of his social theory, which includes his view of social action.

13. Horvath, "Organization of Social Action," 221–31; also see Townley et al.,"Performance Measures," 1045–72.

14. What is being advocated for throughout these six studies is *biblical social action* that addresses the needs of economically vulnerable individuals and families and activities that seek to reduce the causes of poverty. Although this book does not intend to endorse any particular method or specific type of activity for evangelistic social action, I feel compelled to stress the importance of community development models over paternalistic methods of charity or wealth distribution. I am grateful to Doran Wright, pastor of Grace City Church Bridgeport (CT), for recommending to me *A Heart for the Community: New Models for Urban and Suburban Ministry* (John Fuder and Noel Castellanos, eds.) as a text that underscores the importance of Christian community development for addressing the needs of poor neighborhoods and communities. Also, see Lupton's *Toxic Charity*. For a catalog of various social action and anti-poverty related ministries see Mae Elise Cannon's *Social Justice Handbook*.

Introduction

What, then, is evangelistic social action? Throughout the following studies I frequently reference Mark's programmatic[15] use of OT contexts regarding the economically vulnerable and the land, particularly contexts that reference Exodus land-laws (e.g., Exod 21–23; Mal 3:1–5; Jer 5:2; 7:9; Amos 4:1–2; etc.), which, for Mark, informs his understanding of the gospel (Mark 1:1–3; note Exod 23:20; Mal 3:1). The Exodus land-laws are operating behind his programmatic theme, informing the reader/listener of the gospel's content (i.e., what the gospel is and what it means). Land-laws were given to ensure that the economically vulnerable (i.e., the land-less) were full participants in the benefits of living in the land.[16] This supports the importance of considering the poor in relationship to the Christian community's social context.

In light of Mark's association of the kingdom with the gospel (1:14–15) and the gospel's programmatic association with the Exodus land-laws, I propose that *biblical social action is a means to ensure that the blessings and benefits of living in society reach to the poor.*[17] Stephen Mott, former Professor of Christian Social Ethics at Gordon-Conwell Theological Seminary, points out that the Bible speaks of what is called "social action" in terms of carrying out justice and caring for the needs of the weak.[18] In her book, *Social Justice Handbook*, Mae Elise Cannon affirms a similar understanding of the biblical concept of social justice:

> The resources that God provides were made available to his people from the very beginning. Justice is expressed when God's resources are made available to all humans, which is what God intended. Biblical justice is the scriptural mandate to manifest the kingdom of God on earth by making God's blessings available to all.[19]

As the following studies affirm, social action is a relevant and legitimate evangelistic activity when it promotes actions and outcomes that demonstrate the inaugural presence of God's rule and reign over creation.

15. By "programmatic" I mean that a concept, phrase, or an event described in the text contains a main theme of Mark's Gospel, which offers a referent for meaning, definition, and/or content (an internal hermeneutical orientation) that Mark sets forth, assisting his audience to understand more clearly the parts or plotline of the story in view of the whole story.

16. See Brueggemann's *The Land* regarding the biblical responsibilities of God's people to the land and to the land-less (i.e., the economically vulnerable and the poor).

17. See chapter 2, "Wasted Evangelism."

18. Mott, "Evangelism and Social Action."

19. Cannon, *Social Justice Handbook*, 22.

Thus, social action, the advocacy and activities on behalf of the economically vulnerable, should be an intentional component of a church's task of evangelism.

BARRIERS MILITATING AGAINST AN OPEN DISCUSSION ON EVANGELISM

We do not typically approach the subject of *evangelism* and *social action* impartially, but with political, demographic, and religious preconceptions and biases. Opening up a conversation to re-assess the nature of evangelism is difficult, especially when social action and issues of poverty are injected into the discussion. The intent of this volume is not to debate the subject, or to review the history of the various positions regarding evangelism and social action,[20] but to offer an exegetical and biblical theological approach to the question, *Can social action be evangelism?* It is important, nonetheless, to recognize there are barriers that can militate against an open discussion on the subject of evangelism and social action.

For many, the meaning of evangelism is self-evident because of its association with "proclamation" activities (e.g., preaching, proclaiming, witnessing, etc.). Evangelism's etymological relationship to the term "good news" (i.e., the *evangel*) can box one into defining evangelistic activity as passing on *information*, that is, to tell, preach, or share the *news* of Jesus Christ—that is, *to evangelize*. For many conservative evangelical Christians defining evangelism any other way causes the gospel (i.e., the *news*) to lose its meaning, robs the people of this important information, and diminishes the work of salvation in Jesus Christ. Evangelism's strong association to the *news* of the gospel suggests to some that anything outside verbal, cognitive-based activities is a threat to the fundamentals of the faith.

Additionally, those who have the highest interest in evangelism are often those least interested and least skilled in critical, theological reflection.[21] Since evangelism is understood as a self-evident activity, rarely is the subject examined exegetically or evaluated theologically, but is usually consigned to matters of practical theology (e.g., missions, preaching, personal

---

20. Note the following volumes that offer material that review the various positions and tensions regarding evangelism and social action: Nicholls, ed., *In Word and Deed*; Moberg, *The Great Reversal*; and, Schlossberg et al. eds., *Christianity and Economics in the Post-Cold War Era*.

21. Abraham's *Logic of Evangelism* for a more in-depth discussion on this point.

Introduction

witness, church outreach programs, and church growth). (*Meaning* is often confused with *application*.)[22] This, then, does not promote biblically relevant criteria *to precede* the discussion and, thus, limits the possibility of new, creative, and potentially sound understandings of biblical evangelism.

Within evangelical circles, to advocate that social action can be evangelism is challenging, for such subjects as poverty and the poor are often relegated to the private sphere. Therefore, anything related to the public arena of rights, laws, and taxes or the confronting of social or governmental systems on behalf of the poor are often associated with the "social gospel" and the theologically liberal church.[23] Although historically the church was deeply involved with issues of poverty, a "great reversal" took place between 1900 and about 1930.[24] Evangelical fundamentalists turned away from their social responsibilities as a reaction against the social gospel that was perceived to be aligned with liberalism, which had diminished Bible infallibility and inspiration and weakened biblical views of sin, hell, salvation, and the deity of Jesus. When civic and political social concerns became suspect in the minds of evangelical academics and popular revivalists, social action responsibilities took on a minor role for much of the evangelical Christian community.[25] Anything associated with the social gospel was considered a distraction and, to some, a betrayal to the fundamental essence of the gospel (i.e., the information, that is, the *news* of Jesus Christ).[26] This history spills over into any contemporary discussion on evangelism and social action.

There are also demographic barriers to an open discussion regarding the association between evangelism and social action. Over the last seven decades, people have been moving out of urban centers and into the suburbs, including Christians and their churches. The twin demographic forces of urban flight and suburban sprawl contribute to the evangelicals' disassociation with issues of poverty and the poor. As a result, this social

---

22. See chapter 6, "Significance *Before* Application," for a model on developing relevant and authoritative application, particularly as it relates to the Christian's faithful obedience to the gospel.

23. For a review of the history and some of the causes for the rise of the "social gospel" and the history of its inherent tension with conservative Christianity see Ken Wytsma, *Pursuing Justice*, 203–18.

24. Marsden, *Fundamentalism and American Culture*, 86; also Moberg, *Great Reversal*; Henry, *Uneasy Conscience*; Nicholls, ed., *In Word and Deed*.

25. Marsden, *Fundamentalism and American Culture*, 86.

26. Adeyemo, "Critical Evaluation," 48–49.

transformation helped reinforce a one-dimensional understanding of the gospel,[27] which determines, for many, the nature of evangelism. Suburbanization of American society has moved much of the evangelical communities of faith outside populations affected by poverty. Rather than church communities promoting social action on behalf of poorer communities, the (upward) mobility of American families toward the suburbs demand that suburban churches serve a socializing and stabilizing function. Not a very likely set of social forces that will generate social change on behalf of the economically vulnerable hidden outside their neighborhoods and unknown within their circles of friends and acquaintances.[28]

The barriers reviewed here are not exhaustive, but are limited to those most relevant to the arguments and conclusions of the following studies. To overcome these barriers, we will turn our attention to the text of Scripture, particularly the Gospel of Mark, as a basis for entering into a discussion on the biblical relationship between evangelism and social action.

THE PICTURE OF WASTED EVANGELISM AND THE SIX STUDIES

I am indebted to Donald Juel's two works *A Master of Surprise* and *The Gospel of Mark*, which offer a tempered reader-response approach to interpreting the Gospel of Mark.[29] Though I do not fully subscribe to such a hermeneutical method, we as readers/listeners are still *to respond* to the portrait of the gospel Mark has drawn for us through his narrative of the events, ministry, and teachings of Jesus Christ. In these two volumes, Juel presents a "wasted seed" interpretation of the Mark 4 parables, which helped to foster my initial thoughts regarding the link between the gospel as Mark presents it and the nature of evangelism.[30]

---

27. A one-dimensional gospel indicates solely a person/God dynamic relationship; whereas a multi-dimensional gospel includes the person/God dynamic and, also, creation/God, person/creation, and person/person. *Wasted evangelism* considers the multi-dimensional gospel more representative of a biblically sound narrative definition of the gospel.

28. See chapter 5, "Idolatry and Poverty," for a fuller discussion on Christians, urban flight, and suburban sprawl.

29. Juel, *Master of Surprise*, 3–30 and *Gospel of Mark*, 15–42.

30. Juel, *Master of Surprise*, 45–63 and *Gospel of Mark*, 120–29.

Introduction

Evangelism is the sowing of the word (Mark 4:14) that Jesus likens to a Master Farmer who sows his seed "lavishly, carelessly,"[31] allowing it to land, indiscriminately, on both poor and good soil. Juel concludes that the Mark 4 Sower-soil-seed parable (which I call *the parable of the Sower who sows*) describes "how it is" with the church's task of evangelism, that is, the reality illustrated by the Farmer, his sowing of seed, the poor and good soils, and the pathetic and bountiful harvests.[32] The portrait depicted in the parable teaches us not to render judgment on what is poor soil and what is good soil, but simply to sow indiscriminately like the Master Farmer, that is, to "waste" the seed of the gospel. This is the picture of evangelism and, thus, a portrait of our story as communities of believers: The church's task of *wasted evangelism*.

The six studies in this book (i.e., the chapters) form an exegetical argument through Mark's Gospel that seeks to demonstrate that *social action can be evangelism*. The order of the chapters is intentional. The series reflects the sequence in which the studies were developed; as a result of research and conclusions, one study led to the next. The first chapter, "Widows in Our Courts," was my first exegetical venture into the subject of evangelism and social action. The poor widow scene in Mark 12 (vv. 38–44) seemed a good place to begin, for it placed me, the reader/listener, in a context where there was a poor widow, people who were taking advantage of her, and a structure (i.e., the temple system) that made the situation possible—all the ingredients that social action seeks to address. The Mark 12 poor widow episode shapes our understanding of discipleship: Our patterns of discipleship should include the Christian community's role as advocates for the poor and for confronting the structures that are harmful to the economically vulnerable.

As I began to draw conclusions regarding discipleship and the issues of poverty from my study of the Mark 12 poor widow text, I came to realize the need to develop my own exegetically-based "theory of evangelism" in order to determine how the Christian faith relates to the issues of poverty. This led me back to the Mark 4 parable of the Sower (chapter 2), which ultimately contributed the title to this volume, "Wasted Evangelism." Mark 4 is a logical text for determining the meaning and nature of biblical evangelism because Jesus' parable is specifically about the spread and increase of the word, which is the gospel (note 1:1, 14–15; 2:2; 4:14, 33). Typically,

---

31. Juel, *Master of Surprise*, 57.
32. Ibid., 56–57.

the "soil" parables are understood individualistically (*what kind of soil are you?*). However, while uncovering the OT background of the Mark 12 poor widow scene (12:38–44), I discovered another, more likely, paradigm for interpreting the meaning of the Mark 4 parable (vv. 1–8; 14–20): much of the redemptive, exile, and restoration language and imagery in the OT is agricultural (as is the Mark 4 parable of sowing the word). The parable is less about people (i.e., individual soils) and more about God's redemptive plan and the nature of evangelism—the case I make throughout the following studies. The "wasted seed" depicted in the parable is the sowing (i.e., spreading) of the word of the gospel (4:14), which Mark tells us is directly linked to the OT (1:1–3) and is, by Jesus' own explanation (4:11–12), related to OT exile-theology.[33] Interestingly, these connections are programmatically associated with OT contexts that include references to the poor, the economically vulnerable, and issues of justice. The Mark 4 "wasted seed" parable shows there is a biblical link between evangelism (i.e., the spread of the word of God's gospel) and social action (God's concern for the poor and for justice), which contributes to a narrative definition of biblical evangelism and its potential outcomes.

What we learn from Mark's Gospel comes to us in stories, not lectures; meaning is determined through narrative, not argued through propositions or syllogistic logic. The roles and interactions of the characters, which are strategically embedded into the narrative, play an important part in developing Mark's themes, and thus are instructive for the reader/listener. Chapters 3 ("You will Appear as *Fishers*") and 4 ("A Prelude to Judgment") focus on characters in the storyline that continue to establish the relationship between the gospel, Christian discipleship, the church's task of evangelism, and social action. As shown in chapter 3, the meaning of the Mark 1:17 *fisher*-promise links the disciples' role as agents of God's inaugurated kingdom to social action outcomes. In chapter 4, an analysis of the Mark 3 Beelzebul episode (vv. 20–35) reveals the narrative implications of the conflict-thread in 2:1—3:6 between Jesus and the Jewish leadership. This study turns our attention toward the role of church leaders who are to be

---

33. Refer to chapter 2, "Wasted Evangelism," for the foundational OT background to Mark's understanding of the gospel (1:1–3; Exod 23:20; Mal 3:1; Isa 40:3). Note, additionally, Jesus' reference to the Isaiah 6 idolatry-taunt (Isa 6:9–10) in 4:12, a clear reference to OT exile-theology. See Beale, "Isaiah VI 9–13," 257–78; Caneday, "He Wrote in Parables," 35–67; Keegan, "Parable of the Sower," 501–18; McComiskey, "Exile and the Purpose of Jesus' Parables," 59–85.

faithful *insiders* who do *the will of God* (3:35), which includes the deliberate incorporation of social action into a church's evangelistic activities.

The significant role the OT plays in Mark's Gospel cannot be overlooked as we seek to understand how he defines *the gospel of Jesus Christ* (1:1) and its relationship to the church's evangelistic task. The extensive work throughout all these studies shows Mark's consistent and programmatic use of OT texts and contexts that reference the poor and issues of justice. This strongly suggests that the issues of poverty and justice are intrinsically linked to the gospel. While encountering the numerous OT texts that Mark utilizes throughout his Gospel narrative, a common thread emerged: there are multiple and consistent inter-related OT references that contain the issue of idolatry and many of these same OT texts, directly or within the context, mention the issue of poverty or justice. Mark harnesses these very OT texts to give programmatic content to the gospel, which further defines the nature of biblical evangelism. Chapter 5 ("Idolatry and Poverty") examines the juxtaposition of OT idolatry texts with texts that contain references to the poor and issues of poverty and, as well, Mark's use of them throughout his narrative. This study presents an apologetic paradigm for defining the biblical nature of evangelism, which, legitimately and necessarily, includes social action outcomes in a church's evangelistic activities.

Leading up to chapter 6, it should be noted that in the previous *fishers of men* study (chapter 3) I concluded that the Mark 1:17 *fisher*-promise finds its inaugural fulfillment in Jesus' commission of the twelve (Mark 3:13–15). Chapter 6 ("Significance *Before* Application"), the final in the series, continues the implications of the *fisher* study by examining the Mark 3 commission *to preach* and *to have authority to cast out the demons* (vv. 14c–15) in order to decipher its significance for the reader/listener on this side of the text. The commission indicates that *fisher*-followers are to mirror Jesus' ministry, which demonstrated the inauguration of God's dominion over the realms of humankind. Thus, the church should incorporate deed-parables (i.e., the significance of Jesus' *casting* ministry) into its evangelistic activities. In view of the *fisher* concept's association with OT contexts that reference the poor and issues of justice, the Mark 3 commission implies that social action is a relevant and appropriate response of obedience to the gospel.

THE AIM AND GOAL OF WASTED EVANGELISM

There is a sense of urgency to these *Wasted Evangelism* studies and their assertion that *social action can be evangelism*, for the lives of the economically vulnerable and generations of poor families are at stake. The end of these exegetical studies is not simply to win an argument and certainly not to present a political position. They are to dissuade us—particularly non-poor, suburban and exurban evangelicals—from settling for a one-dimensional understanding of the gospel that tends to endorse our own personal security and happiness and promotes the sustainability of our local church communities instead of advocating on behalf of those affected by the issues of poverty.

With some fear and trembling, my aim throughout these six studies is to contribute to the discussion and add light to the sometimes heated debate on the relationship between evangelism and social action. The goal of *Wasted Evangelism* is, then, to provide an exegetically-based narrative understanding of biblical evangelism, which, according to Mark's Gospel, includes God's care for the economically vulnerable and concern for the issues of poverty. The close examination of Mark's Gospel and the biblical texts associated with idolatry, poverty, and justice provides an opportunity for Christians, especially evangelical church leadership in America, to rethink the evangelistic activities of their churches and reconsider what it means to engage the surrounding communities as agents of God's kingdom.

At a very personal level, the exegetical process reflected in these chapters caused me to think more deeply about my own Christian faith and to reassess my understanding of the gospel and, as well, my view of the church's task of evangelism. My prayer is for a wider audience to stand before the text of Mark's Gospel, hear my exegetical arguments, and, as a result, more deeply connect their faith to those whose lives are affected by the issues of poverty. Thus, my desire is to let the text of Scripture speak, show how I arrived at my exegetical and interpretive conclusions, and present a case for what I discovered, namely, that social action ought to be a component of a church's evangelistic activities.

1

Widows in our Courts (Mark 12:38–44)
The Public Advocacy Role of Local Congregations as Discipleship

"If I look at the masses, I will never act. If I look at the One, I will."
—MOTHER TERESA

"The prophet announces the end, the end of haughtiness in which one takes priority over another, the one who has forgotten about covenant partners. It is clear that this is not simply gentle concern for poor folks, but it has to do with Yahweh, with his character and his commitments. He is allied with the poor against the rapacious wealthy. That is who he is and no royal wishing will have it otherwise."
—WALTER BRUEGGEMANN, *THE LAND*

"It is delicate work, I have found, establishing authentic parity between people of unequal power."
—ROBERT D. LUPTON, *TOXIC CHARITY*

Wasted Evangelism

THE EVANGELICAL COMMUNITY EXISTS at a time of great opportunity. Although there is often an uneasiness between the evangelical church and much of the public square, the general opinion of religion's and the church's role has taken on a more positive perception regarding the care and help for our poor. But, of course, there are still some limitations.

Throughout history the church has always been involved at some level with caring for the poor—with and without government partnership. However, more recently there has been a devolution in how American society undertakes care for its poor and vulnerable populations, a shifting of roles and responsibilities from the public-government arena back toward the private sector, which includes religious communities. There are practical reasons for this, such as the lack of government resources and the shallowness of its social capital. There are also cultural reasons, such as a postmodern climate that promotes more openness to spirituality. As a result, Americans by and large support the role of religion in addressing the issues of poverty and caring for its poor.

The acceptance of the church's role as an advocate for the poor in the public square and, as well, for social action are not necessarily for spiritual reasons, but for very practical ones. Although there are exceptions, government and private social service systems look more favorably today upon the church as a partner, which can include conservative and evangelical churches as well. Many acknowledge that the church's social capital, resources, and concepts of reciprocity can benefit the poor. Additionally, religion's role in providing social services is welcome because it relieves some of the burden on government and the public to provide for the poor. In this environment, churches can be legitimate brokers of community interests, offering wider networks and deeper social ties across all political, socioeconomic, and demographic categories. Communities of faith represent a significant resource for social action because of their unique capacity to motivate and mobilize a network of human, financial, and social capital for public ends (i.e., for the public good).

Along with the aforementioned devolution, there continues to be a tension caused by a deep-seated American cultural resistance to promoting religious change in others. There seems to be a general acceptance of faith-based organizations and churches to provide social services; but this support drops significantly when asked whether faith-based organizations can encourage their "clients" (the beneficiaries of faith-based or church-centered social services) to have a religious conversion. The acceptance of church-based partners in social action, therefore, has limitations: there is approval of utilizing the church's inherent social capital and, as well, some of its moral dimensions and principles of reciprocity in the public square, but not for proselytizing for church membership or promoting religious conversion.

As Christians we recognize that the church exists in the tension between its earthly social dimensions and its spiritual essence as the body of Christ—in the world, but not of it. In order for the church, however, to be formed more by its relationship to Christ than by the prevailing political and modern cultural pressures, that is, its cultural-social location,[1] there needs to be an intentional commitment by church leaders to biblical discipleship. Today, the local Christian congregation is presented with a timely opportunity to fulfill its responsibilities toward the poor. The Mark 12 *poor widow* episode provides a window into the gospel's relationship to the issues of poverty that will provide biblical patterns for Christian discipleship, which, I will argue, include a public advocacy role on behalf of those living with the effects of poverty.

MARK 12:38–44: THE POOR WIDOW EPISODE AND ITS SOCIAL LOCATION

The scene depicted in Mark 12:38–44 is a powerful slice of life that is now part of recorded redemptive history, challenging those who stand before the text to respond in faithful obedience. But what does this obedience look like? The Mark 12 story of *the poor widow* calls local communities of faith to incorporate an advocacy role into their patterns of discipleship, which should move the church away from its preoccupation with the private sphere and compel it toward the public square as purveyors of and partners in social action.

> In His teaching He was saying: "Beware of the scribes who like to walk around in long robes, and like respectful greetings in the market places, and chief seats in the synagogues and places of honor at

---

1. A "cultural and social location" encompasses the mores, attitudes, and prevailing cultural norms, that is the cultural and social texture, at a specific time (or era) and demographic/geographic location. It is the context within which people/groups experience the forces that impact how they live and think, including the development of everyday habits and behaviors; it is also the way or lens people understand and even mediate their worldview.

> banquets, who devour widows' houses, and for appearance's sake offer long prayers; these will receive greater condemnation."
>
> And He sat down opposite the treasury, and began observing how the people were putting money into the treasury; and many rich people were putting in large sums. A poor widow came and put in two small copper coins, which amount to a cent. Calling His disciples to Him, He said to them, "Truly I say to you, this poor widow put in more than all the contributors to the treasury; for they all put in out of their surplus, but she, out of her poverty, put in all she owned, all she had to live on" (Mark 12:38–44).

The woman in the story is not just a widow; she is a poor widow. This strengthens her identification with a group of economically vulnerable people that were to have special protection and provision by those who rule, serve as priests, and own property as prescribed in the Torah and reinforced through prophetic voice.[2] Geoffrey Smith reminds us that in the OT "widows, along with the fatherless and aliens, were the most vulnerable and dependent class of people in the land."[3] The poor widow is also in the temple and placed in a scene amid individuals that, as a group, have been opposing Jesus from the very start (1:22; 2:1—3:6; note 11:1—12:37); yet, they should have been *her* chief advocates. As a minor character in Mark's Gospel story, the *poor widow* is strategically placed in the narrative's plot and, as well, is pregnant with OT Torah and prophetic significance.

There are two general interpretations posited for this story: 1) It is a paradigm of Christian commitment that focuses on the widow's action as an example of devotion and sacrificial giving; 2) it represents "the last straw" of Torah disobedience before judgment falls on the temple (Mark 13:2), with the focus, then, on Jesus' conflict with temple authorities.[4] Though this episode does appear to offer a paradigm for Christian discipleship, it is the latter interpretation that seems most appropriate to the text and its context. The purpose here is to demonstrate a reading of this familiar Bible story that posits a negative interpretation rather than the more positive one that is typically put forward (i.e., sacrificial giving), thereby affecting how this text ought to inform and form Christian discipleship.

---

2. Evans, *Mark 8:27—16:20*, 277.
3. Smith, "Widow's Offering," 27–36.
4. Some argue for a variation of the two views (see Smith, "Widow's Offering"); see comments on Mark 12:38–44 by Evans (*Mark 8:27—16:20*) and Gundry (*Mark*).

The failure of interpretation—an erroneous example for discipleship

There is some irony to these two reactions (that is, the two interpretations) to the story, which I call *the poor widow vs. duplicitous scribes* episode: one holds it up as an example of faithful devotion and sacrificial giving, while the other sees judgment, lament, and tragedy.[5] Everything about this short story suggests that the widow is being taken advantage of by a temple leadership that does not have her best interests in mind. Although it might be advantageous for churches and Christian ministries to see the *poor widow* as an example of sacrificial giving, this interpretation, however, turns the text 180 degrees contrary to its context and is disconnected from the plot Mark has developed through his Gospel narrative. This leads to a failure of interpretation that distracts the Christian community from developing biblically authoritative and analogous application from this text.[6]

This episode fits within Mark's paradigm for Christian discipleship; but, what does it require of the Christian community? How does it inform the Christian call to discipleship? Is the widow the focal point, or is the failure of temple leadership the crux of the story that should form the church's understanding of discipleship? Mark does draw a narrative correspondence between the widow giving *her whole life* (*holon ton bion autēs*, 12: 44c)[7] and Jesus' imminent sacrifice, the giving of *his* own life. Some take this to mean that "we, too, should give our lives and resources sacrificially like the widow and Jesus." No. This is an inappropriate analogy and is an ill-fitted correspondence to the text and its context. While the link to Jesus is certainly there in the Gospel story, the larger issue is the burden that was improperly, even maliciously, laid on the *poor widow* by the temple establishment—the *poor widow* should not have had to give *her whole life* (v. 44c). This is the point here: as God's representatives, the scribes and, as well, the whole of temple leadership should have been her advocates, not the cause of her destitution. The link to Jesus is simply that he will step up to be her advocate and will give his life on her behalf.

Furthermore, interpretation of this scene should not be dependent on the inner disposition of the widow. Addison Wright insightfully points

---

5. Wright, "Widow's Mite," 256–65.

6. See chapter 6, "Significance *Before* Application," for a discussion regarding making appropriate application.

7. Author's translation. The NASB renders this phrase, *all she had to live on* (Mark 12:44c).

out that the "inner disposition and outward bearing of the widow are not described or hinted at in the text" and in the end "there is no praise of the widow in the passage and no invitation to imitate her, precisely because she ought not to be imitated."[8] We do not know her inner motivation—faith, love of God, works, despair, fear, guilt, or obligation? At this point, this is all speculation. Any comment about the inner disposition or motivation of the widow is achieved only by reading *into* the text. Thus, any application that stems from "her motivation for giving all that she had" will be misguided.

Nowhere does this text describe the widow's piety. It seems more reasonable to assume that Mark is drawing our attention to the duplicitous character of the scribes and the sad state of the *poor widow*, which are *in* the text. Concentrating on the widow as an example fails to take into account the obvious thread of opposition that Jesus has with many of the existing temple activities and his conflict with its leadership (e.g., Mark 1:21–22; 2:1—3:6; 7:1–13; 11:1—12:37). Such a positive reading also neglects to take into account the final destination of the widow's coins—that is, the temple that will be destroyed (13:2)—and the eventual judgment on temple authorities (12:40c; 14:53–65). In the end, our reading of this text should cause, at a minimum, a reaction of displeasure because the "widow's donation to the temple is a misguided gesture,"[9] a waste, and a contributor to her continued impoverishment.

Jesus' observation of a *poor widow* who had given the last of her financial resources for which *her whole life* depended can just as equally be read as "downright disapproval"[10] and not as praise. The contrast between the scribes and the widow is not about piety, but for illustrating and emphasizing the duplicitous conduct of the scribes. It is lamentable to watch this act of the *poor widow* in the presence of such wealth and religious duplicity. We can fail to notice there is a tragedy happening that day, right there in the temple courts.

Character stories in Mark's Gospel

For examples or paradigms of Christian discipleship, appeal is often made to incidents and episodes in which minor characters in the Gospels receive affirmation from Jesus for their "faith" or in which Jesus calls attention to an

---

8. Wright, "Widow's Mite."
9. Ibid.; see also Waetjen, *Reordering of Power*, 183–96.
10. Wright, "Widow's Mite."

act of faithful devotion. Even though we can only speculate on the widow's inner intentions, it is reasonable, nonetheless, to see "an example" is happening here in this story. But as a minor character, how does the widow function in this text?

Mark does not capitalize on "examples" of faithful devotion as do the other Gospel writers. The few occasions, however, are worth reviewing, for there are observable patterns. First, when it is clear that Mark intends the minor character to be an example of faith or discipleship, in each case Jesus says something *to* the individual, commending their response or act.

- The four men who lower the paralytic down through the roof (2:3–5): "And Jesus seeing their faith said to the paralytic, 'Son, your sins are forgiven'" (v. 5).
- The healing of Jairus' daughter (5:21–24, 35–43): "But Jesus, overhearing what was being spoken, said to the synagogue official, 'Do not be afraid any longer, only believe'" (v. 36).
- The woman who touched Jesus to heal her flow of blood (5:25–34): "And He said to her, 'Daughter, your faith has made you well; go in peace and be healed of your affliction'" (v. 34).
- The healing of the child of a Syrophoenician woman (7:24–30): "And He said to her, 'Because of this answer go; the demon has gone out of your daughter'" (v. 29).
- The two-phase healing of the blind man (8:22–26): "Taking the blind man by the hand, He brought him out of the village; and after spitting on his eyes and laying His hands on him, He asked him, 'Do you see anything?'" (v. 23).
- The man in the crowd whose daughter could not be healed of demonic possession by the disciples (9:17–27): "And Jesus said to him, '"If You can?" All things are possible to him who believes'" (v. 23).
- Bartimaeus receives his sight (10:46–52): "And Jesus said to him, 'Go; your faith has made you well.' Immediately he regained his sight and began following Him on the road" (v. 52).

Second, there are occasions where "lessons" from the minor characters are for the benefit of Jesus' opponents or in contrast to his opponents: forgiving, then healing the paralytic, 2:3–12; the calling of Levi the tax-collector, 2:14–17; healing the man with the withered hand on the Sabbath,

3:1–6; and freeing the man of the legion of demons, 5:1–19. In these stories, any interaction with the minor character is incidental to the scene for the point is directed toward Jesus' opposition or to set up a contrast to or with or for them, which is "the lesson." Third, in some instances Jesus responds to a request and asks (commands) the minor character to say nothing to others about their encounter (e.g., cleansing of the leper, 1:40–45; also 8:22–26). Fourth, in a few scenes where Jesus interacts with or calls attention to a minor character, the emphasis on discipleship is not necessarily on the minor character, but on *why* Jesus interacts with or calls attention to that minor character: Jesus' encounter with the leper (1:40–44), Levi the tax collector (2:14–17), the gentile Jairus (5:21–24, 34–43), the legion-possessed man (5:1–19), and the Syrophoenician woman (7:24–30)[11] all indicate something about the inauguration of the kingdom rather than simply as examples to be imitated. The Mark 12 poor widow episode fits into this last category (given its relationship to the wider context, which will be discussed below) and is similar to the episodes in which Jesus addresses his opposition or seeks to make a contrast to them.

In Mark 12 Jesus does not address the *poor widow*, nor does he comment on the *poor widow's* faith; but, he does address his disciples. In fact, the people and activities to which Jesus calls attention (i.e., the appearance and actions of the scribes and the presence and activity of the *poor widow*) hinge on what he had commanded his disciples at the opening of the scene: *Beware of the scribes* (v. 38b; note earlier *Beware of the leaven of the Pharisees and the leaven of Herod*, 8:15b). The *poor widow* is not the object of the lesson, but is a juxtaposed minor character to highlight the duplicitous scribes that *are* the lesson to be observed. In Mark 12:38–44 there is no dialog or words directed to the widow, only an observation made by Jesus and pointed out to his disciples. There is "no invitation in the text to imitate the widow, no statement that Jesus looked on her and loved her, no command to go and do in like manner, no remark that she is not far from the kingdom."[12] She is *not* the example. The duplicitous scribes and the situation exposed in this scene are *the* example.

---

11. The Syrophoenician woman obviously is commended for her persistence (7:24–30); the lesson, however, is for the reader/listeners to understand that those outside of Israel have access to the gospel: the implications of Jesus' arrival reach beyond Israel ("as far as the curse is found"). What Jesus commends in the Syrophoenician woman is what is deficient in the disciples, and possibly the readers/listeners.

12. Wright, "Widow's Mite."

Widows in our Courts (Mark 12:38-44)

Our *poor widow vs. duplicitous scribes* episode is, indeed, for discipleship, but its lesson and example are not drawn from reading into the text some inner disposition of devotion in the widow. The appearance of the *poor widow* in the scene supports Jesus' warning to the disciples in 12:38-40: *Beware duplicitous scribes who parade around as if they are close to God, but are actually the very reason for this widow's impoverishment in the first place* [author's paraphrased interpretation]. It seems more reasonable to understand that the paradigm for discipleship is related to *why* Jesus points out the duplicitous scribes and the *poor widow* to his disciples. The command is clearly marked: *Beware of the scribes* (12:38b). The warning to beware of the duplicitous scribes who are juxtaposed with a *poor widow* gives the reader/listener a direction to consider what it means to obey the command (*Beware of the scribes*, v. 38b) and for "applying" the episode as a whole (i.e., what discipleship includes).

Mark 12:38-44—what stands behind the text?

The *poor widow vs. duplicitous scribes* episode confronts the reader/listener from its own place in time; so, its own social and cultural location will help us determine how it should shape the church's patterns of discipleship. As a text, it still remains a part of the society and culture from whence it originated, thus the descriptions and character interaction place expectations upon the reader/listener. It is legitimate to ask, *What stands behind the text?* Recent commentaries[13] and articles[14] acknowledge that OT Torah and words from the prophets concerning God's and Israel's relationship to the poor stand behind this text. There is also recognition that the temple had functioned as a commercial-banking center and the scribes as managers for the estates of Israelite widows.[15] These historical symbols that shed light on the episode's setting will help us to read the text more effectively in order to decipher its value for discipleship.

---

13. E.g., Edwards, *Gospel According to Mark*, 378–82; Evans, *Mark 8:27—16:20*, 276–85; France, *Gospel of Mark*, 488–92; also see Watts, *Isaiah's New Exodus*, 315.

14. E.g., Derrett, "'Eating Up the Houses of Widows,'" 1–9; Hamilton, "Temple Cleansing," 365–72; Smith, "Widow's Offering"; Sugirtharajah, "Widow's Mite Revisited," 42–43; Wright, "Widow's Mite."

15. Derrett, "'Eating Up the Houses of Widows'"; Hamilton, "Temple Cleansing"; France, *Gospel of Mark*, 491.

Since arriving in Jerusalem, Jesus has been involved in a series of confrontations with temple authorities (Mark 11:1—12:37).[16] In fact, from the beginning, as France points out, "all the scribes we have met in this gospel have been critics, if not openly enemies, of Jesus, and here in Jerusalem their hostility has come to a head as he predicted (cf. 8:31; 10:33)."[17] The *poor widow vs. the duplicitous scribes* episode reflects this animosity; afterward, Jesus brings his public journey to Jerusalem and the temple to a close with a warning:

> "Beware of the scribes who like to walk around in long robes, and like respectful greetings in the market places, and chief seats in the synagogues and places of honor at banquets, who devour widows' houses, and for appearance's sake offer long prayers; these will receive greater condemnation" (12:38-40).

Why this warning to *Beware of the scribes*? Why does Jesus give this particular description of the scribes? Is the warning for his disciples (and future reader/listeners) to guard against being taken advantage of by such duplicitous scribes or those like them? Or, is it a warning to note their duplicity and not repeat or imitate it? The latter seems most reasonable, for in the next set of verses, with no change of scene, Jesus juxtaposes the warning to beware of scribes *who devour widow's houses* (v. 40a) with an unnamed *poor widow* whom Jesus portrays as giving her last two coins (vv. 41–44). The widow's house-estate is actually devoured right before their eyes.

The temple was not only the religious center in Israel, it also had become the economic hub for the nation as well. Jesus' warning is related to the temple leadership's association to commerce and, in this particular text, the scribal role as estate trustees for Israelite widows. Neill Hamilton notes, "It was to this temple with this bank and these historical, political associations that Jesus came for the 'cleansing' episode" (11:15–18).[18] Overturning the tables of the "money changers" (*kollybistēs*, 11:15) probably refers to "the banking operation that Jesus suspends." It should not be a surprise to find the same banking function present in the widow story as well.[19]

---

16. Additionally, it should be noted that such conflict with temple authorities has been a hallmark of Mark's Gospel narrative (note 1:21–22; 2:1—3:6).

17. France, *Gospel of Mark*, 489; also see Evans, *Mark 8:27—16:20*, 277–80.

18. Hamilton, "Temple Cleansing."

19. It is possible that 2 Macc 3:10–11 offers a background for the story in the first place. There is also evidence of a "banking" context in Sirach and Tobit (see Hamilton, "Temple Cleansing").

Widows in our Courts (Mark 12:38–44)

Jesus' warning (*Beware of the scribes*, 12:38b) finds its basis (i.e., its social and cultural location) in the scribes' function as bankers and estate trustees. The scribe's rather elaborate appearance is, as Jesus describes them, neither happenstance, nor arbitrary. The purpose of their public presentation was not for celebration or remembrance of God's glory or his redemption, but was designed to impress onlookers. Their appearance and positioning were not merely for social standing, but served a commercial purpose: they were demonstrating in public their credibility as "trustees" of people's funds and estates.[20] However, Jesus points out that their appearance was fraudulent—the scribes' pious activities and appearance were merely a religious façade.

The description of the scribes is not a pretext for introducing the *poor widow* episode or to set up a proof text on "sacrificial giving." While we do not know the widow's inner disposition, we do have indications of such for the scribes.[21] Here there is no speculation, for Jesus supplies plenty of information to assess "their hearts." The scribes walk about in their priestly robes as a way "to draw attention to themselves and to be associated with the prestigious temple establishment."[22] Their dress, public appearance, and status were all calculated to show their "religiosity," a sign of their trustworthiness because they *appeared* as associates of the priests and, thus, "very pious." Everything was designed to indicate "they were close to God." Their lengthy prayers were also a means to an end, for such "long prayers" in public indicated a pious reputation that met the requirement needed to be entrusted with maintaining and overseeing the properties of others. The scribes, if they were considered honorable, could function as *epiteropos* who were "guardian, custodian, manager, and trustee, all in one."[23] Duncan Derrett notes:

> Once the office was secured the misappropriation of funds could begin . . . [the scribes] misappropriate it only through their public reputation for piety. Thus we must translate: ". . . those that 'eat

---

20. Derrett, "'Eating Up the Houses of Widows.'"

21. Jesus interjects his comments into an already existing cultural dialog: "'impious' men of professed piety and fastidiousness who are 'devourers of the goods of the poor, saying that they do so on the ground of their justice, but to destroy them'" (Derrett, "'Eating Up the Houses of Widows'").

22. Evans, *Mark 8:27—16:20*, 278.

23. Derrett, "'Eating Up the Houses of Widows'"; also France, *Gospel of Mark*, 429.

away' the estates of the widows, and, with such an end in view, indulge in lengthy prayers: they shall suffer a heavier sentence."[24]

Scribes managed the estates for their own advantage and promoted "the temple cult which 'eats of' the resources of the pious poor, or more generally through exploiting their hospitality and trust."[25] Mark, through the detailed description, ensures that the reader/listener fully understands the duplicity of these scribes toward the *poor widow* in the temple court (12:42a).

The description of the scribes is not simply a contrast with the *poor widow*, but is to point toward a cause and effect: the cause (a system/structure and its duplicitous authorities) leads to the effect (the impoverishment of a widow). After the tragedy of losing her husband, a widow in Israel would entrust her assets to the banking trustees, that is, "worthy" scribes, who dressed just right and publically offered long-prayers. But the first tragedy is made worse by the second. The scene explicitly implies that the scribes caused the *poor widow*'s destitution by fraudulent management of her estate and, now, she gives the last of her resources to support and to participant in the very system, ironically, that had caused her impoverishment.

The word used to depict the scribes' action "to devour" (*katesthiō*, 12:40; also Matt 23:14; Luke 20:47) the houses/estates of widows means more than just "sponging off" their assets. The devastating impact of this word can be seen in other NT texts:

> "The sower went out to sow his seed; and as he sowed, some fell beside the road, and it was trampled under foot and the birds of the air ate it up [*katephagen*]" (Luke 8:5; also Mark 4:4; Matt 13:4).

> "but when this son of yours came, who has devoured [*kataphagōn*] your wealth with prostitutes, you killed the fattened calf for him" (Luke 15:30).

> And if anyone wants to harm them, fire flows out of their mouth and devours [*katesthiei*] their enemies; so if anyone wants to harm them, he must be killed in this way (Rev 11:5).

> And his tail swept away a third of the stars of heaven and threw them to the earth. And the dragon stood before the woman who

---

24. Derrett, "'Eating Up the Houses of Widows.'"
25. France, *Gospel of Mark*, 491.

was about to give birth, so that when she gave birth he might devour [*kataphagē*] her child (Rev 12:4).

And they came up on the broad plain of the earth and surrounded the camp of the saints and the beloved city, and fire came down from heaven and devoured [*katephage*] them (Rev 20:9).

Jesus' use of this term indicates that the duplicitous scribes and the corrupt estate-management and religious system had rendered the widow's assets completely consumed.[26] She is left devastated by the very hands of those who were to protect her and who were to speak on her behalf.

Often much is made of the coinage in the story (v. 42). Many assume, too quickly, that the widow's offering is placed "voluntary" in one of the thirteen trumpet-shaped vessels used to receive the various offerings by those entering the temple courts. Some offerings were obligatory, related to the temple tax and sin offerings; some were free-will and contributions of charity. Nothing in the text necessitates that the widow's offering was voluntary. In fact, the scene and the wider context suggest that the two coins (*leptons*), which equaled a *quadran*, were more likely related to the temple tax or sin offering than to the voluntary free-will offering. The widow's offering was worth less than one hundredth of a *denarius* or one hundredth of a day's wage. This amount was capable of purchasing a "handful of flour."[27] According to OT Levitical provisions, if someone's *means are insufficient* for even the *two turtledoves or two young pigeons*, then a *tenth of an ephah of fine flour* may be substituted for the sin offering (Lev 5:11; 14:21–32). Interestingly, there is also evidence that some temple authorities had viewed the offering of flour with contempt:

> Once a woman brought a handful of fine flour, and the priest despised her, saying, "See what she offers! What is there in this to eat? What is there in this to offer up?" It was shown to him in a dream: "Do not despise her! It is regarded as if she had sacrificed her own life" (*Lev. Rab.* 3.5).

The presence of the two coins in the scene emphasizes the widow's condition of poverty and suggests her disadvantage (her standing or status) before the leaders in the temple courts, who were to be her advocates, but only had contempt for her.

---

26. Derrett, "'Eating Up the Houses of Widows'"; Smith, "Widow's Offering."
27. Evans, *Mark 8:27—16:20*, 283.

Wasted Evangelism

In addition to experiencing the loss of her spouse, making the widow one of the more vulnerable in Israel, she had been placed into this humiliating predicament by the established authorities and their banking system. The people and system had rendered her estate/house "devoured" by requiring the widow to contribute to that very system her remaining means (i.e., the last of her funds) to live. Jesus condemns the duplicitous temple leadership, their malicious behaviors (12:40c), and the temple system (13:2) that worsened the *poor widow*'s condition (12:44c) and left her resources now completely "devoured," which was represented in the *poor widow* giving her last two coins.[28]

"The widow" bracket[29]

Mark is known for his bracketing structures that help guide his readers/listeners through the narrative.[30] There is an overlooked bracket in the Jerusalem-temple entrance-exit segment of the Gospel (Mark 11–13). The maltreatment of *the widow* brackets Jesus' entrance into the temple area and his exit (Mark 11:11—13:2). These brackets can be seen in how the OT frames this segment of Mark's Gospel.

---

28. Wright, "Widow's Mite." Another possible reading for the contrast Jesus made between the surplus of the wealthy and the widow's last two coins might suggest that those with the surplus have an oblivious detachment (malicious or banal) from the plight of the *poor widow* whose life was about to be *devoured*—they have *surplus* and her whole life will be *devoured*—and that those who are called to observe the contrast (i.e., disciples and readers/listeners) are not to do the same.

29. Unless otherwise indicated, throughout this section *the widow* or simply *widow* is meant as a synecdoche, indicating the whole of vulnerable widows and, if the context allows, the larger group of vulnerable people: orphans, foreigners, the poor, the fatherless, etc.

30. Edwards, "Markan Sandwiches," 193–216.

Widows in our Courts (Mark 12:38-44)

Gospel of Mark 11-13: Jerusalem-Temple Entrance-Exit Segment	OT Framework	"the widow"
Jesus enters the temple (11:11)		
Cursing the fig-tree/overturning tables of commerce/the withered fig-tree (11:12-21)	Jer 7-8 Also: Lev 5:11 Lev 12:8 Lev 14:22, 30	"Do not trust in deceptive words, saying, 'This is the temple of the Lord, the temple of the Lord, the temple of the Lord.' For if you truly amend your ways and your deeds, if you truly practice justice between a man and his neighbor, if you do not oppress the alien, the orphan, or the widow, and do not shed innocent blood in this place, nor walk after other gods to your own ruin, then I will let you dwell in this place, in the land that I gave to your fathers forever and ever. Behold, you are trusting in deceptive words to no avail" (Jer 7:4-8).
Jesus warns of scribes (12:38-44)		
Beware duplicitous scribes who devour widow's houses/the poor widow put in all she owned (12:38-44)	Exod 22:22-24 Also: Deut 14:28-29 Deut 24:19-21 Lev 19:9-10 Lev 23:22	"You shall not afflict any widow or orphan. If you afflict him at all, and if he does cry out to Me, I will surely hear his cry; and My anger will be kindled, and I will kill you with the sword, and your wives shall become widows and your children fatherless" (Exod 22:22-24).
The temple destroyed (13:1-2)	Mal 3:1-5	"'Then I will draw near to you for judgment; and I will be a swift witness against the sorcerers and against the adulterers and against those who swear falsely, and against those who oppress the wage earner in his wages, the widow and the orphan, and those who turn aside the alien and do not fear Me,' says the Lord of hosts" (Mal 3:5).

Through this bracket we find an underlying theme: the impoverished *widow*. The Mark 12 poor widow episode is intentionally crafted into a storyline that begins with the cursing of a fig-tree (11:12-14, 19-20); then, leads immediately into the overturning tables of commerce in the Court of the Gentiles (11:15-17); and, then, ends with the promised destruction of the temple (13:1-2). The actions of Jesus in this segment are "consistent with the classic tradition of Israel's prophets, who criticized the political and religious policies of the nation's leaders."[31] Jesus' words and activities in Mark 11–13 are calculated to imply OT prophecy was being fulfilled right before their eyes. The *Lord* had come *suddenly*[32] into his temple (Mark 11:1–11).[33] The people had welcomed him gladly. The leaders, however, were not prepared; they were even absent at his appearance.[34] After a series of conflict scenes in Mark 11–12,[35] Mark ends the Jerusalem-temple entrance-exit segment with Jesus announcing that *not one stone* of the temple *will be left upon another* (13:2c) and, then, he leaves the temple, never to return.

As the table above shows, *the widow* is embedded throughout this section in key events. When Jesus had interrupted the commerce in the Court of the Gentiles (Mark 11:15–18), reference is made to Jeremiah's temple sermon (Jer 7):

> And He began to teach and say to them, "Is it not written, 'My house shall be called a house of prayer for all the nations'? But you have made it a robbers' den" (Mark 11:17).

The indictment comes from Jeremiah 7:11 in which Yahweh declares that his house/temple had *become a den of robbers*. The preceding context (Jer 7:4–8) indicates the foundation for the charge (v. 11) and offers a fuller background to evaluate the significance of the thread of conflicts in Mark 11–12, as well as the presence of the economically vulnerable widow (12:41–44) in the temple courts and her presence behind the temple-threat (13:2). In the Jeremiah context, the *widow* is present (as well as *the alien* and *the orphan*) as the nation of Israel is called to repentance, a return to Exodus covenant land-laws (e.g., Exod 22:22–24; Lev 19:9–10; 23:22; Deut 14:28–29; 24:19–21) that would forestall judgment on the temple:

> Do not trust in deceptive words, saying, "This is the temple of the Lord, the temple of the Lord, the temple of the Lord." For if you truly amend your ways and your deeds, if you truly practice justice between a man and his neighbor, if you do not oppress the alien,

---

31. Evans, *Mark 8:27—16:20*, 182.

32. I take the term *suddenly* to mean "unexpectedly," as if unprepared.

33. In Mark's opening (1:1–3), he begins with this same Malachi reference (Mal 3:1), which implicitly warns of the Lord's *sudden* coming to his temple. See chapter 2, "Wasted Evangelism," for more elaboration on the Malachi 3 reference.

34. Watts, *Isaiah's New Exodus*, 315.

35. Watts notes that the "controversy stories of 2:1—3:6 resemble those in 12:13–44" (*Isaiah's New Exodus*, 133).

the orphan, or <u>the widow</u>, and do not shed innocent blood in this place, nor walk after other gods to your own ruin, then I will let you dwell in this place, in the land that I gave to your fathers forever and ever. Behold, you are trusting in deceptive words to no avail (Jer 7:4–8).

Israelite leadership had a false sense of security. They had ignored the covenant warnings (e.g., Exod 22:22–24). Yet, despite their neglect of Torah land-stipulations regarding the care of the impoverished and their disregard for justice, the leaders believed the temple would receive special protection from God's judgment because it was his dwelling (Jer 7:4–8). Such faith was misplaced and *to no avail* (Jer 7:8) for the temple will be destroyed (Jer 7:12–15; Mal 3:1–5; Mark 13:2). Additionally, the OT reference in Mark 11:17 also reflects Isaiah 56:7 (*My house will be called a house of prayer for all the peoples*) in which the prophet exhorted, *Preserve justice and do righteousness* because Yahweh's *salvation is about to come* and *His righteousness to be revealed* (56:1). Yet the prophetic voice goes unheeded (note 56:10–12).

The *widow* connection is further confirmed by Mark's reference to *selling doves* as part of the description of the "buying and selling in the temple" (11:15).[36] Mark draws upon the maltreatment of the poor through an obvious OT reference to a Levitical provision for the impoverished:

> But if he cannot afford a lamb, then he shall bring to the Lord his guilt offering for that in which he has sinned, two turtledoves or two young pigeons, one for a sin offering and the other for a burnt offering (Lev 5:7).

Could it be that Jesus is condemning the "concept of a Temple tax"?[37] Robert Gundry infers as much when he writes regarding the table-turning scene:

> The sellers sell sacrificial animals guaranteed to be clean to pilgrims who live too far away to bring their own and to locals who do not want to risk having their own animals declared unclean by priestly inspectors. The moneychangers give acceptable Tyrian currency for other currencies in order that worshipers may pay the temple tax and buy sacrificial animals (*m. Seqal.* 1:3, 47–8; 5:3–5 *et passim*). Doves are sold to worshipers who cannot afford animals (Lev 1:14; 5:7, 11; 12:6, 8).[38]

36. Note Lev 5:11; 12:8; 14:22 (a poor leper!); 14:30.
37. Watts, *Isaiah's New Exodus*, 326.
38. Gundry, *Mark*, 636.

Mark certainly implies that Jesus has something against the activities taking place in the temple courts and their effect on the economically vulnerable, for there is a clear link between the poor and Jesus' living parable of judgment (i.e., overturning the tables). The overturning tables event, along with the disturbing scene of the Mark 12 *poor widow* left devastated at the hands of the scribes, was part of an elaborate commerce-banking system that was taking advantage of the poor.

The cursing of the fig-tree brackets the scene of Jesus overturning the tables. But why does Jesus curse a fruitless fig-tree that was not in season anyway? There are two aspects of this scene that are helpful for our discussion of the duplicitous scribes and the Mark 12 poor widow. First, the scene fits the OT expectations that the *Lord* would arrive *suddenly* ("unexpectedly") at his temple (Mal 3:1). R. T. France and Rikki Watts recognize this potential in the cursing of the fig-tree, namely that it mimics the entry of Jesus into Jerusalem in which his "initial visit to the temple has found all leaves, but no fruit."[39] France puts it: "A tree in full leaf at Passover season is making a promise it cannot fulfill; so, too, is Israel."[40] The fig-tree—overturning tables—fig-tree sandwich parallels the final episode in which Jesus warns of duplicitous scribes:

A	B	C	D
11:11	11:12–14	11:15–17	11:20
Jesus arrives at the temple	Curses fig-tree	Judgment—overturning of the tables	The fig-tree is withered/destroyed
12:34	12:38–44	13:1–2	Future time
Jesus teaches in the temple	Condemns scribes	Judgment—*no stone left on another*	Future destruction of the temple

---

39. France, *Gospel of Mark*, 441; also Watts, *Isaiah's New Exodus*, 315.

40. France, *Gospel of Mark*, 441.

Widows in our Courts (Mark 12:38-44)

The closing fig-tree bracket—*the fig-tree withered from the roots up*, 11:20—indicates that the table-turning was judgment and a harbinger to the eventual destruction of the temple as Jesus affirms and foretells (13:2).

Second, the fig-tree scene is also an allusion, if not a direct referent to Jeremiah 8:13:

> "I will surely snatch them away,"
> declares the Lord;
> "There will be no grapes on the vine
> And no figs on the fig tree,
> And the leaf will wither;
> And what I have given them will pass away."

Watts demonstrates that the fig-tree episode is closely linked to the table-turning scene in that Jesus' OT references are in close proximity. He notes that the cursing of the fig-tree is "a dramatic invocation" of Jeremiah 7–8. Moreover, the prophetic words of judgment are acted out as a living parable when Jesus overturns the tables in the temple courts, which points to the temple's end.[41] The enactment is complete when the fig-tree, afterward, is *withered from the roots up* (Mark 11:20b), which prophetically ensures the temple's eventual demise. To make the Jeremiah 7–8 correspondence to Mark's Jerusalem-temple entrance-exit segment more vivid, it is interesting to note that Jeremiah even adds an indictment against scribes:

> How can you say, "We are wise,
> And the law of the Lord is with us"?
> But behold, the lying pen of the scribes
> Has made it into a lie (Jer 8:8).

The *chief priests and the scribes* (Mark 11:18a) found themselves the targets of Jesus' indictments and the object of his judgment parables (activities). They understood his action-parable, for they *began seeking how to destroy Him* (11:18b; note 3:6; 12:12). Yet, ironically, Jesus will soon make the same predication of the temple (13:2).[42] (Note the pattern set out by Mark in the grid above.)

Finally, the closing *widow*-bracket is Jesus' exit from the temple (13:1–2) in which there is an OT referent that includes *the widow*. Following the warning about duplicitous scribes (12:38–40) and the observation

---

41. Watts, *Isaiah's New Exodus*, 317–18.
42. France, *Gospel of Mark*, 446; also note the impact of the parable given in Mark 12:1–12.

regarding the *poor widow* (vv. 41–44), Jesus, then, declares that judgment would befall the temple (13:2). Here in the final scene, Mark ends the Jerusalem-temple entrance-exit segment (Mark 11–13) with a link to the Malachi 3 threat. First, the Lord had come *suddenly* ("unexpectedly") to his temple, bringing judgment (portrayed in the judgment-action-parables).[43] We read in Malachi:

> "Behold, I am going to send My messenger, and he will clear the way before Me and the Lord, whom you seek, will suddenly come to His temple; and the messenger of the covenant, in whom you delight, behold, He is coming," says the Lord of hosts (Mal 3:1).

Second, *the widow* is in close proximity to this announcement of judgment, which provides a basis for the Malachi threat (3:1), that is, the reason the temple will be destroyed:

> "Then I will draw near to you for judgment; and I will be a swift witness against the sorcerers and against the adulterers and against those who swear falsely, and against those who oppress the wage earner in his wages, the widow and the orphan, and those who turn aside the alien and do not fear Me," says the Lord of hosts (Mal 3:5).

The Malachi threat is related to the maltreatment of *the widow* (i.e., not fulfilling the covenant land-laws of Exodus toward the economically vulnerable), thus clearly signifying Mark's intention for drawing upon the *poor widow* in Mark 12 just prior to Jesus' pronouncement of judgment on the temple (13:2).

The association between Mark 11–13 and the Malachi 3 threat is made more poignant to the reader/listener, for in the wider context of Malachi's prophetic pronouncement there are charges against the leadership of Israel. They have disregarded God's "statutes" (Mal 3:7; also 4:4). They are charged with "robbing" God through the misappropriation of temple tithes and offerings (Mal 3:8–9). Interestingly, the temple authorities who were to receive the tithes and offerings were to share it with *the widow*:

> When you have finished paying all the tithe of your increase in the third year, the year of tithing, then you shall give it to the Levite, to the stranger, to the orphan and to the widow, that they may eat

---

43. Danker, "Double-entendre in Mark XII 9," 162–63; Watts, *Isaiah's New Exodus*, 315.

in your towns and be satisfied (Deut 26:12; also note 14:29; Lev 27:30).

"Robbing God" was related to the misuse of *the widow*'s share of the tithe—a state of affairs similarly portrayed in the Mark 12 poor widow episode.

The subtle incorporation of *the widow* into the Mark 11–13 narrative confronts the reader/listener with the OT promise-threats of judgment on those who do not care and advocate for the poor: *the widow*'s presence is set within scenes of Jesus overturning the tables; she is behind the cursing of the fig-tree; and, she is prophetically tied to Jesus' comments regarding the eventual destruction of the temple. This string of *widow*-allusions is made concrete and personal when she is identified amid the duplicitous scribes in the temple courts (Mark 12:42). The *widow* context represents a serious breach of covenant-keeping. The violation of explicit land-laws and her presence throughout the Jerusalem-temple entrance-exit segment (i.e. the judgment-parable scenes of overturned-tables and the cursing of the fig-tree, the climactic poor widow scene of chapter 12, and the Malachi threat at the temple) indicate the final nail in the coffin for Israel, the result of extensive and continuous disobedience. This is the significance of the Mark 12 *poor widow vs. duplicitous scribes* episode, which presents a negative interpretation (i.e., a warning to beware) and should cause concern for us on this side of the story as we consider how this text offers a paradigm for Christian discipleship.

AWAKEN TO THE ADVOCACY ROLE IN A CHURCH'S DISCIPLESHIP

Gospel narrative is not merely informational in nature; it is meant to move an audience to respond. Mark expected his readers/listeners, that is, the community of believers, to respond to his Gospel—to hear and be affected by the stories and teachings and events that shape his narrative. This is equally true regarding the Mark 12 scene under discussion. The *greater condemnation* (12:40)[44] of the temple establishment and the end of the temple (i.e., its destruction, 13:2) should not be dismissed as mere historical information or relevant only to the Israel of old. Mark crafts his narrative in such a way that pulls his readers/listeners into the story so they would hear

---

44. Mark uses *krima* here, which means *judgment* and is most likely drawn from the Malachi reference (Mal 3:5).

that their end can have a similar outcome if they are likewise unprepared, for they, too, *do not know when the master of the house is coming* (Mark 13:35).[45]

The warning to *beware* of duplicitous scribes is soon followed by Jesus' disciples pointing out the "wonderful stones" and "wonderful buildings" of the temple (13:1). It is to this which Jesus replies, "Not one stone will be left upon another" (13:2). This is ironic and disappointing. The disciples didn't get it; they had missed the point. They have not been listening—a dangerous place to be, for this is the OT charge against Israel's unprepared leadership.[46] Yet all readers/listeners are to guard against their own unpreparedness at the (re)appearance of the Master of the house.

> "Therefore, be on the alert—for you do not know when the master of the house is coming, whether in the evening, at midnight, or when the rooster crows, or in the morning—in case he should come suddenly [*elthōn exaiphnēs*] and find you asleep. What I say to you I say to all, 'Be on the alert!'" (Mark 13:35–37).

Jesus' words and Mark's use of the discourse seem intentionally calculated to draw future readers/listeners into the story, commanding their readiness, their preparedness to be "caught" doing the will of the Master (13:28–37; note 3:35). It is not coincidental that Jesus uses wording reminiscent of Malachi's threat that the *Lord of hosts* would *suddenly come* (*exaiphnēs ēxei*, Mal 3:1 LXX; note Mark 13:37 above) to his temple, bringing judgment (Mal 3:1–5).[47] Those who will fall before his righteous anger are the leaders *who oppress . . . the widows* (Mal 3:5)—the very background embedded into the Jerusalem-temple entrance-exit segment (i.e., the Mark 11–13 context.).

Unlike the temple establishment, the readers/listeners on this side of the story need to be prepared for his sudden (re)appearance (*let the reader understand*, Mark 13:14b; note also 13:35–37). Like the duplicitous scribes and unprepared temple leadership in the days of Messiah's first appearance, there will also be fraudulent messiahs and deceptive prophets who will seek to cause stumbling and disobedience among the elect (Mark 13:3–37).

---

45. The drawing in of the readers/listeners can also be seen in the "hardening" texts directed at the disciples (Mark 6:51–52; 8:14–21).

46. See Watts, *Isaiah's New Exodus*, 311–37.

47. A link between Mark 11:1—13:36 and the Mal 3 threat is also seen with the appearance of the Mal 3:1 "messenger" in Mark's Gospel (*My messenger*, 1:2) and, as well, the question regarding John the Baptist in the Mark 11–13 context, specifically in Mark 11:30–32.

Nonetheless, despite the opposition, conflicts, and obstacles between the first and future appearances of Jesus, the church is called to awaken from sleep (i.e., its lulled complacency), remain always alert, and live out faithful obedience (13:33–37). As the Mark 13 discourse suggests the Christian community will continue experiencing the conflict between the old age and its structures and the inauguration of the new age. Yet, the church is reminded that they will *always have the poor* in their midst (Mark 14:7). In light of the Mark 12 poor widow episode (12:38–44) and the wider embedded *widow*-background (11–13), there is good reason to integrate advocacy and social action on behalf of the poor into our own patterns of church discipleship while we await the return of the Master of the house (13:35).

Jesus' warning (*beware, blepō*, 12:38) against duplicitous scribes (12:38–40) and, then, calling attention to the presence of the *poor widow* (vv. 41–44) imply a negative, rather than a positive, paradigm for Christian discipleship. The "negative" implication is not surprising, for the poor widow scene (12:38–44) is followed by a series of "be on guard," "watch," and "take heed" exhortations in Mark 13, all using the same word, *blepō* (*see*, vv. 2, 5; *be on guard*, v. 9; *take head*, vv. 23, 33). In this case, Christians should beware and guard against religious structures and habits that contribute to the causes of poverty—this "application" seems appropriate and analogous in light of Mark's embedded *widow* references throughout the Jerusalem-temple entrance-exit segment of his Gospel narrative (11–13) and, in particular, the Mark 12 poor widow episode. It seems reasonable that acting as an advocate for the poor in the public square would offer constructive patterns of discipleship that would guard against the warning and implications of *the poor widow vs. duplicitous scribes* episode, while also fulfilling expectations inherent in the gospel.[48]

Our ways of doing church are not neutral

In light of *the poor widow vs. duplicitous scribes* episode, church leaders should, at least, question who benefits and who does not benefit from current church structures and bureaucracies (i.e., church life and function). The building-centered and business-centric models that most contemporary church-systems emulate can result in duplicitous habits, which can be suggestive of a protective posture for its leaders and for the cultural

---

48. This is the very aspect of the gospel that I will argue for throughout the next 5 studies/chapters in this volume.

status-quo. Our ways of doing church are not neutral. The temple system and its leadership, as the conflict stories in Mark indicate, were antithetical to the arrival of the kingdom that had been inaugurated by Jesus' arrival.[49] Perhaps it is not the construction of temples or the development of religious bureaucracies per se, but the energy and resources used to maintain these systems that promote the status of their own authorities and stakeholders, which can distract (to put it blandly) from a church's responsibility toward the poor. Rather than laboring to maintain current church systems and structures, contemporary church leaders need to promote the church's responsibilities to the poor. Otherwise, they may replicate the social and cultural location described in Mark 12:38–44.

The cost of doing church business and maintaining church bureaucracies are not neutral to the church's role as advocates for the poor. This includes the allocation of human, financial, and social capital available in and through a church or a consortium of churches for use in the public square. Such allocations of financial and human capital could be used for advocating and caring for the economically vulnerable and the poor. The resources and capacity of the local church need to be evaluated, not by our contemporary cultural expressions of church life, but in terms of the kingdom of God, which certainly includes addressing the causes of poverty and advocating for the poor.

Andrew Davey, in his book *Urban Christianity and Global Order*, insists that a church concerned about "its own sustainability must have strategies other than the growth paradigm."[50] Contemporary church growth models are multimillion-dollar business ventures with huge marketing campaigns and an elite celebrity leadership of its own that promote costly expectations for a local church. There should be consideration whether such growth expectations divert resources and human capital away from a church's responsibilities regarding the poor. While a church's sustainability should be directed outward and toward the future, it should also have positive, redemptive consequences for the community, with special consideration for its vulnerable populations.

Readers/listeners on this side of the text are not only urban[51] congregations that have a natural association with vulnerable populations, but

---

49. Sugirtharajah, "Widow's Mite Revisited"; also see chapter 4, "A Prelude to Judgment," for an analysis of the Mark 2:1—3:6 conflict thread.

50. Davey, *Urban Christianity*, 112.

51. The principles and significance concluded from this study, as well as the remaining

Widows in our Courts (Mark 12:38-44)

suburban and exurban church communities, as well, stand before the Mark 12 *poor widow vs. duplicitous scribes* episode. Churches located outside of urban settings are not exempt from being readers/listeners of this story because they are removed from urban poverty. In fact the suburban and exurban church's departure and distance from poverty might actually be a cause of poverty. Suburban churches should consider whether they are participating in the same socio-economic system that has removed social, financial, and human capital from the social service, housing, labor, healthcare, and workforce development systems that should be available to the poor in urban centers.[52]

The Mark 12:38-44 episode does not contrast the conduct of the scribes with the supposed faith of a *poor widow*. Rather it exemplifies how religious appearances can mask duplicity and camouflage defective systems that can actually cause poverty and/or perpetuate it. Jesus was condemning a religious and civic system that had lost its redemptive reason for existence. He also called out its duplicitous leaders who had developed a religious and social structure that shaped behavioral values that actually contributed to the conditions of the poor.[53] In his commentary on this passage, Ched Myers writes:

> The temple has robbed this woman of her very means of livelihood (12:44). Like the scribal class, it no longer protects widows, but exploits them. As if in disgust, Jesus "exits" the temple—for the final time (13:1a).[54]

As contemporary readers/listeners to *the poor widow vs. duplicitous scribes* episode, a local congregation ought to question whether its current organizational bureaucracy (i.e., a church's structures and system, that is, the way it works) and its resultant habits and behavioral values reflected by its leaders and members contribute to the causes of poverty, or whether they promote advocacy for the poor.

---

studies in this volume, are applied to and focused on urban, suburban, and exurban demographics; however, they may be applied and adapted to our rural and country areas as well as they relate to the issues of poverty and the church's association to the poor.

52. See chapter 5, "Idolatry and Poverty."
53. Myers, *Binding the Strong Man*, 262, also 321.
54. Ibid., 322.

Discipleship demands a self-less public advocacy dimension

The faith community is publically relevant, not when it acts as a critic of societal patterns, but when it engages in advancing positive and adequate alternatives to public issues. The question is, to borrow from Richard John Neuhaus, "no longer about relevance but about relevance *to what* and *toward what end*."[55] A church's public voice must promote the interests of more than its own membership for it to actually be a public voice.[56] Raymond Knighton, in his report on the "Social Responsibility of Evangelization" to the 1974 Lausanne Committee for World Evangelism, alluded to what Colin Morris wrote in *Include Me Out*: "If the church turns a blind eye to the injustices around it, the world will turn a deaf ear to everything else the church tries to say."[57] Knighton concluded that "[s]ocial action is simply obedience to the command of God" and is part of the evangelizing task of the church. Os Guinness, in his report to the same committee on "Social Responsibility," rebuffed the church's tendency to concentrate on minor and private issues to the "virtual ignoring of major principles and issues" related to justice, mercy, violence, race, and poverty.[58] Elsewhere Guinness wrote that the "highest American good is more than the struggle over who gets what, when, and how."[59] A worthy thought that confronts the local church. Too often involvement in the public square for the church is limited to issues that threaten its existence, comfort, and the status quo.

To advocate for others is to speak on their behalf and for their interests, and sometimes at the expense of one's own self-interests (including a congregation's own self-interests). Discipleship that intentionally moves the church into the public square can guard against the perils of self-interest that seek to protect the status quo of its own "religious system" and its established authorities. In light of the church's intrinsic biblical association with the poor and its accompanying responsibility to care for the vulnerable, it is essential for discipleship to have a dimension of public advocacy. Discipleship that advocates for the interests of the poor rather than its own

---

55. Neuhaus, *Naked Public Square*, 42–43; my emphasis.

56. Ibid., 27, also 36.

57. Knighton, "Social Responsible," a paper presented at the 1974 Lausanne Conference on World Evangelism, published in *Let the Earth Hear His Voice*, 710–12.

58. Guinness, "Evangelicals Among Thinking People" a paper presented at the 1974 Lausanne Conference on World Evangelism, published in *Let the Earth Hear His Voice*, 713–15.

59. Guinness, *American Hour*, 154.

Widows in our Courts (Mark 12:38-44)

sustainability is a faithful application of the Mark 12 *poor widow vs. duplicitous scribes* episode.

When a church affirms its relationship to Jesus Christ as the Lord over every sphere of life, this should thrust the church outward into the public square. However, faith and church life for much of the evangelical church is turned inward, experiencing Christianity in individualistic terms and within the self-interests of its members, which narrows the patterns and activities for discipleship. From this perspective, church-life becomes privatized and vague, and society at large becomes invisible.[60] The presence of the conservative church in the political arena and in the public square, however, does not necessarily reflect "a shift from a protective goal to a redemptive goal but an increase in the perceived level of threat."[61] A renewed attention by the evangelical church to the public square can actually represent an increased desire to protect the church's status-quo in American life. The injustices in the public square that are of interest to conservative church congregations are often those which are perceived as threats to their privatized lifestyles, economic comfort, and theological plausibility. In other words, injustices that are not "personally threatening" can receive "much less of their attention."[62]

Keeping it local; creating new listeners[63]

Robert Chambers wrote that "poverty is entanglement," that is, the poor are caught in a web of relationships—some by design (social and political sin), some from personal failure (adamic and personal sin), some by inheritance (intergenerational poverty), and some because of structural limitations (institutional sin)—that cause community and personal poverty.[64] The causes of poverty can be personal, social, or structural. The poor will find the potential to be freed from poverty when all causes are addressed. This is the task of advocating for the vulnerable and the reason for a church's intentional participation in social action on behalf of those living with the effects

---

60. Budziszewski, *Evangelicals in the Public Square*, 17.
61. Ibid., 46.
62. Ibid.
63. "Listener" listed alone indicates those who hear the gospel and are outside of the church community.
64. See Christian's *God of the Empty-Handed* for a review of the causes of poverty from a Christian perspective.

of poverty. The church that incorporates a truly public dimension into its pattern of discipleship surrenders its need to maintain and protect its status quo and its established leadership. It is now free to focus its resources, energies, and habits toward the needs of the economically vulnerable. This kind of discipleship imitates the Head of the church and demonstrates the presence of the gospel of the kingdom rather than affirming patterns of behavior and systems that simply maintain church structures that might be harmful to the economically vulnerable (e.g., Mark 12:38–44).

The *poor widow* episode, informed by the surrounding narrative, should shape a local church's patterns and activities of discipleship (i.e., its church life and, in particular, the behavior and values of its leadership). This is significant, for there is an emphasis, today, on pushing social issues, concerns, and solutions toward local public squares and smaller institutions. It has been acknowledged that smaller-scale institutions are needed at the local level, for this allows ordinary citizens to participate in issues facing the community around them in meaningful and safe spaces.[65] This is an opportune time for the local church to adopt a more gospel-centered discipleship that focuses the congregation outward, making itself available to serve in the public square.[66]

Most church-centered charitable activities concentrate on small-scale, tangible, short-term effects "rather than those that are ongoing, extensive, and directed at underlying causes of social problems."[67] Assessing a community's needs, especially as they relate to vulnerable populations, and making an audit of available community resources are a good place to start in making a church's discipleship reflect its advocacy responsibilities toward the poor. However, ameliorating immediate needs (as important as that may be) is only a beginning. Beyond that, a church's discipleship pattern should include taking action (i.e., social action) that seeks to alleviate the causes of poverty and move people (individuals and families) out of poverty, first in the local context, but also extending to the wider

---

65. Stockwell, "Cathedrals of Power," 80–93.

66. Studies suggest and government policies recognize that community-based organizations, including faith-based organizations, are in "the best position to allow citizens to rediscover their power, define their dream, and work out strategies so that such dreams can become realizable." But, this acknowledgement implies partnerships with local stakeholders and the use of government and, as well as, private resources (Stockwell, "Cathedrals of Power," 92).

67. Baggett, "Congregations and Civil Society," 425–54; also see Fuder and Castellanos, eds. *A Heart for the Community* and Lupton, *Toxic Charity*.

community and, even, global contexts.[68] Such advocacy and social action on behalf of the poor is a just and faithful application of the significance of the *poor widow vs. duplicitous scribes* episode. Church leadership should create discipleship patterns that promote the availability of a church's or a church consortium's social capital[69] (e.g., member-volunteers, financial and space resources, and social support network) to entities and non-profits that are involved in the social service and workforce development network in the local and wider community.

A public advocacy dimension of discipleship is not intended to recruit new church members, but it does enable new listeners to hear the gospel story. When a congregation or church consortium connects its social capital and resources to the wider community, such action pulls others outside of the membership into the story and, thus, creates new listeners. Such a view of discipleship allows the invading kingdom of the gospel, that is, the rule and reign of God in Christ to influence, not only the poor in the church's midst, but also municipal leaders, social service leadership and workers, local non-profits, area Workforce Investment Boards, politicians, and other community stakeholders.

POSTSCRIPT—DO NOT SQUANDER THE OPPORTUNITY TO GIVE LIFE TO THE WIDOW

How we hear this story of duplicitous scribes and a *poor widow* will make us good or poor readers/listeners, which will have a bearing on how a church understands the biblical nature of Christian discipleship. Questions arise from the story: *Who will save this widow? Who will come and stand between this widow and the cause of her poverty? Who will make a way to restore her? Who will give her life so she does not have to give her whole life?*

To read this text and see the widow as an example of Christian devotion and sacrificial giving is to limit our view of the situation encountered in the Mark 12 poor widow passage, which can distract a church from being shaped into the community Mark is imagining through his Gospel narrative. Such a reading minimizes the significance of a story about how,

---

68. See Mae Cannon's *Social Justice Handbook* for a catalog and review of various justice and anti-poverty related ministries and organizations that a church or consortium of churches can participate.

69. See Cnaan's *The Invisible Caring Hand* for a good discussion regarding the definition of social capital as it relates to church-life and social action, 261–75.

at the least, misplaced religious values, and, at worst, fraud, deception, and greed can cause a person's poverty and can enable that condition to continue. It will take God's judgment against the enablers of her impoverishment (12:40) and against the system that perpetuates it (13:2) to remove the causes of this widow's poverty. This episode is a part of God's Word to the church, thus Christ's decisive action not only redeems the widow's plight, the story's significance ought to move the church into the public sphere: God in Christ will bring about a new social order of justice and righteousness (i.e., the inaugural presence of the kingdom)[70] through the creation of a new people shaped by a discipleship that incorporates advocacy for the poor.

In *The American Hour*, Os Guinness argues for the necessary and important role of faith in the American public square. He writes:

> At stake are the authorities and moral assumptions that will prove decisive in shaping the public and private lives of Americans, and thus in determining how America tackles its lengthening list of serious problems.[71]

In order for a local evangelical church to have an authoritative, moral voice in the public square on the serious problems facing our society, it needs to be perceived, not as a special interest group or self-interested political voting base, but rather as a community that puts the interests of others above its own (Phil 2:3–4). Its voice cannot enter the public square solely to discuss social matters on "the basis of private truths"[72] designed to protect a congregation's (i.e., its members') cultural status and private lifestyles. For the church to have a public voice that affects the public square with kingdom values, it needs to have public *actions* that demonstrate the interests of the community and, in particular, *actions* that reflect advocacy and social action on behalf of the poor.

There will be expected tensions in advocating for the poor in the public square, including opposition from within and from outside the church community. The political process is rarely comfortable for those with deep, conservative biblical convictions and is often beset with estranged alliances

---

70. Interestingly, I made this conclusion before I made a similar exegetical observation regarding the meaning of the term "fishers of men" used in Mark 1:17. See chapter 3 for a fuller explanation of the Mark 1:17 *fisher*-promise and its implications for the church and its role in social action.

71. Guinness, *American Hour*, 4.

72. Neuhaus, *Naked Public Square*, 36.

Widows in our Courts (Mark 12:38–44)

and awkward compromises. Additionally, the very poor we seek to serve will not always appreciate or rise up to the advocacy afforded to them.[73] Nonetheless, as Dietrich Bonhoeffer said, we need to "smudge" ourselves with "the hard complexities of the world."[74]

The church's current social and cultural location and, as well, the surrounding contemporary political realities present the church with great opportunities in the public square to fulfill its role as advocates for the poor. We, however, should be mindful of the reprimand Guinness directs toward the Christian community his *The Last Christian on Earth* (formerly entitled *The Gravedigger File*):

> We are at the point where there may actually be more Christians in America than ever before, with more money at their disposal, more powerful technologies to use, more positions of national influence to fill, and a global opportunity with which to respond. But with corruptions from within, the opportunities will be squandered. With many Christians little or no different from their "pagan neighbors," much of American Christendom is more modern and more American than it is any longer decisively Christian.[75]

Today, it is lamentable to see *the widows* in our courts amid such wealth and resources (i.e., church-based social, financial, and human capital). We, too, can fail to notice there is tragedy happening, today, right before our own eyes. Church discipleship, shaped by *the poor widow vs. duplicitous scribes* episode, should reflect the kingly proverb:

> Open your mouth for the mute,
> For the rights of all the unfortunate.
> Open your mouth, judge righteously,
> And defend the rights of the afflicted and needy (Proverbs 31:8–9).

---

73. As with the aim of the theory of religion and politics, discipleship that incorporates advocacy for the poor in the public square does not necessarily do away with the tension, but should create solutions that recognize and accommodate the tensions in order for the poor to find relief, dignity, self-sufficiency, and, ultimately, a restored God-image (see Conchran, "Sacramental Theology").

74. Elshtain's "Afterward" in *Evangelicals in the Public Square* by Budziszewski, 197.

75. Guinness, *Last Christian on Earth*, 55.

2

Wasted Evangelism (Mark 4)
Social Action Outcomes and the Church's Task of Evangelism

"In the *corpus christianum* the different tasks of the community were distributed between state, society, family and church. As the *corpus christianum* decays, the congregation will again recollect the wealth of its own charismata and thrust forward to the total testimony of salvation which leaves no sphere of life without hope, from faith to politics, and from politics to economics."

—Jürgen Moltmann, *The Church in the Power of the Spirit*

"It may be an overstatement that almost all contemporary study of Mark 4 is an attempt to reign in a narrative too difficult to control—but if overstated, it is not far off the mark."

—Donald Juel, *A Master of Surprise*

"If the land is not to be wrongly handled, the king must remember barrenness and birth, slavery and freedom, hunger and manna, and above all the speeches at the boundary."

—WALTER BRUEGGEMANN, *THE LAND*

A NUMBER OF YEARS ago my pastor had a great idea to get people to come to church. One Sunday morning he asked us to list on the 3 x 5 card in our bulletin topics that our friends would like to hear. He was planning a "relevant and practical" sermon series during the evening services. The pastor hoped the topics would interest our non-churched friends if there were some "practical" value to them. This was a no-brainer for me, so, without hesitation, I wrote down "workforce development" and "poverty," topics that would interest *my* friends.

Some weeks later, I asked the pastor if he had seen my 3 x 5 card. He acknowledged he saw my topics and then made this comment, "That's *your* area." For sure, these areas are *mine* in the sense that for the last sixteen years I have been a grant writer and a planner for a number of social service agencies, particularly two Community Action Agencies, whose mission is to alleviate the causes of poverty and move families toward self-sufficiency. At that moment, I realized I needed to develop my own "theory of evangelism" as it relates to the Christian faith and issues like "workforce development" and "poverty."

The pastor's comment to me was in line with a history of dissonance over the church's social responsibilities and how the Bible speaks to issues of poverty. For the last century and a half there has been a rather impassioned debate and divide among evangelicals on these subjects. This dispute plays a major part in George Mardsen's renowned *Fundamentalism and American Culture*, originally published in 1980.[1] Perhaps as an outcome of the 1960s Jesus movement, the 70s and early 80s reflected a renewed interest in the subject of Christianity and social responsibility. Through intellectual associations and convening bodies, evangelicals wrestled with the relationship of salvation and evangelism to social responsibilities and the poor.[2]

---

1. Marsden, *Fundamentalism and American Culture*; also Henry, *Uneasy Conscience*.

2. E.g., Douglas, ed., *Let the Earth Hear*; Moberg, *Great Reversal*; Stott, *Christian Mission*; Henry, *Politics for Evangelicals*; Nicholls, ed., *Word and Deed*; also, Neuhaus, *Naked Public Square*; also, Richardson, *Social Action vs. Evangelism*; and more recently, Schlossberg et al., eds., *Christianity and Economics*.

Wasted Evangelism

Christians, today, cannot avoid the renewed attention—in and outside the institutional church—given to issues of poverty[3] and the church's relationship to socio-economic structures.[4] This interest is everywhere—in the political arena (both among conservatives and liberals), among younger college graduates who ask, "How does your company serve the needs of the community?" when they consider job opportunities, and within the emergent community.[5]

It is time, again, for the Christian community to wrestle with the relationship between evangelism and social action[6] as the church seeks to be both biblical and socially relevant. Lacking, however, is a theory of evangelism that addresses the church and its social responsibilities.[7] Although a biblical theology for evangelism deserves to be more fully developed, the scope of this chapter will concentrate on the narrative role of Mark's parable of *the Sower who sows the word of the gospel* (Mark 4:3–8; 4:14, 33),[8] which offers a relevant text for defining evangelism that includes the plausibility of social action outcomes.

---

3. E.g., Cnaan, *Invisible Caring Hand*; *Newer Deal*; Christian, *God of the Empty-Handed*; Kahl, "Christian social doctrines and the welfare state"; "Religious Roots"; Metzger, *Consuming Jesus*; Myers, *Walking with the Poor*; Sider, *Just Generosity*; *Rich Christians*; *Scandal of the Evangelical Conscience*.

4. E.g., Baggett, "Congregations and Civil Society," 425–54; Budziszewski, ed., *Evangelicals in the Public Square*; Olasky, *Tragedy of American Compassion*; Salamon, *Partners in Public Service*; Stockwell, "Cathedrals of Power," 80–93; Sugirtharajah, ed., *Voices from the Margin*; Unruh and Sider, *Saving Souls*; Van Til, "Basic Sustenance," 441–66.

5. E.g., Kinnaman and Lyons, *unChristian*; McLaren, *Everything Must Change*; Samson and Samson, *Justice in the Burbs*.

6. See the introduction, "Evangelism and Social Action: An Exegetical Argument," for the relationship between evangelism and social action and, as well, for my working definition for "social action."

7. William Abraham offers a theory in his *Logic of Evangelism* in which he affirms the importance of an eschatological foundation for evangelism.

8. I refer to the Mark 4 parable (vv. 3–8, 14–20) as either the parable of *the Sower who sows* (4:3b) or the parable of *the Sower*. Whatever parts the *soil* and *seed* play, or their significance, *the Sower* is the central character. The parable does not begin, "There are seeds a sower sows," or "There is soil that is sown with seed"; but does begin, *Behold, the sower went out to sow* (4:3).

DEFINITION, GOALS, AND OUTCOMES & THE PARABLE OF THE SOWER WHO SOWS

In the field of social services, of which I am vocationally related, outcomes are an important element in determining what actions are needed. So, likewise with *evangelism*—if an outcome of evangelism is "personal decisions for Christ," then activities of soul-winning, witnessing, crusades, and salvation-centered preaching are reasonable; if numerical church-growth is the outcome, then activities that promote such "growth" are acceptable; and, as I will posit here, if addressing the issues of poverty and social-righteousness are outcomes, then social action is a valid evangelistic activity.

Those who have the highest interest in evangelism usually appear to be those least interested in "critical, theological reflection."[9] Since evangelism seems mostly self-evident, rarely is the subject examined or evaluated theologically, but consigned to matters of church praxis. This does not promote biblically relevant criteria to precede the discussion, and thus limits critical analysis, biblical evaluation, and creative thinking regarding evangelism.[10]

There is a tendency to define *evangelism* etymologically and stop there. Since the Greek noun *euaggelion* means "good news" and the Greek verb *euaggelizō* means "to proclaim the good news," evangelism, then, is simply "proclaiming the good news." With this *definition*, proclamation-centered activities are *the* valid forms of evangelism: Preaching, teaching, witnessing, or sharing a testimony. The hoped for outcomes of a proclamation-centered evangelism are individual-centered and number-oriented: confessions of faith, increased church attendance, etc. However, does the Gospel narrative itself allow this definition to go unchallenged?

The narrow, proclamation-centered definition only succeeds if solely based on word-studies and isolated proof-texts. It is not entirely clear that the NT presents "a vision of evangelism merely from verbal consideration" related to the etymology of the word "evangelism."[11] The early church, especially reflected in the Gospels, seems more interested in creating a narrative so future church generations could imagine what it means for the gospel of the kingdom to have been inaugurated.[12] Any attempt to develop a coherent

---

9. Abraham, *Logic of Evangelism*, 1.

10. Ibid., 17.

11. Abraham, "Theology of Evangelism," 117–30.

12. Although not intended as a foundation for evangelism, Beale in his *The Temple and the Church's Mission* offers a biblical theology for the church's mission that should be considered as any theory of evangelism is developed.

theory of evangelism must begin with the implications of the presence of the kingdom, which is wholly constitutive of the gospel.[13] The remainder of this chapter will explore how the parable of *the Sower who sows*, which fits within this framework, offers a narrative definition of evangelism that includes social action outcomes.[14]

THE SET-UP: RE-HEARING THE "BEGINNING OF THE GOSPEL" (MARK 1:1–3)

Mark does not begin his narrative as do the writers of the other synoptic Gospels: *The beginning of the gospel of Jesus Christ, the Son of God* (Mark 1:1).[15] Many recognize that Mark's *heading* is similar to the Priene Calendar Inscription[16] honoring Caesar Augustus (9 BC):

> Because providence has ordered our life in a divine way . . . and since the Emperor through his epiphany has exceeded the hopes of former good news [*euaggelia*], surpassing not only the benefactors who came before him, but also leaving no hope that anyone in the future will surpass him, and since the birthday of the god was for the world the beginning of his good news . . .[17]

In close historical proximity to Jesus' own birth, Caesar Augustus' birthday (in 9 B.C.) was declared as *euaggelia* (*Good News*), and thus the political and social significance must have had some bearing on Mark's Gospel *heading*.[18]

---

13. The kingdom of God and the parable are "inseparable" (France, *Gospel of Mark*, 184); "God's rule is sown" (Waetjen, *Reordering of Power*, 102); also, Abraham, *Logic*, 17; Abraham, "Theology of Evangelism."

14. See excursus at the end of this chapter.

15. *Son of God* (*huiou theou*) read by ℵa A B D K L W Δ Π 33, as well as other authorities, however Metzger et al. decided on brackets, i.e., [*huiou theou*], and as well do the UBS Greek text (4th ed.) and NA27. Guelich argues for possible omission through scribal error. France suggests there is good reason to view *huiou theou* (*Son of God*) as original (*Gospel of Mark*, 49). Noted by Evans, even if the words *huiou theou* are omitted "nothing of Mark's Christology is lost," for Jesus is identified as "son" or "son of God" throughout Mark's Gospel (1:11; 3:11; 8:38; 9:7; 12:6; 13:32; 14:36, 61; 15:39). Also see Evans, "Inscription," 67–81.

16. Witherington (*Gospel of Mark*, 69) referring to Dittenberger, *Orientis graeci inscriptiones selectae*, II, no. 458, pp. 48–60, lines 40–42; see also Evans, "Inscription."

17. *OGIS* 458; ca. 9 BCE.

18. Witherington suggests that *Son of God* in 1:1 is highly likely in light of the Priene inscription (*Gospel of Mark*, 69).

Wasted Evangelism (Mark 4)

No doubt Mark harnesses the association with Caesar—his appearance, the celebration of his birth as a god, his epiphany as "good news" to the world, all appearing extremely relevant.[19] What is drowned out by the excitement of this association, with all its "implied" (and applied) anti-imperialism[20] (i.e., Jesus vs. imperial Rome, Jesus vs. imperial America, etc.), is that by the time the small church had become established throughout the Roman Empire[21] the rule of the Caesars had begun to deteriorate.[22] Perhaps this explains, at least in part, the hostility between the political and religious powers and the new sect with a powerful new "gospel" with a different Caesar.

While harnessing the political significance, Mark takes his narrative in a different direction to show how a better "gospel" is invading the realms of humanity—i.e., Caesar's domain. In Mark's introduction, we are creatively drawn into an intriguing, and yet overlooked, thematic thread woven into his Gospel that should inform our concept of evangelism.

First things: the beginning and foundation

Mark starts his Gospel abruptly with *archē*, usually translated *beginning*, but it should not be taken temporally—that is, "this is *the beginning of the history* of the story *of the gospel.*" Here, *archē* suggests more the idea of *foundation, essence,* or *first principle*.[23] It is not sequential or temporal, but descriptive of origin: *The essence and foundation of the gospel of Jesus Christ, the Son of God, just as it is written . . .* (1:1–2a).

Without much knowledge of the OT, readers/listeners can sense the "essence" of this story is somehow connected to ancient promises.[24] Mark's Gospel *header*[25] (v. 1) is linked to verses 2–3, where *kathōs gegraptai* (*as it*

---

19. Edwards, *Gospel According to Mark*, 24.

20. E.g., Horsley, *Hearing the Whole Story*; *Jesus and Empire*; Myers, *Binding the Strong Man*; Resner, ed., *Just Preaching*; Waetjen, *Reordering of Power*; also see Benson and Heltzel, eds., *Evangelicals and Empire*.

21. Though a minor point, for the purposes of this study, I take the destination of Mark's Gospel to be Rome.

22. Evans, "Inscription."

23. *Louw-Nida* (68.1) designates the Mark 1:1 reference as *Beginning* (aspect), however there are some who suggest that *foundation* (58.20 in *L-N*) is a more apt nuance. See also Boring, "Mark 1.1–15," 43–82; Hooker, *Beginnings*, 19–22; also Edwards, *Gospel According to Mark*, 23–24.

24. Juel, *Gospel of Mark*, 54.

25. Most likely the summary extends from 1:1 to 1:8, with some pushing the end of

is written, v. 2a) does not begin a new thought, but connects *the gospel of Jesus Messiah*[26] (1:1) to a "tapestry" of three OT passages (vv. 2b–3): Exodus 23:20, Isaiah 40:3, and Malachi 3:1.[27] *Kathōs* (*as, just as*) links what follows with what precedes, as is regularly the case with *Kathōs gegraptai* (*as it is written*).[28] Verses 2–3 draw on a programmatic OT foundation, setting-up themes Mark will harnesses and develop throughout his narrative: the exodus/exile, the issue of idolatry, and the threat of judgment for not keeping the land-laws.[29]

Refers to Isaiah	As it is written in Isaiah the prophet:	Mark 1:2a
Blended citation: Exod 23:20/Mal 3:1	"Behold, I send My messenger ahead of you who will prepare Your way;	Mark 1:2b
Reference to Isa 40:3	the voice of one crying in the wilderness, 'Make ready the way of the Lord; make his paths straight'"	Mark 1:3

The context of each element of the citation sets-up a framework for *relistening* to the parable of *the Sower who sows* and, as well, is also crucial for shaping a definition of evangelism and its potential outcomes.

Yahweh's Dominion

Alluding to Isaiah 40:3, Mark appears to be tying together "two disparate, potentially antagonistic theologies"[30] intrinsic to his Gospel: The imperial

---

the "summary" to v. 13, some to v. 18. I hold the introductory matters to extend to v. 20, for v. 21 begins the events of the Galilean mission. Noting the possible range to the opening "summary" is sufficient for the purpose of this study. See chapter 3, "You Will Appear as *Fishers*," for further explanation on Mark's introductory section.

26. I will often throughout the studies render the NASB "Christ" as "Messiah," in order to stress Jesus' role in appearing as God's agent who inaugurates his kingdom and time of redemption.

27. *Just as it is written* (*Kathōs gegraptai*) points the reader/listener to the Hebrew Bible as "the beginning of the gospel about Jesus Messiah"; see Caneday, "He Wrote in Parables," 35–67; also Edwards, *Gospel According to Mark*, 26.

28. France, *Gospel of Mark*, 50. Note that *Kathōs gegraptai* (*just as it is written*) is used as a technical way of introducing an OT quotation, but never starting a new thought—in fact, interestingly, 1QS 5:17 introduces Isa 40:3 this way.

29. Watts, *Isaiah's New Exodus*, 57.

30. Evans, "Inscription."

cult of Caesar and OT expectations. Isaiah 40:1 foretells an era of *comfort*[31] after exile (Isa 36–39), indicating, in eschatological promise, Yahweh was about to act in history. It is from this Mark makes a correspondence (i.e., a fulfillment, a *typos*) to his Gospel: *A voice is calling, "Clear the way for the Lord in the wilderness; make smooth in the desert a highway for our God"* (Isa 40:3; cf. Mark 1:3). The imagery is common to Isaiah's world, reflecting the ceremonial procession of Babylonian and other Ancient Near Eastern victor-kings. Here, it is Yahweh who comes as Victor-King for his people. The event is *Good News*:

> Get yourself up on a high mountain,
> O Zion, bearer of good news,
> Lift up your voice mightily,
> O Jerusalem, bearer of good news;
> Lift it up, do not fear.
> Say to the cities of Judah,
> "Here is your God!" (v. 9).

The *Good News* (*euaggelion*) is associated with Yahweh, who comes *with might* (*meta ischys*, v. 10 LXX) to demonstrate his reign, dispensing his *reward* and *recompense* (Isa 40:10; cf. Mark 1:7). John the Baptist refers to Jesus as the *mighty one* (*ho ischypoteros*, Mark 1:7), extending the connection also to the Beelzebul conflict, for Jesus is the "Stronger man" who binds strongman-Satan (*tou ischyrou/ton ischyron*, Mark 3:27). There is also mention of the Spirit (*Who has directed the Spirit of the Lord,* Isa 40:13), which in Isaiah is related to Yahweh and his actions. Isaiah 40:13 begins a series of texts associating the Spirit to the eschatological promises of Yahweh's "coming."[32] In Isaiah 63:10 Israel's rebellion against Yahweh is seen as *grieving of the Holy Spirit* (63:10)—a harbinger/*typos* of the Beelzebul confrontation (Mark 3:22–30). The presence of the Spirit in Mark signals the inauguration of the Isaianic promises associated with the in-breaking of God's reign (Mark 1:8, 10).[33] There are five Isaiah passages with reference to

---

31. In the latter half of Isaiah the term and concept of *comfort* marks the anticipated outcomes of God's deliverance and the exercise of his Lordship and dominion to redeem his remnant—Isa 40:1; 49:13; 51:3, 12, 19; 52:9; 57:18; 61:2; 66:11, 13. Note in Isa 51:3, the concept of God's *comfort* is related to God's action to restore his community, which is pictured prophetically as a return to the garden-like conditions of Eden's creation.

32. See Isa 42:1; 44:3; 48:16; 59:21; 61:1; 63:14. Note the connection of the Spirit, Israel's rebellion against Yahweh, and the *grieving of the Holy Spirit* (Isa 63:10)—a harbinger/*typos* of the Beelzebul confrontation (Mark 3:22–30).

33. Watts, *Isaiah's New Exodus*, 5.

good news (euaggelion),[34] furthering the correspondence between Yahweh as the Victor-King and the gospel of the kingdom of God.[35]

Mark indicates the *time is fulfilled,* namely *the kingdom of God is at hand (ēggiken hē basileia tou theou,* Mark 1:15). Although *it is near (ēggiken,* v. 15) is frequently used throughout the LXX, Isaiah links it to "the promise of the nearness of God's righteousness."[36] The texts themselves are parallel to Isaiah 40 (cf. Isa 46:13) and offer further significance to the announcement of God's arrival.

> Thus says the LORD,
> "Preserve justice and do righteousness,
> For My salvation is about to come[37]
> And My righteousness to be revealed" (Isa 56:1).

In light of the future "new exodus," the mention of God's righteousness (cf. Isa 46:13) and the call to *preserve justice and do righteousness* (Isa 56:1) echo the covenant faithfulness expected for living in the land (Exod 23; also see Deut 4:8; 32:4).

Mark is announcing the long awaited "new exodus."[38] Now, Jesus' words and deeds become the content of the *gospel,* the *Good News (euaggelion,* Mark 1:1, 14, 15), as both the fulfillment of the expected Isaianic promises of the new exodus and the indicator that the presence of the kingdom has been inaugurated.[39]

The poor, idolatry, and the threat of judgment

Within the contexts of the blended OT citation, our attention is drawn to the presence of the poor and vulnerable. There are direct references to the poor in the fused Exodus 23:20/Malachi 3:1 element of the citation. In fact preceding the Exodus 23:20 referent we are, for the first time, introduced

---

34. See Isa 40:1–11; 41:21–29; 52:7–12; 60:1–9; 61:1–11.

35. Note Mark 1:14–15; Isa 40:9d; Isa 52:7, *announcing good news* that *Your God reigns*—Isa 41:21–29, associated with idolatry; 52:7–12, God's arrival to rule; 60:1–7, God's redeemed City where the nations are drawn to its light; 61:1–11, Jesus' commencement of his mission. Evans ("Inscription") notes that three of the references are pivotal texts (Isa 40; 60; 61) used to develop Jesus' and the early church's theology of mission.

36. See Isa 46:13; 51:5; 56:1; also see Watts, *Isaiah's New Exodus,* 100.

37. The LXX has *ēggisen* for the English rendering *is about to come.*

38. Watts, *Isaiah's New Exodus,* 87.

39. Ibid., 98.

to the vulnerable trio, *the widow, orphan,* and *alien/stranger,*[40] and their relationship to the fabric of society as part of the land-laws (e.g., social, economic):

> You shall not wrong <u>a stranger</u> or oppress him, for you were strangers in the land of Egypt. You shall not afflict any <u>widow</u> or <u>orphan</u>. If you afflict him at all, and if he does cry out to Me, I will surely hear his cry; and My anger will be kindled, and I will kill you with the sword, and your wives shall become widows and your children fatherless. If you lend money to My people, to <u>the poor</u> among you, you are not to act as a creditor to him; you shall not charge him interest. If you ever take your neighbor's cloak as a pledge, you are to return it to him before the sun sets, for that is his only covering; it is his cloak for his body. What else shall he sleep in? And it shall come about that when he cries out to Me, I will hear him, for I am gracious (Exod 22:21–27).

We also learn the poor are not to be given deference in matters of law just because they are needy (Exod 23:3), while *You shall not pervert the justice due to your needy brother in his dispute* (v. 6) or *oppress a stranger* (v. 9). Then in 23:11, the basis for the seventh year rest is *so that the needy of your people may eat.*[41]

Moving to the Malachi 3 referent, we also see "the poor" as we are confronted with the harsh realities of God's judgment on those who oppress the vulnerable trio: *Then I will draw near to you for judgment . . . against those who oppress the wage earner in his wages, the widow and the orphan, and those who turn aside the alien . . .* (Mal 3:5).

Although there is no direct mention of "the poor" in the Isaiah 40 context, we should not overlook the concept of Yahweh's kingship and the imagery of the coming Victor (vv. 3, 9). This Victor-King who comes *with might* (v. 10) is also likened to a Shepherd (v. 11):

> Behold, the Lord GOD will come with might,
> With His arm ruling for Him.
> Behold, His reward is with Him
> And His recompense before Him.

---

40. The *widow, orphan,* and *alien/stranger* trio is a frequent reference throughout the OT, particularly in contexts that concern God's covenant with his people or a reaffirmation of that covenant: Exod 22:21, Deut 10:18–19; 14:29; 16:11, 14; 24:17, 19, 20, 21; 26:12, 13; 27:19; Jer 7:6; 22:3; Zech 7:10; Mal 3:5; cf. Lev 19:34; Isa 1:17, 23; 10:2; Ps 94:6; Hos 14:3.

41. See Exod 23:12; Lev 19:10; 23:22; Deut 14:29; 15:9–11; 24:19–22; 26:12.

> Like a shepherd He will tend His flock,
> In His arm He will gather the lambs
> And carry them in His bosom;
> He will gently lead the nursing ewes (Isa 40:10–11).

The beneficent shepherd-king described in ancient Near Eastern texts suggests some degree of correspondence between Yahweh as Shepherd and the care of the powerless, a task given by the gods to the king.[42]

The issue of idolatry also makes a strong appearance in the OT contexts of Mark's "foundational" citation:

> You shall have no other gods before Me. You shall not make for yourself an idol, or any likeness of what is in heaven above or on the earth beneath or in the water under the earth. You shall not worship them or serve them; for I, the LORD your God, am a jealous God (Exod 20:3–5b).

> He who sacrifices to any god, other than to the LORD alone, shall be utterly destroyed (Exod 22:20).

> Now concerning everything which I have said to you, be on your guard; and do not mention the name of other gods, nor let them be heard from your mouth (Exod 23:13).

> You shall not worship their gods, nor serve them, nor do according to their deeds; but you shall utterly overthrow them and break their sacred pillars in pieces (Exod 23:24).

> You shall make no covenant with them or with their gods. They shall not live in your land, because they will make you sin against Me; for if you serve their gods, it will surely be a snare to you (Exod 23:32–33).

> As for the idol, a craftsman casts it,
> A goldsmith plates it with gold,
> And a silversmith fashions chains of silver.
> He who is too impoverished for such an offering
> Selects a tree that does not rot;
> He seeks out for himself a skillful craftsman

---

42. Dey, "Poverty," 1–8; also see chapter 5, "Idolatry and Poverty," for an expanded discussion on Yahweh, the god's, and the poor.

To prepare an idol that will not totter (Isa 40:19–20).[43]

In Malachi, there is a direct reference to idolatry: Judah is rebuked *for profaning the sanctuary of the Lord which He loves and has married the daughter of a foreign god* (Mal 2:11). Also, the segment on *profane sacrifices* and *polluted offerings* (1:7–12) consists of idolatrous attitudes and practices of temple priests. Meanwhile the Malachi 3:1 element of the citation contains judgment language appropriate for the idolatrous practices of temple leadership (Mal 3:2–4). The references to *sorcerers* and *those who swear falsely* are also related to idolatry (Mal 3:5; note Exod 22:18).

What is of interest and overlooked is that *the poor* and the issue of idolatry are associated in the Exodus/Malachi contexts.[44] In the Exodus context, laws and stipulations are given to prepare Israel for living "in the land" (Exod 20–23).[45] Interestingly, in the midst of a series of land-requisites and social ordinances that culminates in a warning against idolatry (23:32–33), there is a caution against afflicting *the stranger, widow*, and *orphan* trio:

> He who sacrifices to any god, other than to the LORD alone, shall be utterly destroyed. You shall not wrong a <u>stranger</u> or oppress him, for you were strangers in the land of Egypt. You shall not afflict any <u>widow</u> or <u>orphan</u>. If you afflict him at all, and if he does cry out to Me, I will surely hear his cry; and My anger will be kindled, and I will kill you with the sword, and your wives shall become widows and your children fatherless. If you lend money to My people, to <u>the poor</u> among you, you are not to act as a creditor to him; you shall not charge him interest (Exod 22:20–25).[46]

The juxtaposition here is significant, for the issue of idolatry (*You shall not have any gods before Me*, Exod 22:22) is intimately connected to how the world is to work relationally and socio-economically (Exod 21–23), with an emphasis on social responsibilities toward the vulnerable and the poor.

---

43. See 42:17; 44:9–10; 45:16, 20; 46:1; 48:5; 57:13; 66:3. The Isaianic references to idolatry are usually in the context of Yahweh's incomparableness to the other powers in creation.

44. Chapter 5, "Idolatry and Poverty," elaborates on the juxtaposition of idolatry with poverty in the OT, as well as the association of these two themes in Mark's Gospel.

45. Watts, *Isaiah's New Exodus*, 63.

46. Exod 22:18 and 19 are also related to pagan worship and idolatry.

The association suggests that a form of idolatry is the marginalization or disregard of the vulnerable and poor.[47]

Mark's Exodus reference is located in what "constitutes a final warning [just] prior to the sealing of the covenant (24:1–18)."[48] They are to remember "Yahweh's presence at the founding moment,"[49] which includes (necessitates) ensuring that the poor are protected and full participants in the benefits of the land. Exodus 23:20 introduces a series of reminders and warnings that the land-stipulations are to be obeyed. Idolatry is the antithesis to obeying the "voice" of the angel (for *God's name is in him*, v. 21):

> Behold, I am going to send an angel before you to guard you along the way and to bring you into the place which I have prepared. Be on your guard before him and obey his voice; do not be rebellious toward him, for he will not pardon your transgression[50] [cf. Mark 3:29; 4:12], since My name is in him. But, if you truly obey his voice and do all that I say, then I will be an enemy to your enemies and an adversary to your adversaries. For My angel will go before you and bring you in to the land of the Amorites, the Hittites, the Perizzites, the Canaanites, the Hivites and the Jebusites; and I will completely destroy them. You shall not worship their gods, nor serve them, nor do according to their deeds; but you shall utterly overthrow them and break their sacred pillars [reference to idols] in pieces. But you shall serve the LORD your God, and He will bless your bread and your water; and I will remove sickness from your midst. There shall be no one miscarrying or barren in your land; I will fulfill the number of your days. I will send My terror ahead of you, and throw into confusion all the people among whom you come, and I will make all your enemies turn their backs to you. I will send hornets ahead of you so that they will drive out the Hivites, the Canaanites, and the Hittites before you. I will not drive them out before you in a single year, that the land may not become desolate and the beasts of the field become too numerous for you. I will drive them out before you little by little, until

---

47. Refer to chapter 5, "Idolatry and Poverty," for an expanded explanation of the relationship between the issue of idolatry and the poor.

48. Watts, *Isaiah's New Exodus*, 65.

49. Ibid., 66; also note *Ex. Rab.* 32:6, 9; *Midr. Ps* 90:9; as well, Gen 24:7; 48:16; Exod 3:2; Judg 6:11–14; Mal 3:1.

50. Note *rebellious* and *no pardon* references in v. 21; cf. Mark 3:29; 4:12. See chapter 4, "A Prelude to Judgment," for a fuller discussion on the relationship between Mark's introductory, blended OT quote and the *blasphemy against the Holy Spirit* in Mark 3.

Wasted Evangelism (Mark 4)

you become fruitful[51] and take possession of the land. I will fix your boundary from the Red Sea to the sea of the Philistines, and from the wilderness to the River Euphrates; for I will deliver the inhabitants of the land into your hand, and you will drive them out before you. You shall make no covenant with them or with their gods. They shall not live in your land, because they will make you sin against Me; for if you serve their gods, it will surely be a snare to you (Exod 23:20–33).

The mixed Exodus 23:20/Malachi 3:1 element recalls God's social ordinances, indicating a threat to those not obeying them. The Malachi referent (3:1) and its immediate context refers back to the Exodus land-laws and, as well, looks forward to the new exodus.

"Behold, I am going to send My messenger, and he will clear the way before Me and the Lord, whom you seek, will suddenly come to His temple; and the messenger of the covenant, in whom you delight, behold, He is coming," says the LORD of hosts (Mal 3:1).

The similarities to Isaiah 40:3 are obvious.[52] The verbal similarities between Malachi 3:1 and Exodus 23:20 are also apparent, marking a *typos* or fulfillment of judgment for breaking the requisite land-laws related to the vulnerable trio:

"Then I will draw near to you for judgment; and I will be a swift witness against the sorcerers and against the adulterers and against those who swear falsely, and against those who oppress the wage earner in his wages, the widow and the orphan, and those who turn aside the alien and do not fear Me," says the LORD of hosts (Mal 3:5).

A composite of idolatry and the disregard for the marginalized form the basis of the judgment. Mark prepares the reader/listener, first, for John the Baptist (1:4–8), and, then, the eventual "sudden" appearing of Jesus in judgment at the temple in Jerusalem (Mark 13).[53]

51. *Auxēthēs, fruitful* in the LXX; compare Mark's use of *auxanomena* in the *Sower who sows* parable (Mark 4:8).

52. On the correspondence between Isa 40 and Mal 3 see Watts, *Isaiah's New Exodus*, 82–83. Also, note Mal 3:1 (LXX), *he will clear the way*; cf. Isa 40:3; Mark 1:2.

53. Interesting, this *appearing* at the temple comes first in parable *as deed* in Jesus cursing the fig tree (Mark 11:12–14, 20 21) and overturning of the tables in the temple courts (11:15–18), and then in prophetic word (and eventual reality) as he spoke of its destruction (Mark 13). See chapter 1, "Widows in Our Courts," for a discussion of the fig-tree/overturning tables as parable; also Watts, *Isaiah's New Exodus*, 86–88.

Wasted Evangelism

The programmatic summary

R.T. France concludes that "Mark has declared his hand" in the opening verses of his Gospel, setting the framework in which we are to understand his whole story.[54] We accept that Mark has drawn into his Gospel the motifs of God's dominion, the Exodus, exile, the Spirit, and idolatry. What is undervalued, overlooked, or even ignored is that the same context that contains these obvious correspondences, likewise, includes direct references regarding socio-economic relationships and community responsibilities toward the poor and vulnerable.

THE PARABLE OF THE SOWER WHO SOWS: THE REALITY OF THE KINGDOM'S PRESENCE

We turn our attention to the Mark 4 parable where the Sower sows seed with six different results.[55] The parable of the *Sower who sows* begins Mark's highest concentration of parables.[56] This chapter of parables, although centering on the *sowing of the word* (4:14), rarely is utilized for developing a foundation or theory for evangelism. At best the parable is employed for its "practical" value to explain why individual "soils" (i.e., people) reject the gospel or abandon the faith, and then to make some appeal for individuals "to be more receptive soil." However, this seems like putting the cart before the horse—the application before significance. Before "applying" this parable, some attention must be given as to why Jesus gave the parable in the first place. Agreeing with Ben Witherington, I think this parable ought *not* to be dissected "into specific parts," for it is a parable, not "a syllogistically driven speech."[57]

We seem to "use" parables to interpret the Christian life. Parables in the NT are often read and preached mythically, as if they explain our place in the world, reinforce our "traditions," and help explain our relationship

---

54. France, *Gospel of Mark*, 50.

55. It should be noted that the seed producing little to no results are *not* separate individual harvests; whereas, the 30-, 60-, and 100-fold results are harvests.

56. See 4:3–8, 13–20, 21–25, 26–29, 30–32; the explanation/parable theory—4:10–12, 33–34; other parables in Mark—2:21–22; 12:1–9; 13:28–29; 13:34–37. Also, Marcus, *Mystery of the Kingdom*, 1.

57. Witherington, *Gospel of Mark*, 163n66.

to the world around us.[58] There is a tendency to use one's own "plausibility structures" (i.e., the things, ideas, and habits that help us make sense of our world and our place in it) to form a paradigm for interpreting them and "smuggle them into" our understanding of the parables.[59] In Rabbinic literature and the writings of Qumran (i.e., Jewish extracanonical material) parables were used to clarify or interpret OT texts, as well as, to explain meanings, often hidden, in OT stories and how they apply to that day. But not so in the OT itself, where parables usually are a form of judgment-speech—many times with a subversive twist. It is interesting that the context of Isaiah and Ezekiel, both used in Mark 4, have judgment-parables in their own OT contexts (see parables in Isa 5, Ezek 17, Ezek 31; and note Ezek 20:49 and chapters 21–24). Parables are spoken to the disobedient, rebellious, and idolaters. Mark's parable chapter falls within this framework.

Often overlooked, the imagery of the parable of *the Sower who sows* "the word" continues the themes established at the beginning of Mark's Gospel—covenantal faithfulness, warning against idolatry, social righteousness, and the vulnerable and the poor.[60] The parable of *the Sower who sows* assists the readers/listeners to understand the nature of the gospel and how they are to imagine what it means for the gospel of the kingdom to be present (1:14–15).

Why Jesus came

There is little doubt that the *Sower* is Jesus.[61] Before the parable begins (4:2), Jesus' authority as a *teacher*[62] is recognized. Mark's use of *exēlthen* (*went out*, 4:3) in the parable's opening line draws the reader/listener back to Mark 1:38–39 and the purpose for which Jesus came:

> He said to them, "Let us go somewhere else to the towns nearby, so that I may preach there also; for that is what I came for [*eis*

---

58. Herzog, *Parables as Subversive Speech*, 43; also see Crossan, *The Dark Interval*, 33–44.

59. Herzog, *Parables as Subversive Speech*, 14–16.

60. Refer to the *Set-up* above on Mark's summary, 1:1–3, and its association with Exodus, Isaiah, and Malachi.

61. Witherington, *Gospel of Mark*, 164–65; Marcus, *Mystery of the Kingdom*, 37–39.

62. Witherington, *Gospel of Mark*, 164. Also see 1:21, 22, 27; 3:13; 4:1, 2; afterward—4:38; 5:35; 6:1, 6, 34; 7:7; 8:31; 9:17, 31, 38; 10:17, 20, 35; 11:17, 18; 12:14, 19, 32, 38; 13:1; 14:14, 49.

touto gap exēlthon]." And He went [*ēlthen*] into their synagogues throughout all Galilee, preaching and casting out the demons" (Mark 1:38–39).[63]

Later, Mark tells us that Jesus *went out [exēlthen] . . . and all the people were coming to Him, and He was teaching them* (2:13). Furthermore, Mark's narrative depicts Jesus as the herald (1:14–15) and doer of the kingdom (Mark 1:21–27—*teaching, casting out demons, doing miracles*). Thus, it is reasonable to conclude that the parable presents the reality of the in-breaking of God's kingdom in Jesus, who is the sower of the word of the gospel.[64]

The word (logos)

Jesus' use of *logos* (*word*, Mark 4:14, 33) for the seed is significant: "One might have expected Jesus to talk about sowing the good news of the coming dominion of God rather than the 'Word.'"[65] Some argue that *logos* (*word*) is a term for the gospel later developed by the church, and thus influenced its use in Mark's interpretation, rather than originating from Jesus. However, there is no reason the reverse cannot be the case—that is, Jesus' use led to the early church's association of *logos* with the gospel.[66] Already in Mark 2:2, Jesus *spoke the word* (*ton logon*), an obvious reference to the gospel of the kingdom (1:14–15).

Additionally, it is reasonable for Jesus to have used *logos* in light of his pending use of Isaiah 6, for *logos* is used by the LXX throughout the preceding Isaiah 1–5 context. The rulers are commanded to *hear the word* (*logos*, 1:10). It is the *word* (*logos*, 2:1) that Isaiah *sees* concerning Yahweh's reign among the nations and it is God's *word* (*logos*, 2:3) that the nations long to hear and obey. Furthermore, following the Isaiah 5 vineyard parable and the threat of exile (*My people go into exile for their lack of knowledge*, 5:13),

---

63. See Mark 1:35; also note *aperchomai* (*went up*) in 3:13 at the first reference to the calling of the twelve and then at the close of the periscope, 6:12, *exerchomai* (*went up*), both indicating the purpose of Jesus' and their mission; note Edwards, *Gospel According to Mark*, 130.

64. See Mark 4:14; 4:33; cf. 1:14–15; Matt 4:23; Luke 16:16; see Edwards, *Gospel According to Mark*, 129; McComiskey, " Exile and the Purpose of Jesus' Parables," 59–85; Marcus, *Mystery of the Kingdom*, 26.

65. Witherington, *Gospel of Mark*, 161n60.

66. Taking the reverse, namely Jesus' use of *logos* (*word*) provides the eventual use of *logos* (*word*) in the early church, which might also help in connecting the meaning of "gospel" in Paul, Luke-Acts, etc. to its use in the Gospels.

the prophet imagines judgment in agricultural terms similar to the parable of *the Sower who sows*:

> Therefore, as a tongue of fire consumes stubble
> And dry grass collapses into the flame,
> So their root will become like rot and their blossom blow away as dust (5:24a).

Then the stanza concludes with an ironic twist regarding "poor soil," for unlike the Gentiles, who come to listen to God's law and obey his *word* (*logos*, 2:3), Israel has *rejected the law of the Lord of hosts and despised the word [logon] of the Holy One of Israel* (Isa 5:24c).[67]

The use of *logos* (*word*) to identify *the seed*, which is the gospel of the kingdom, is an appropriate word for Jesus to have used, especially for importing the Isaiah 1–5 context into the parable of *the Sower*.[68]

The parable's rhetorical function

The parable's rhetorical function is to answer the question *Why the opposition?* The dynamic presence of God's reign had arrived (1:14–15), displayed in Jesus' teaching, exorcisms, and healings—so why the decline in positive response?[69] Although the parable of *the Sower* offers an explanation,[70] it is a faulty generalization to suggest the parable is about the toughness of the mission, or why people in general reject the Good News. Rather than focusing on individuals in general, as the narrative moves from baptism to the parable, the crowd's attraction to Jesus is contrasted to the temple-leadership's rejection of or stumbling over Jesus and his kingdom-gospel (both his teaching and his deeds).

There is great response from the crowds (1:16–45), even contrasting Jesus' authority (teaching and deeds) with the authority of the scribes (1:22,

---

67. Elsewhere God brings judgment and curse on his people for their lack of *knowing* and *understanding* (Isa 1:3, *lack of understanding*; 27:11, *not a people of discernment*; Hos 4:6, *My people are destroyed for lack of knowledge*).

68. Elsewhere the LXX utilizes *logos* (*word*) for God's word (e.g., Exod 4:28; 19:7, 8; 20:1; Deut 9:10; Jer 1:4, 11, 13). There is little difference between *hrēma* (*word*) and *logos* (*word*), for in many places the two are parallel—Exod 4:15 (*ta hrēmata mou*); Exod 4:28 (*tous logou kyriou*); Exod 19:6 (*hrēma*); Exod 19:7, 8 (*logos*); Exod 20:1 (*logous*); Exod 24:3 (*all the words [hrēmata] of the Lord*).

69. France, *Gospel of Mark*, 189.

70. Ibid., 182.

27). As Jesus continued to speak *the word to them* (*elalei autois ton logon*, 2:2), he is accused of blasphemy (*only God can forgive sins*, 2:7)—a set-up for the Beelzebul controversy (3:22–30). This marks a turning point in the opposition, not from the crowds, but from the leadership. There is distaste for the company Jesus keeps (*eating and drinking with tax collectors and sinners*, 2:16). Apparently, they did not like *the soil* where Jesus was sowing his seed. Afterward, the Pharisees are offended that the disciples do not fast (2:18). To make matters even worse, Jesus and his disciples eat grain on the Sabbath (*why are they doing what is not lawful on the Sabbath?*, 2:24). Eventually Jesus is *grieved at their hardness of heart* (3:5).[71] And soon, the *Pharisees went out and immediately began conspiring with the Herodians against Him, as to how they might destroy Him* (3:6). Yet, despite the antagonism, *a great multitude* (3:7) from Galilee, Judea and Jerusalem continue to come to Jesus (vv. 7–8a); even those from "outside" Jerusalem, that is *Idumea, beyond the Jordon, and the vicinity of Tyre and Sidon, a great number of people heard of all that He was doing and came to Him* (3:8b).[72]

The parable is not a lesson about the general public (i.e., *individual* soils), but reflects the reality concerning those who are the maintainers and guardians of Israel's religious and socio-economic structures. The parable affirms God's judgment and ensures that God's word will not return empty (i.e., the harvest among the crowds and, even, outsiders; see Isa 2:1–4; 55:1–13).[73] The lavished seed of the kingdom (word and deed) sown by the Master Sower is wasted on some, yet still produces a good crop among the crowds and "outsiders," a harvest of 30-, 60-, and 100-fold.

Analogous to the Isaiah 6 idolatry-taunt

After the parable of *the Sower who sows*, the twelve asked Jesus "about the parables" (4:10).[74] Affirming the association with the *kingdom of God*

---

71. An obvious reference and harbinger of the Isaiah idolatry-taunt reference (Isa 6:9–10) in Mark 4:12.

72. With Mark's reliance on Isaiah, could the picture of these outsiders beyond Jerusalem and Judea (3:7–10) be an inaugurated fulfillment of Isa 2, where the nations gladly come to hear the *word* of God? Note the following story concerning the Syrophoenician woman in Tyre who comes to Jesus concerning her possessed daughter (7:24–30).

73. There might be an association, or background to Isa 55, which presents imagery similar to the parable of the Sower (Isa 55:10–13).

74. Note the disciples ask about *the parables*, plural. There are at least multiple parables in the narrative thus far—the Beelzebul parable (3:22–27) and *the Sower who sows*

(4:11), Jesus reaches back to the Isaiah 6 idolatry-taunt to explain: *those who are outside get everything in parables, so that [hina] while seeing, they may see and not perceive, and while hearing, they may not hear and not understand, otherwise they might return and be forgiven* (Mark 4:11b–12; cf. Isa 6:9–10). The *so that* (*hina*, Mark 4:12a) introducing the Isaiah 6:9 referent provides difficulty for many, however, the telic (expressing end or purpose) use should not be rejected or evaded, for "Jesus adopts a meaning for Isaiah 6:9–10 virtually identical to the original meaning in Isaiah."[75] The parable of *the Sower* is the reality of God's judgment; the consequences are in play even now.[76] Reviewing the context of Isaiah 1–5 will bear this out even further.

While recognizing the "difficult theology" and harshness of Isa 6:9–13, G. K. Beale points out that the text "functions as a pronouncement of judgment on Israel's idolatry" and is a consequence "of the nation's covenantal disobedience."[77] This is clear from the preceding where Israel's leadership is indicted for idolatry (Isa 1:29–31; 2:6–9; 2:12–13; 2:18, 20). The rulers had persistently rebelled against God; his patience reaching the limit. There is a match—a *lex talionis*[78]—between their condition and the judgment, for *Israel does not know . . . My people do not understand* (Isa 1:3) and the taunt pronounces *Keep on listening, but do not perceive; Keep on looking, but do not understand* (Isa 6:9; cf. Mark 4:12).[79] In fact, the mark of exile is the *lack*

(4:1–8). The disciples are not necessarily asking about *these* parables, but about Jesus' use of parables. Readers/listeners assume the disciples had not connected the parables as a form of judgment. Perhaps they did, and, therefore, are asking about the nature of the kingdom. This would be similar to the question asked of the temple in Mark 13:1, just prior to the long teaching on the judgment on the temple and the "end of days."

75. McComiskey, "Exile and the Purpose of Jesus' Parables"; also Caneday, "He Wrote in Parables."

76. McComiskey ("Exile and the Purpose of Jesus' Parables") argues that the exile judgment is the background to Jesus' use of Isa 6:9, demonstrating that the rejecters of the gospel are in exile (continue in exile) and under the hardening judgment of God, whereas those who accept the message of Jesus move *from* exile *to* remnant. The potential for a continuous judgment of "exile" is also argued by Beale ("Isaiah VI 9–13," 257–78); also see Beale's *We Become What We Worship*, 51–57.

77. Beale, "Isaiah VI 9–13" and see McComiskey, " Exile and the Purpose of Jesus' Parables." See Ps 115:1–4, 135:15–18; Isa 46:7; Jer 10:5.

78. Beale, *We Become What We Worship*, 57.

79. The issue of *hearing* is central to the parable of *the Sower who sows* (Mark 4:3, 9, 12, 23, 24), thus it is no surprise that the idolatry-taunt, as well, brings up *hearing* (Isa 6:9–10; Mark 4:12). Ironically, it is the stormy sea that *listens* (*hypakouei*, 4:41) to Jesus' word.

of knowledge (Isa 5:13). Mark picks up the issue of *knowledge* and *perception* throughout his narrative (Mark 4:12, 13; 7:14, 18; 8:17[80]; 9:32; 12:24; cf. 11:33; 12:33; 13:14).

Although the whole nation falls under judgment, it is specifically the leaders whom God holds accountable for provoking rebellion (Isa 1:10, 23), despising the word of the Holy One (Isa 5:24; cf. 1:4), and abandoning social responsibilities toward the poor (Isa 1:17, 23; 3:14–15).[81] This is analogous to the incessant confrontations Jesus has with the Jerusalem temple-leadership throughout Mark's narrative. Following on the heels of the Beelzebul confrontation (Mark 3:22–30), the judgment reflected in the parable and implied by the Isaiah 6 referent is appropriate for Israel's unprepared leadership.[82] As with the temple leaders addressed by Isaiah, there will be no forgiveness for the temple-leadership who reject Jesus and his kingdom-word (*do not forgive them*, Isa 2:9; cf. Isa 6:10; Mark 3:29; 4:12).[83] The allusion is strengthened in that Jerusalem had stumbled and rebelled against God's *presence* (Isa 3:8) and had called *evil good, and good evil*, substituting *darkness for light and light for darkness* (5:20).

Along with the theme of *justice* and *righteousness* (Isa 1:17, 21, 26, 27; 3:10; 5:7, 16), there are also direct references to the poor:

> "Wash yourselves, make yourselves clean;
> Remove the evil of your deeds from My sight.
> Cease to do evil,
> Learn to do good;
> Seek justice,
> Reprove the ruthless,
> Defend <u>the orphan</u>,
> Plead for <u>the widow</u>" (1:16–17).

---

80. Note the accusation and warning to the disciples: *"Do you not yet see or understand? Do you have a hardened heart?"* (Mark 8:17).

81. The reference to the *whole head is sick* and *the whole heart is faint* is most likely a reference to Israel's leadership (1:5). Also, the temple-leadership is implied in the case against the sacrilege of worship.

82. Watts, *Isaiah's New Exodus*, 183.

83. Note *no healing*, Isa 3:7; cf. Mark 4:12: *No forgiveness* and *no healing* might be interchangeable. The concept of *forgiveness* and *healing* are parallel in Isa 53. In Isa 1–5 there is promise of *no forgiveness* (2:9) and *I will not be your healer* (3:7). This might explain why some readings of Isa 6:10 indicate the lack of *forgiveness* and some the lack of *healing* (note Isaiah Targum 6:10 uses *forgiven* rather than *healed*). Perhaps this is also why in Mark, Jesus and his critics link healing and forgiveness elsewhere (e.g., Mark 2:1–12).

> Your rulers are rebels
> And companions of thieves;
> Everyone loves a bribe
> And chases after rewards.
> They do not defend <u>the orphan</u>,
> Nor does <u>the widow's</u> plea come before them (1:23).
>
> The LORD enters into judgment with the elders and princes of
> His people,
> "It is you who have devoured the vineyard;
> The plunder of <u>the poor</u> is in your houses.
> What do you mean by crushing My people
> And grinding the face of <u>the poor</u>?"
> Declares the Lord GOD of hosts (3:14–15).

The mention of the vulnerable trio, the *orphan*, the *widow*, and the *alien/stranger*, is an obvious reflection of the covenant stipulations of Exodus 21–23. The Israelite's idolatrous behavior is not only apparent in the adopting of "foreign influences" (note Isa 2:6–11) and reflected in the profanity of their worship (Isa 1:10–15), but also evident in not fulfilling their covenant social responsibilities to the poor.

The agricultural imagery is also present

The imagery of the parable of *the Sower who sows* is also analogous to the agricultural imagery developed in Isaiah 1–5.[84]

> Your land is desolate,
> Your cities are burned with fire,
> Your fields—strangers are devouring them in your presence;
> It is desolation, as overthrown by strangers.
> The daughter of Zion is left like a shelter in a vineyard,
> Like a watchman's hut in a cucumber field, like a besieged city (1:7–8).
>
> Surely you will be ashamed of the oaks which you have desired,
> And you will be embarrassed at the gardens which you have chosen.
> For you will be like an oak whose leaf fades away

---

84. The two follow-up kingdom parables in Mark 4:26–29 and 4:30–32 also contain imagery analogous to OT references.

> Or as a garden that has no water.
> The strong man[85] will become tinder,
> His work also a spark.
> Thus they shall both burn together
> And there will be none to quench them (1:29–31).

> The Lord enters into judgment with the elders and princes of His people,
> "It is you who have devoured the vineyard;
> The plunder of the poor is in your houses.
> What do you mean by crushing My people
> And grinding the face of the poor?"
> Declares the Lord GOD of hosts (3:14–15).

Additionally, the agricultural imagery of *oaks* (1:29–30; 2:13; cf. 6:13) and *gardens* (1:29–30) is associated with idolatry.[86] Idolatry is associated with the dissonance between the function of worship and the nation's community life and to its social responsibilities (1:12–15; 1:16–17; cf. 1:21). The people's idolatry created attitudes, as well as, religious and socio-economic structures (2:6–8; 2:20) and habits that discouraged or hindered them from their responsibilities toward the poor.[87] God's description of this failing and his judgment (e.g., *the Lord will have a day of reckoning*, 2:12) throughout Isaiah 1–5 are expressed in or followed by agricultural images (e.g., 2:13).[88]

The parable of God's vineyard

There is also a connection, rarely noticed, between Mark 4 and Isaiah 5. In Isaiah, the parable of the vineyard is sandwiched between indictments (Isa 1–3) and the idolatry-taunt (Isa 6:9–10.). The owner of the vineyard is Yahweh and the vineyard represents his people (vv. 1–2). It was expected to produce good grapes, but only produces worthless ones (v. 2). As a result,

---

85. Note in v. 31, *the mighty one* (*hē ischys*, LXX), who is under judgment (cf. Mark 3:27).

86. Beale, "Isaiah VI 9–13."

87. Whether intentional or an unintended consequence, idolatry is linked at the religious and social levels, influencing how community members (the poor and non-poor) relate to each other. This was the antithesis of the Exodus covenant and land-laws, and formed, at least in part, a reason for divine punishment (i.e., the Isaiah 6 idolatry-taunt). See chapter 5, "Idolatry and Poverty," for an expansion on idolatry, habits, and the non-poor's disassociation with the poor.

88. See also Isa 1:7–8, 19, 28–31; 2:12–15; 3:14; 5:8–10, 17, 24; cf. 2:4.

God foretells judgment for his vineyard similar to the imagery in Mark's parable:

> I will lay it waste;
> It will not be pruned or hoed,
> But briars and thorns will come up.
> I will also charge the clouds to rain no rain on it (Isa 5:6).

Then, as with the parable of *the Sower*, after the parable of the vineyard an explanation is offered (vv. 7–30). Amid the rebellion and idolatry is the continued charge that justice and righteousness is absent from God's vineyard:

> For the vineyard of the LORD of hosts is the house of Israel
> And the men of Judah His delightful plant,
> Thus He looked for justice, but behold, bloodshed;
> For righteousness, but behold, a cry of distress (5:7).

In summary, there is a corresponding pattern seen in both Isaiah 1–6 and Mark 3–4:

Indictments against the leaders of Jerusalem	Isa 1–4	Mark 3:22–30
Agricultural parable of judgment	Isa 5:1–7	Mark 4:1–8
Explanation and idolatry-taunt/promise-threat/judgment	Isa 5:8ff./Isa 6:9ff.	Mark 4:10–13, 4:13–30

The rhetorical function of the parable continues the programmatic themes established by Mark at the opening of his Gospel. The parable of *the Sower who sows* and its place in Mark's Gospel narrative is analogous to Isaiah 1–6. The parable presents the realities of the inaugurated gospel of the kingdom, not simply how hearts need to change. The spreading of the *word*, that is the gospel of the kingdom, is not limited to the religious realm or to individual salvation, but ought to include outcomes that Mark draws upon that give content to his Gospel, which include social righteousness that addresses the needs of the vulnerable and the poor.

THE WASTED SEED AND THE HARVEST OF THE KINGDOM: IMPLICATIONS FOR EVANGELISM

Often referred to as *the Parable of the Soils*, this story is frequently turned into a metaphor for human psychological attitudes, exploiting the text to get people to change.[89] This is somewhat understandable, for the word-count favors the soils, so getting soils to change is a reasonable outcome—at first glance. Most critical commentary review ancient Palestine plowing methods, usually to show plowing was done *after* sowing.[90] Making correspondences to farming can be useful, but it can also obscure the subversive nature of the parable.[91] Plowing is noticeably absent in the parable. The soil is passive[92]—it is what it is: shallow, rocky, weed/thorn infested, or good. Like the first follow-up parable (vv. 26–29), where the man does nothing but *cast seed upon the soil*, growth happens without the aid of *the Sower*.[93] The parable does not rhetorically ask, "What kind of soil are you?" nor is there an implied command, "Soil, be more receptive—change!" In fact, the Isaiah referent implies the soil cannot change (Mark 4:11–12). We are, however, to imagine that the seed is sown without regard to where it lands; nothing else is done. We are moved *away* from human intervention to manipulate a harvest *to* a picture of a *Sower who sows* despite the outward realities of the conditions where the seed lands. He sows indiscriminately, lavishly, almost carelessly.[94] All the while, the readers/listeners become aware that some seed will be wasted and yet there will be a good harvest.[95] In a retelling of the parable a century after Mark's Gospel, Justin Martyr exhorts Christians to sow every corner "in hopes that good soil might somewhere be found."[96]

89. France, *Gospel of Mark*, 189.

90. Ibid., 191; also Payne, "Order of Sowing and Ploughing," 123–29; Myers, *Binding the Strong Man*, 174–76; Edwards, *Gospel According to Mark*, 128. Meyers (*Binding*, 176) notes Jeremias's comment on the parable: "he sows intentionally on the path . . . since he intends to plough the seed in when he ploughs up the path . . ." (*The Parables of Jesus*, 11f.).

91. Herzog argues that Jesus' parables should be interpreted as "a form of subversive speech" (*Parables as Subversive Speech*, 9).

92. Juel, *Master of Surprise*, 60; Marcus, *Mystery of the Kingdom*, 40.

93. Often ignored is that the harvests of 30-, 60-, and 100-fold are not explained. They just seem to happen. No reason is given why there is a crop (similar to the parable of the ignorant farmer in 4:26–29). On the other hand, the obstacles and hardships not only drive people away from the gospel, but sometimes they are the very things that draw people to it.

94. Juel, *Master of Surprise*, 57.

95. I am indebted to two works by Juel, *Master of Surprise* and *Gospel of Mark*, for offering a tempered reader-response approach to interpreting the Gospel of Mark (*Master of Surprise*, 3–30; *Gospel of Mark*, 15–42). These two volumes presented a case for "wasted seed" which formed the beginning and basis of my link between the gospel and the nature of evangelism (*Master of Surprise*, 45–63; *Gospel of Mark*, 120–29).

96. *Dial. Trypho* 125:1–2 (Edwards, *Gospel According to Mark*, 128).

The imagery of increasing harvest

Among the prophets, harvest imagery is stock language for God restoring his remnant, as a metaphor for the in-breaking of his dominion, and in texts of judgment and eschatological promise.[97] The imagery links the parable to the inauguration of the kingdom of God and provides an image of continuous growth. There are not six fields (three poor; three good), but four[98] areas where seed falls with six different results—"a crescendo of momentum,"[99] an obvious progression: No germination (v. 4; v. 15); some growth, but lacking root quickly withers (vv. 5–6; vv. 16–17); growth, but no fruit (v. 7; vv. 18–19); and then three escalating harvests of 30-, 60-, and 100-fold (v. 8; v. 20).[100] The unsuccessful seed are described with the aorist as to what is done to them (*eaten by birds, scorched by the sun, choked by weeds*) or what they failed to do (*gave no fruit*). Whereas, the seed that falls in good soil is the subject of an active sentence, with imperfect verbs (*edidou, yielded; epheren, produced*) and present participles denoting continuous growth (*anabainonta* and *auxanomena*).[101] The harvest imagery supports a realized eschatology, giving the sense of the reality of the kingdom as it rolls out and increases.[102]

The harvest motif is continued by NT authors writing about the church's growth.[103] In Acts, Luke pairs up *logos* (*word*) and *auxanō* (*increase*)

---

97. See Ps 126:6; Isa 9:3; 17:5; 55:10–13; 60:21; 65:21–22; 66:20; Jer 2:3; 31:27–28; Hos 2:9; 6:11; Isa 16:9; 17:11; 18:5–6; 24:13; Jer 5:17, 24; 8:20; 12:13; 48:32; 50:16; 51:32–34; Joel 1:11; 3:13 (cf. Mark 4:29); Amos 4:7. A number of these texts reflect the language of Exodus stipulations, as well. The language in Jeremiah 5 is very similar to Isa 1–5, where God's indictment of his people/rulers reflects God's concern for their social neglect of the poor.

98. Note the connection of the "four soil types" and "four kingdoms" in Daniel's visions (Dan 2; also 7:13; 8:17) (see Higle, "Seeds of Subversion").

99. Edwards, *Gospel According to Mark*, 129.

100. Perhaps a rhetorical device for remembering the "lesson." France observes this, but does not expand (*Gospel of Mark*, 191).

101. Also note in the first follow-up parable (4:26–29), the progression of the plant—*first the blade, then the head, then the mature grain in the head* (v. 28b)—and the crop, governed by a present tense verb (*bear fruit, karpophorei*, v. 28a), supporting a picture of continued growth of the kingdom. See France, *Gospel of Mark*, 192.

102. Note the numerous references to the increasing borders of Israel (i.e., the Davidic kingdom) and the promise to be able to contain the plethora of the remnant among the exiled Jews and the Gentiles at the "end of time."

103. Both the geographic/demographic growth and maturity (i.e., discipleship, sanctification).

to indicate the gospel's geo-demographic expansion from Jerusalem to the Gentile world (*ho logos tou theou ēuxanen, the increase of the word*, Acts 6:7; 12:24; 19:20). Paul utilizes *auxanō* (*increase*) in the context of church-growth (Eph 2:21; 4:15; Col 1:10; 2:19).[104] Paul also picks up the Mark 4 imagery to explain his own ministry where *God causes the growth* (*auxanō*, 1 Cor 3:6–7).

Sowing and the mustard bush

In the second follow-up parable (Mark 4:30–32), *the Parable of the Mustard Bush*, the imagery is consistent with Mark's programmatic themes and reinforces a public dimension to evangelism:

> And He said, "How shall we picture the kingdom of God, or by what parable shall we present it? It is like a mustard seed, which, when sown upon the soil, though it is smaller than all the seeds that are upon the soil, yet when it is sown, it grows up and becomes larger than all the garden plants and forms large branches; so that the birds of the air can nest under its shade" (4:30–32).

The picture of the proverbial small mustard seed producing a comparably large bush for the size of the seed is suggestive of small beginnings vs. large results. However, this, too, can obscure the subversive nature of this kingdom-parable. First, the mustard plant is not a tree; it is a large bush.[105] Second, this bush is an uncontrollable plant that tends to take over the garden. Finally, what farmer in his right mind wants birds[106] in his garden?

Like Mark's opening verses, *the parable of the mustard bush* "mingles"[107] three OT texts: Ezekiel 17:23, Ezekiel 31:6, Daniel 4:12:

> On the high mountain of Israel I will plant it, that it may bring forth boughs and bear fruit and become a stately cedar. And birds of every kind will nest under it; they will nest in the shade of its branches (Ezek 17:23).

---

104. Paul uses both *karpophoreō* (*bear fruit*) and *auxanō* (*grow, cause to grow*) to indicate that *the word of truth, the gospel* had expanded into the Colossae region (Col 1:5b–6); also note 1 Pet 2:2; 2 Pet 3:18.

105. In the Matthew and Luke versions the bush is portrayed as a tree.

106. *Birds* are equated with the nations, i.e., Gentiles in the OT imagery, and probably carry similar imagery here; thus, the term adds to the continued, increasing harvest of the *gospel of the word* imagery.

107. Marcus, *Mystery of the Kingdom*, 203.

> All the birds of the heavens nested in its boughs,
> And under its branches all the beasts of the field gave birth,
> And all great nations lived under its shade (Ezek 31:6).

> The tree grew large and became strong
> And its height reached to the sky,
> And it was visible to the end of the whole earth.
> Its foliage was beautiful and its fruit abundant,
> And in it was food for all
> The beasts of the field found shade under it,
> And the birds of the sky dwelt in its branches,
> And all living creatures fed themselves from it (Dan 4:11–12).

What is of interest is the contrast between the *trees* in the OT referents and the *bush*[108] in the Markan parable, and, as well an overlooked reference to the poor in the Daniel 4 context.

The two Ezekiel referents are judgment-parables, while in Daniel the context is a parabolic vision of judgment on the king of Babylon. All three references utilize the *tree* motif,[109] which is OT imagery for kings and their kingdoms, and the *branch* imagery represents how a kingdom offers protection and sustenance to its subjects.[110] Jesus, on the other hand, alters the OT imagery, ever so slightly, replacing the noble *Cedars of Lebanon* and the *large and strong tree* of Babylon with a domesticated mustard bush. "It is hard to escape the conclusion that Jesus deliberately links the rule of God to a weed."[111]

Daniel's interpretation (4:19–26) indicates that Nebuchadnezzar's dominion would be taken away until he recognizes that *the Most High is sovereign over all kingdoms on earth* (i.e., the true sovereign ruler of all the trees, v. 25 NIV). Then, in light of the branch imagery, there is

---

108. Here in Mark "the seed grows into the greatest of all *shrubs*, but in Matthew (13:32) and Luke (13:19) it becomes a tree" (Funk, "Looking Glass," 3–9). To someone knowledgeable of the OT, where great trees symbolize great kings and empires, Mark's reference to God's dominion as a large bush "comes as a jolt, even a joke. The birds of heaven are taking shelter here under a tree of about eight feet. The great tree of God's kingdom has gone domestic" (Funk quoting M. Sabin).

109. Along with the political connotations, the tree motif also carries a cultic and/or idolatrous connection as well.

110. Ezekiel's cedar-trees, as well as Nebuchadnezzar's vision, represent the power and growth of two non-Israelite empires, and the birds that find rest/nesting in them are the nations (see Ezek 31:6).

111. Witherington (*Gospel of Mark*, 172) quoting Oakman (*Jesus and the Economic Questions*, 127).

an interesting juxtaposition between the pending judgment and Daniel's advice to the king of Babylon:

> Therefore, O king, may my advice be pleasing to you: break away now from your sins by doing righteousness and from your iniquities <u>by showing mercy to the poor</u>, in case there may be a prolonging of your prosperity (Dan 4:27).

This advice reflects the Exodus land stipulations concerning righteousness and the poor. Ironically, the warning is to a non-Israelite, anti-Yahweh king, ruling a Gentile empire.

The OT trees vs. the Markan mustard bush, along with Daniel's reference to *showing mercy to the poor* (4:27), infuse the concept of the "in-breaking of the kingdom" with a broader sense than simply individual conversion. The kingdom of God, having taken root and growing mysteriously, subverts "existing kingdom visions and power structures."[112] *The Parable of the Mustard Bush* expands our understanding of evangelism to include issues regarding the dominions of mankind (i.e., socio-economic and power structures) and the poor.

Poor soil and the deeds that follow (Mark 5)

The reader/listener leaves the sowing parables and encounters Jesus in a series of miracle events (5:1–43) with noticeably very little "proclamation." A structural clue in Mark's Gospel story-line indicates that Jesus' actions themselves are a "sowing" of the gospel of the kingdom. Note the chiastic structure suggested by the apostle-commission texts that form the obvious bookends:

> A. The twelve and their kingdom task (3:13–19)
>   B. Conflict, the Beelzebul story, true family (3:20–35)
>   C. *Word parables (4:1–34)*
>   D. The authoritative, mysterious One (4:35–41)
>   C. *Action parables (5:1–43)*
>   B. Conflict, extended family/hometown rejection (6:1–6)
> A. The twelve and their kingdom task (6:7–13)[113]

---

112. Witherington indicates the existing structures in Israel are in Jesus' mind; however, the parable and the rest of the Gospel seem to point toward the dominion of God reaching well beyond the borders of Israel. And, as the "pigs" story is about to suggest, certainly the existing structure in place is there by the power of Rome itself (*Gospel of Mark*, 172).

113. Watts offered a possible chiastic structure; however, I slightly amended it

Wasted Evangelism (Mark 4)

The bookends (A) indicate that the commissioning of the twelve includes proclaiming and doing, word and deeds.

> (A) "And He appointed twelve, so that they would be with Him and that He could send them out to preach, and to have authority to cast out the demons" (3:14–15).

> (A) "They went out and preached that men should repent. And they were casting out many demons and were anointing with oil many sick people and healing them" (6:12–13; also 7b).

Along with the noticeable chiastic structure, these passages suggest that the deeds that follow are parable-deeds, demonstrating that evangelism, that is the sowing of the kingdom, includes both proclamation and action (deeds).

Furthermore, some have also noted that the miracles function in a similar way to the spoken word (i.e., Jesus' teaching). It has been observed that "the kind of amazement and awe that result from Jesus' miracles (2:12; 7:37) also result from his teaching (9:32; 11:18)."[114] The nature of the parables is noticeably parallel to the miracles in "their overall function" and "in many specific details of their contents."[115] The results are similar: both conceal and reveal, both are received and rejected, both reveal the in-breaking of God's reign. The miracles are "another mode of language (more dramatic certainly, but in its own way more ambivalent), communicating like parabolic teaching the mystery of God's action in the world."[116]

The stories in Mark 5 also portray the Master-Sower sowing the gospel in what appears to be unpromising soil. Everything about the three miracle vignettes hints at wasted seed that ought not to yield a crop. Immediately,

---

(*Isaiah's New Exodus*, 217n161).

114. Marcus (*Mystery of the Kingdom*, 16) referring to Achtemeier, "He Taught Them Many Things," 478–80.

115. Blomberg, "Miracles as Parables," 327–59; also, Myers, referring to G. Theissen (*Miracles Stories*, 264): "The discourse of healing and exorcism is central to this section. G. Theissen, in his study of the social function of primitive Christian miracle stories, points out that most contemporary Hellenistic miracle sources originated from the aristocracy, and through the highly institutionalized practice of divination and technique-magic were 'concerned with the maintenance of the accepted order and way of life.' Other pagan traditions of 'sorcery and magic represent an individualistic reaction to growing social disintegration.' In contrast, the gospel miracles assert the promise and possibility of radical socio-political change in behalf of the disenfranchised. They function to subvert, not legitimate, the dominate order" (*Binding the Strong Man*, 182).

116. Blomberg, "Miracles as Parables." As well, Marcus concludes that Mark's Gospel as a whole functions like a parable (*Mystery of the Kingdom*, 110).

Jesus is confronted by a man with an unclean spirit, in Gentile territory, who dwells among the dead (*among the tombs*, v. 3). Afterward on the return trip, Jesus is touched by a woman who has a hemorrhage and he touches a dead child. The *field* where Jesus immediately sows the kingdom is beyond the borders of the sacred. The *garden* where the domesticated bush of God's kingdom extends its branches, immediately attracts the unwanted—the unholy, unclean, the sick, and the dead—to find the protection and sustenance of its shade. The Master-Sower wastes his seed, yet, there is harvest.

EVANGELISM AND SOCIAL ACTION OUTCOMES

An etymologically based proclamation-centered evangelism is insufficient to reflect the reality of the presence of the kingdom of God, and, as well, disconnects evangelism, not only from the full life of the church, but also from the public and social implications of the kingdom.[117] True, it might be anachronistically incorrect to jump completely from Jesus' deeds straight to social action,[118] but it is equally wrong to turn Jesus' parables into mythic stories that affirm "traditional" American values, limited government, and a political and legal agenda that seeks to promote "our way of life."[119] Although leaping from the text to "Christian humanitarianism" is an oversimplification, we cannot ignore that Jesus engaged social institutions, nor overlook that Jesus had immense theological conflicts with temple leadership that reached back to Exodus stipulations and their social implications regarding the vulnerable.[120]

The kingdom context places evangelism directly in the midst of the public realm where the Christian community is obligated to deal with structural sin and be an advocate for the vulnerable and the poor. Also, to not include social action outcomes in evangelistic activities, limits the possible outcomes where God's rule and reign can be expressed, realized,

117. Abraham, "Theology of Evangelism."

118. Actually, it is not altogether inappropriate to make a logical leap from Jesus' deeds—miracles, exorcisms, healing, over-turning temple-trading tables, cursing a fig-tree, and the ultimate temple-destruction announcement—for it has been noted that some of the miracle stories contain references to actual political referents, and the miracles themselves carry a contrast to a social-political dynamic of crowd control.

119. Note Herzog's discussion (in *Parables as Subversive Speech*, 31–34) on Cadbury's *Peril of Modernizing Jesus*.

120. Note the background of the Mark 12 *poor widow* episode discussed in chapter 1, "Widows in Our Courts."

and experienced. Such limiting is the result of a privatized and dualistic understanding of the gospel. Rather, a kingdom-centered evangelism allows for the fullness of the gospel to be realized in individuals, groups, structures, systems, and even culture. Evangelistic strategies and actions ought to enact, demonstrate, fulfill, and advocate for outcomes consistent with God's reign over all the realms of humanity. Evangelistic outcomes ought to include both personal decisions for Christ *and* actions that promote God's righteousness and, in particular, social action that engages the needs and welfare of the vulnerable and the poor.

Almost four decades ago, David Moberg, in his *The Great Reversal: Evangelism and Social Concern*, asked how Christians were to deal with the issues of poverty. This continues to be a pertinent question for the Christian community today—let the debate be lively! However, the topic should not be shrunk to public vs. private, government vs. church, or red vs. blue politics. The gospel of the kingdom is "multidimensional and all-encompassing" and is concerned with both the individual and society.[121] Of course, the gospel calls individuals to a right relationship with God, but it goes beyond private piety, calling Christians, especially Christian leadership, to engage, not only with direct action (i.e., social action) on behalf of the economically vulnerable, but also social and institutional structures that work against fulfilling the church's obligations toward the poor. The Exodus land-laws, operating behind Mark's programmatic theme, were given to ensure that the vulnerable (i.e., the land-less) were full participants in the benefits of living in the land.[122] Social Action is a means to ensure that the blessings and benefits of living in society reach to the poor. The parable of *the Sower who sows* encourages the Christian community to waste its seed, sowing it into every realm and every corner of society "in hopes that good soil might somewhere be found," because it is "our area."

---

121. Arias in his *Announcing the Reign of God* offers one of the more detailed arguments that the "reign of God" ought to be the framework for evangelism.

122. For insight on "the land" and *the land-less* poor, see Brueggemann, *Land*.

EXCURSUS: THE LOGIC OF SOCIAL ACTION AS EVANGELISM

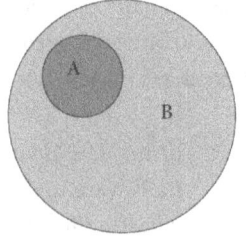

1. Evangelism (A) is Social Action (B)

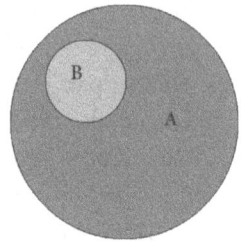

2. Social Action (B) is Evangelism (A)

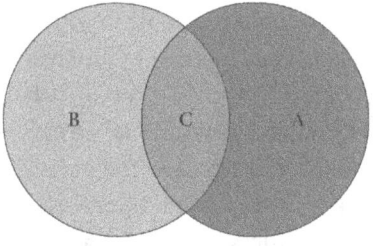

3. Some Social Action (C) is Evangelism (A), or Social Action can be Evangelism.

Is evangelism Social Action? Many simply say *no*. A few say *yes*. To get around actually answering the question, some posit the idea that social action is a consequence of evangelism (after someone is "saved" as it were) or "pre-evangelism." These latter proposals, in my opinion, only skirt the issue and are purely semantics that, actually, miss the point of social action all together. Furthermore, suggesting social action is a by-product of evangelism (i.e., conversion) is to misstate the potential conversion and misrepresent what social action actually is, namely the addressing of social structures to bring about results for those who do not have access to power.

Option # 3 is preferred. It is not that evangelism is a subset of social action (# 1), nor is social action a subset of evangelism (# 2). Evangelism is related to the arrival, revelation, and affirmation of the presence of the kingdom of God, so all social action is not necessarily such a kingdom confirming or promoting activity. However, when social action affirms the principles, intentions, realization and aspirations of the rule and reign of God, it is, as such, evangelism.

When social action promotes the realities of the kingdom of God and seeks to align the world with God's righteous reign, social action is indeed evangelism. This understanding leaves room for other forms of evangelistic activities, which include both word and deed (i.e., action). Furthermore, recognizing that social action is a legitimate form of evangelism also allows a wider range of spiritual gifts, talents, vocations, and personalities within a local congregation to be harnessed to increase the gospel.

3

"You Will Appear as *Fishers*" (Mark 1:17)
Disciples as Agents of Judgment

"Evangelism is not the kind of news that informs, a daily report of the world to be listened to while one goes on eating supper! Instead, it is an emergency bulletin. Table talk stops. The fork clatters to the plate. God has acted; God has provided; one must respond."
—Dr. Stephen Charles Mott

"Christianity conceals within itself a germ hostile to the church. It is far too easy for us to base our claims to God on our own Christian religiosity and our church commitment, and in so doing utterly to misunderstand and distort the Christian idea."
—Dietrich Bonhoeffer, quoted by Eric Metaxas in *Bonhoeffer: Pastor, Martyr, Prophet, Spy*

"We are not commissioned to create a new society; indeed, we are scarcely competent to do so. What the church can do best, though it does so all too seldom, is to delegitimate an unjust system and to create a spiritual counterculture."
—Walter Wink, *Engaging the Powers*

"You Will Appear as Fishers" (Mark 1:17)

AS A NEW CHRISTIAN in 1978, I was promptly placed into a small group of Christian Air Force colleagues for discipleship. Besides encouraging consistent church attendance, a daily prayer-life, and plenty of Bible study, we had a rather tight regimen of Bible verse memorization. For "getting into the Bible," we used the Navigator's *Designed for Discipleship* (or *DfD*s) and for "getting the Bible into us," we used the Navigator's *Topical Memory System* with verse packs and a pocket carrying case to promote regular memorization and self-testing. In the first pack, "Live the New Life," we memorized Matthew 4:19 under the topic, "Witness," *And He said to them, "Follow Me, and I will make you fishers of men."* This memory verse was to encourage our commitment to witnessing, that is, to be "fishers of people" for Jesus.

Many understand the *fisher*-promise to mean that Christians are to *fish* for the unsaved and *catch* them for Christ. Mark 1:17, the text under consideration in this study, and its parallel, Matthew 4:19, are regularly used to promote commitment to evangelism and to being a verbal witness. If one presumes this application, *fishing* is a positive metaphor, an illustration of evangelism, or a "picture of winning people to Christ." Interpreting "fishers of men" in this way assumes that *fishing* is a biblical metaphor for evangelizing (*fishers of men* = evangelism/ witnessing), and would have been understood as such without explanation by the disciples and, later, the readers/listeners of Mark's Gospel. On this reading, the *fishing* metaphor is, then, transferable to today's fishing context, and, thus, can be utilized as an illustration to call Christians to evangelize (i.e., to fulfill being "fishers of men").

It is common for preachers, evangelists, Sunday school teachers, Christian media celebrities, and even Bible professors to repeat Jesus' words in Mark 1:17 (as well as Matt 4:19) as a call and an illustration for evangelism. Messages on evangelism and witnessing using "the different types of fishing" are commonplace, utilizing images to promote the Christian call to evangelize and to exemplify the various ways one can "fish" for people: fly fishing, deep sea fishing, catching fish in nets, and using bigger nets to catch lots of fish (i.e., more people). However, I began to think differently about Jesus' words, *fishers of men*, when a preacher once suggested, "Sometimes you have to use a club, or even throw dynamite in the water to blast the fish out. Likewise, sometimes you have to use extreme methods to win people to Christ." At that moment, many years ago, I knew something was wrong with *that* use of *this* particular biblical metaphor.

While completely appreciating those who *catch* people for Christ, I believe we should pause long enough to reconsider: *fishing* as a metaphor, if fish are unsaved people, imagine evangelism *from the fish's* perspective. Truly, the metaphor seems mismatched. Nonetheless, almost every commentator reflecting on Jesus' words in Mark 1:17 posits a positive interpretation for the use of *fishers of men*. This study seeks to determine Mark's intention in presenting the *fisher*-promise, and, thus, reassess the metaphor's impact on the church's understanding of evangelism, and in particular how the *fisher* metaphor expands the Christian community's role in social action as a legitimate component of evangelism.

THE MISPLACED SELF-EVIDENT FISHERS METAPHOR

Admittedly, evangelism and fishing, at first glance, seem to be a match. So, when we read or hear the biblical phrase *fishers of men*, it appears to be a self-evident metaphor. Or, is it? However neatly these words fit in our stories, illustrations, and anecdotes about witnessing and evangelism, we should not simply assume that *fishers of men* is a self-evident metaphor for the modern reader/listener of the Bible. Think seriously about the *fishers of men* = evangelism/witnessing imagery. Carry it through as a metaphor: Is fishing *ever* good for the fish? The coming of the fisherman for the fish is not good; it is not a blessing. It is dangerous, menacing, ominous, dire, and presents a very life-ending possibility. Fishermen use tricks, cons, lures, hooks, and false hope. If winning souls for Jesus is the meaning of this metaphor, then it loses its seemingly clear metaphorical correspondence when it is transferred to the positive Christian activities of witnessing, evangelism, outreach, and church growth. Fishing is, simply put, not good for fish. The presence of fishermen is not a good sign for them at all. This, all by itself, suggests that we need to look elsewhere for the background that gives meaning (and interpretative depth) to the *fishers of men* metaphor.

Translations don't always help

In order to find meaning in a text of Scripture, there is a temptation to make a leap from the English words or concepts in our translations to whatever corresponds in our contemporary experience. Sometimes it is helpful to turn to various translations. However, in this case, the translations do not help us. In the *New American Standard Bible*, the Mark 1:17 text follows

"You Will Appear as Fishers" (Mark 1:17)

closely to the Greek, nearly word-for-word: "And Jesus said to them, 'Follow Me, and I will make you become fishers of men'" (*Kai eipen autois ho Iēsous, Deute opisō mou, kai poiēsō hymas genesthai halieis anthrōpōn*). Other versions render Mark 1:17 in relatively similar, nearly word-for-word, ways:

> "Come, follow me," Jesus said, "and I will make you fishers of men" (NIV, 1984).[1]

> And Jesus said unto them, "Come ye after me, and I will make you to become fishers of men" (KJV and ASV).

> Then Jesus said to them, "Follow Me, and I will make you become fishers of men" (NKJV).

> And Jesus said to them, "Come ye after me; [and] I shall make you to be made fishers of men" (*Wycliffe New Testament*).

Many translations are very straightforward with little interpretation. However, some modern translations like the *NETBible* reinforce the "fishing = evangelism/witnessing" understanding: *Jesus said to them, "Follow me, and I will turn you into fishers of people" (NETB)*. The *NETBible* expands the Mark 1:17 text, offering more an interpretation than a translation, with little explanation why the text refers to the disciple's vocation rather than a technical term with antecedent, connotative meaning. Other modern or contemporary versions offer similar "interpretations" of Mark 1:17:

> Jesus said to them, "Come with me! I will teach you how to bring in people instead of fish" (CEV).

> Jesus said to them, "Come follow me, and I will make you fish for people" (New Century Version).

> "Come, follow me," Jesus said, "and I will send you out to fish for people" (Today's New International Version).

---

1. While the 1984 version of the NIV keeps the translation closer to word-for-word, the 2011 NIV renders Mark 1:17, *"Come, follow me," Jesus said, "and I will send you out to fish for people."*

Paraphrases lead away from intention

As well, paraphrases and transliterated versions, with few exceptions, go in one direction, offering even less help in deciphering Mark's intent: *fishers of men is a self-evident metaphor for evangelizing* (i.e., *catching people for Jesus*). For example, the *New Living Translation* paraphrases (actually interprets) Mark 1:17: *Jesus called out to them, "Come, be my disciples, and I will show you how to fish for people!"* (NLT). As well, *The Message* paraphrases (again, actually interprets) both Mark 1:17 and Matthew 4:19, not only asserting the supposed self-evident metaphor of "fishing = evangelizing," but also adding words not in the original Greek that provoke the reader/listener to think Jesus actually uttered these words: *Jesus said to them, "Come with me. I'll make a new kind of fisherman out of you. I'll show you how to catch men and women instead of perch and bass"* (MSG). Although all translation involves a measure of interpretation, some versions directly interpret, rather than translate, insisting that Jesus is making a correspondence between fishing and activities of "soul winning." This moves the reader/listener away from what Mark had in mind as he developed his narrative, rather than being compelled by the intent that Mark has crafted into his narrative for those who would hear his Gospel.

As the remainder of this study will bear out, *fishers of men* was a self-evident metaphor when Jesus used it and, then, as Mark utilized it in his narrative, not because some of Jesus' disciples were fishermen or Mark's audience was familiar with fishing, but because there is an OT promised, eschatological expectation which is its referent. The picture Jesus was intending to invoke, perhaps, has little to do with casting out fishing nets or someone casting a fishing pole out in hopes of catching fish. I will suggest that a radically different metaphor is in mind, one that fits Jesus' immediate context and, as well, is consistent with the narrative crafted by Mark. The concept of *fishers* is not so much about Christian activity—though there is action to be taken—but that the metaphorical nature for *fishers* furnishes the definition and content for the range of potential evangelistic outcomes, i.e., the application for *fishing*.

There is a more difficult, harsher interpretation within a negative framework found in the potential correspondence to OT *fisher*-judgment texts and language, which are often traded for the ease of simple word-correspondence at the popular level or hermeneutical umbrage at the more academic level. This hinders hearing the impact that this more difficult, but legitimate, biblical association with the OT concept of *fishers* can have on the nature of evangelism. In the next section, we turn our attention to Mark's text and how *fishers of men* points toward such an OT and eschatological background.

MARK'S GOSPEL SET-UP AND THE MEANING OF THE FISHER-PROMISE

The meaning of the phrase *fishers of men* comes to us in a story, not a lecture; the argument is narrative, not syllogistic. The significance of *fishers of men* first appears within the structure of the introduction to Mark's Gospel story, and then in how this summary is worked out in the narrative world created by Mark. The readers/listeners, with varying degrees, are aware of the story and are familiar with the gospel as it spread throughout the Roman Empire.[2] Even if readers/listeners are unfamiliar with all the potential OT referents, they are already familiar with the gospel story itself and the introduction to Mark's narrative gives the impression that there is an OT background defining the gospel. Mark's introduction is crafted and structured with enough narrative markers to help the reader/listener make sense of the *fisher*-promise and its role in his narrative world. Mark's programmatic summary in 1:1–3 draws on OT eschatological promise-fulfillment and expectation-consummation. This does not stop at verses 1–3, but continues with the verses (4–17) that sets up the narrative world. Although most are comfortable viewing Mark's introduction through verse 15, there is no reason to exclude, as part of his introductory remarks, the initial invitation to join in the administration of the inaugurated kingdom (vv. 16–28).[3]

Preceding the *fisher*-promise, Mark sets the foundation (*the beginning*, v.1) of *the gospel of Jesus Christ, the Son of God* (1:1–3), reaching back to OT contexts (Exod 23; Isa 40; Mal 3) that link the gospel to covenant expectations, judgments regarding land-codes and justice stipulations, and God's actions regarding redemption and remnant.[4] As he begins to shape his Gospel, Mark, then, crafts indicators that highlight characters and the

---

2. I take the destination of Mark's Gospel to be Rome, or a wider church community strongly under Rome's (i.e., Caesar's) direct influence.

3. Henderson, *Christology and Discipleship*; Blakley, "Incomprehension or Resistance?."

4. For the OT backgrounds Mark uses to define *the gospel of Jesus Christ* (1:1) see chapter 2, "Wasted Evangelism."

roles they play (vv. 4–19). Mark's interest in these characters is not necessarily for *the person* (i.e., John the Baptist, 4–8; the Holy Spirit, 9–10; Jesus the Son, 11–13), or for *the group* (i.e., *followers/fishers of men*, 16–18), but for their eschatological significance in relation to the inaugurated kingdom. Mark, indeed, sets up his Gospel introduction in such a way that the readers/listeners should naturally draw such conclusions. The following examines how this helps to decipher the original "self-evident" meaning of the *fisher*-promise in Mark 1:17.

Character introduction: the "happening appearances" (1:4, 9, 11, 17)

There is a grammatical and stylistic clue in Mark's use of an overlooked, yet much used, often un-translated Greek word, *ginomai*, which is strategically embedded in the introduction of his Gospel narrative (Mark 1:4, 9, 11, 17).[5] Each use of a *ginomai* text marks an introduction of a character that is important both for developing the narrative and for explaining the nature of the gospel. Each use helps to reinforce the significance of Mark's programmatic summary (vv. 1–3) and presents or enhances an OT eschatological framework for understanding the gospel of Jesus-Messiah, the Son of God (1:1).

The common Greek word *ginomai* is used throughout Mark's gospel (42x) and typically carries its casual meaning of *be* and/or simply a "happening" in the narrative world. The word, for the most part, helps move the story forward, giving the reader/listener a sense of being *in the present*, pulling the reader/listener along. The common translative significance is along the lines of time, arrival (i.e., *came*), or simply the nuance of narrative movement. Some translations (and commentaries), however, leave out the implications of *ginomai* altogether. Perhaps, this is why the first four times Mark uses *ginomai* very little, if anything, is made of its significance by translators or, even, commentators on the texts. In fact, most translations of Mark 1:4, 9, 11, and 17 gloss over the possibility that there is some intentional significance to be drawn from Mark's use of *ginomai* and, particularly, the significance of verses that set-up the nature of the gospel of Jesus-Messiah, the Son of God (1:1).

---

5. Note, not present in some manuscripts, but a verb needs to be supplied, even if not original, and the choice of *ginomai* is logical.

"You Will Appear as Fishers" (Mark 1:17)

Among translations, the renderings of Mark 1:17 are various. In the NIV, we see a translative range: ". . . so John <u>came</u>"[6] (1:4), "At that time Jesus came" (1:9), "a voice <u>came</u> from heaven" (1:11), and, in 1:17, "I will make you fishers of men," omitting a translation or nuance of *ginomai* altogether. The NASB presents this set of verses: "John the Baptist <u>appeared</u> in the wilderness" (1:4), "In those days Jesus came from Nazareth" (1:9),[7] "a voice <u>came</u> out of the heavens" (1:11), and, in the text under consideration, "I will make you become fishers of men" (1:17). The *Today's New International Version* offers similar translations to the NASB for the first three—"And so John the Baptist <u>appeared</u> in the wilderness" (1:4), "At that time Jesus came from Nazareth" (1:9), "a voice <u>came</u> from heaven" (1:11)—but leaves *ginomai* out of any translative sense in 1:17 ("and I will send you out to fish").

The typical range of *be, happening, came/come,* and even *appear*, all seem plausible renderings here and elsewhere throughout Mark's Gospel. And, the places *ginomai* is left untranslated or is absorbed into the sense of other translated words are, as well, plausible and potentially a fair way to be rendered. Yet, its omission can leave the English reader without an awareness of the importance of the word's presence for determining the meaning and significance *in this particular* context.[8] For those translations that leave out *ginomai* in Mark 1:17 altogether, such translations obscure and hinder hearing its value as Mark sets up his narrative and the possibilities of meaning that assist the reader of English texts to interpret what follows. Most translations conceal the possibility that Mark utilizes *ginomai* to help the reader understand the significance of Jesus' invitation to follow him and *become fishers of men.*

Obviously, context helps determine the sense Mark gives to *ginomai*, nonetheless, there are valid reasons to render *ginomai* in its first four uses as *appear* or more specifically *appear publicly*. In other words, *ginomai* is used, not simply to indicate *being* or to give a present sense for the readers, but *a happening*, and, more specifically, *an appearance* of a character significant to the narrative development. The series of *ginomai* texts in Mark 1:4–17 indicate the *appearance in public* of characters that draw upon and

---

6 I have underlined words directly used to translate *ginomai*.

7. *Ginomai* is not translated directly and is merged with the time reference ("In those days"). Note, in translations of Mark 1:9 offering the English word "came" (*Jesus came*) the word is actually a rendering of the Greek verb *ēlthen* (*he came*) and not *ginomai*.

8. Use of *euthys* (*immediately*) in v. 19 gives a sense of immediate "inauguration."

affirm the programmatic sense Mark developed in his composite OT reference in vv. 2–3.

The sense of *appear* is an acceptable rendering for *ginomai* and should not be eliminated because it does not fit preconceived and popular understandings of the *fishers of men* verse. First, Mark deliberately includes *ginomai* in this text, whereas Matthew leaves it out altogether (as does Luke in his version of the fisher/hunter text, 5:10). Second, the use of *ginomai* carries the idea of "to come into existence," "to become," even "to be born" and, as many translations indicate, can be rendered as *appear* (such as NASB and TNIV). Translating *ginomai* as "appear publicly" is reasonable in these first four instances in Mark's introduction: The range of meaning allows such a rendering or nuance. Third, each of these four *ginomai* texts draw on eschatological and OT themes to introduce the appearance of characters involved with inaugurating the gospel of the kingdom. Mark sets up the introduction to his Gospel-story with a series of eschatological OT expectations that find fulfillment in the "public appearance" of God's kingdom/gospel agents:

> John the Baptist *appeared* (*egeneto*) in the wilderness preaching a baptism of repentance for the forgiveness of sins (1:4).[9]

> And *it appeared* (*egeneto*) in those days Jesus came from Nazareth in Galilee and was baptized by John in the Jordan and immediately coming up out of the water, He saw the heavens opening, and the Spirit like a dove descending upon Him . . . (1:9–10).

> . . . and a voice *appeared* (*egeneto*) out of the heavens, "You are My beloved Son, in You I am well-pleased" (1:11).

> And Jesus said to them, "Come (after) Me, and I will make you *to appear* (*genesthai*) as fishers of men" (1:17).

Character introduction as eschatological agents

We discover in this *ginomai* series the introduction of Jesus as the affirmed Messiah Son of God (1:11) and three characters in supporting roles and relationships to Jesus: John the Baptist, harbinger and way-preparer of Jesus

---

9. These four Mark 1 verses (4, 9–10, 11, and 17) are translated by the author to show the use of *ginomai* (become).

(1:4.), the Holy Spirit, who endows Jesus (1:9), and, then, Jesus' followers, whom he will create to be *fishers of men* (1:17). Each of these *ginomai* texts draw on OT referents, explicit and implied, that offer defining, eschatological distinctiveness to both the gospel and to the characters being introduced.

Mark 1:4.

John the Baptist's eschatological significance is widely recognized, particularly his role as the anticipated forerunner and herald of the kingdom and the Messiah's soon appearance. The immediate reference locating John *in the wilderness* (1:4) links back to Mark's Isaiah 40 reference in verse 3, provoking John's relationship with Yahweh's expected appearance to execute the future, new exodus. John's call to baptism is a harbinger event of the coming of the Spirit (v. 8) and, as well, the time of repentance, before the coming of the kingdom. John's clothing draws on Elijah's appearance in 2 Kings 1:8, as well as in Zechariah 13:4[10] that links *the returning true prophet* with Elijah.[11] Also, there is the obvious link to Mark's opening programmatic summary (vv. 2–3) with the reference to Malachi 3:1, which is associated with Malachi 4:5–6:

> "Behold, I am going to send you Elijah the prophet before the coming of the great and terrible day of the Lord. He will restore the hearts of the fathers to their children and the hearts of the children to their fathers, so that I will not come and smite the land with a curse."

Later in Mark's narrative, this connection is made even more directly:

> They asked Him, saying, "Why is it that the scribes say that Elijah must come first?" And He said to them, "Elijah does first come and restore all things. And yet how is it written of the Son of Man that He will suffer many things and be treated with contempt? But I say to you that Elijah has indeed come, and they did to him whatever they wished, just as it is written of him" (9:11–13).

Additionally, John introduces Jesus as the One who comes after him who is *mightier than I* (1:7), which further links Mark's programmatic

---

10. "Also it will come about in that day that the prophets will each be ashamed of his vision when he prophesies, and they will not put on a hairy robe in order to deceive" (Zech 13:4).

11. France, *Gospel of Mark*, 65–68.

reference in vv. 2–3 to Isaiah 40, where Yahweh is referred to as the Lord God who *will come with might* (Isa 40:10). The Isaiah 40 text is the eschatological promise of Yahweh's new exodus, a redemption that causes his glory to be seen by *all flesh* (Isaiah 40:5). And, it should be noted that John is the eschatological messenger (Mal 3:1; Isa 40:3) who links Jesus to the eschatological expectation of the coming of the Spirit: *I baptized you with water; but He will baptize you with the Holy Spirit* (1:8).

The OT is rich in its material indicating the coming of the eschatological Spirit.

> Until the Spirit is poured out upon us from on high,
> And the wilderness becomes a fertile field,
> And the fertile field is considered as a forest (Isa 32:15).

> "For I will pour out water on the thirsty land
> And streams on the dry ground;
> I will pour out My Spirit on your offspring
> And My blessing on your descendants" (Isa 44:3).

> "It will come about after this
> That I will pour out My Spirit on all mankind;
> And your sons and daughters will prophesy,
> Your old men will dream dreams,
> Your young men will see visions.
> Even on the male and female servants
> I will pour out My Spirit in those days (Joel 2:28–29).

> "Moreover, I will give you a new heart and put a new spirit within you; and I will remove the heart of stone from your flesh and give you a heart of flesh. I will put My Spirit within you and cause you to walk in My statutes, and you will be careful to observe My ordinances" (Ezek 36:26–27).

> I will not hide My face from them any longer, for I will have poured out My Spirit on the house of Israel," declares the Lord God (Ezek 39:29).

Mark 1:4 begins a series of character introductions (cf. vv. 9, 11, 17) that are pivotal in defining the eschatological nature of the gospel, assisting the reader/listener to understand that God's OT types and promises are coming to culmination, fulfillment in the appearance of Jesus-Messiah, the Son of God (1:1). *John the Baptist appeared in history (egeneto) as God's eschatological agent, announcing the inauguration of his kingdom and introducing the Messiah.*

Mark 1:9.

Familiarity with Jesus is assumed in Mark, thus the absence of biographical information (e.g., birth narrative, other family, or current historical record), which Robert Guelich suggests likely stems from Mark's intention "to introduce Jesus in the framework of redemptive history."[12] As suggested by the programmatic summary in 1:2–3 and the eschatological setting established in the introduction of John the Baptist (vv. 4–8), Mark is concerned about placing the reader/listener *immediately* into the realm of redemptive, eschatological fulfillment of OT promises. At the second introductory *ginomai* text (1:9), Mark associates Jesus with the coming of the Holy Spirit, which, too, draws on eschatological expectations regarding the Messiah and/or Yahweh to the Spirit:

> The Spirit of the Lord will rest on Him,
> The spirit of wisdom and understanding,
> The spirit of counsel and strength,
> The spirit of knowledge and the fear of the Lord (Isa 11:2).

> Behold, My Servant, whom I uphold;
> My chosen one in whom My soul delights.
> I have put My Spirit upon Him;
> He will bring forth justice to the nations (Isa 42:1).

> The Spirit of the Lord GOD is upon me,
> Because the Lord has anointed me
> To bring good news to the afflicted;
> He has sent me to bind up the brokenhearted,
> To proclaim liberty to captives
> And freedom to prisoners (Isa 61:1).

This connection enhances the already established link to the Spirit referenced by John (1:8).[13]

Although the role of the Spirit in Mark's Gospel is minimal, an underlying intention is to show the link of the Spirit to the redemptive era that

---

12. Guelich, *Mark 1–8:26*, 31.
13. Also, connected to 1 Sam 16:13; Judg 3:10; 6:34.

has dawned in the coming of Messiah Jesus. It is the Spirit that casts (1:12) Jesus into the desert and Jesus exists in the mode of the Spirit (2:8; 8:12). In Mark 3, we hear that the rejection of Jesus as Messiah is an unforgivable sin *against the Holy Spirit* (v. 29). Later, Mark reveals the presence of the Holy Spirit in Jesus' own apology as the promised and rightful Davidic-Son-King, the type to come (*David himself said in the Holy Spirit, "the Lord said to My Lord, 'Sit at My right hand, until I put Your enemies beneath Your feet,'"* Mark 12:36). After John baptizes Jesus, "the heavens" open and the Holy Spirit, like a dove, descends *upon* Him. The opening of the heavens is reminiscent of Isaiah 64:1[14] (*Oh, that You would rend the heavens and come down, That the mountains might quake at Your presence*) and the reference to the "dove" has connections to Israel and God's act in the flood of Genesis.[15] Later, Jesus' followers will respond to being the misfits, those out of place, misunderstood, persecuted, falsely charged, accused of treason by speaking, not on their own, but by the Holy Spirit (Mark 13:11).

These referents link the Holy Spirit to the promise-fulfillment, type-antitype context that Mark utilizes to indicate the in-breaking of the kingdom into the realm of humanity: *And it appeared publicly (egeneto) in those days that Jesus was baptized by John, one of God's eschatological agents, when the heavens opened and the eschatological Holy Spirit descended upon Jesus.*

Mark 1:11.

After Jesus is introduced by John as the "mightier One who is coming" and who would be baptized with the Holy Spirit, a voice from Heaven announces, "You are My beloved Son, in You I am well-pleased" (1:11). This affirmation has been associated with four significant OT texts:

> Behold, My Servant, whom I uphold;
> My chosen one in whom My soul delights
> I have put My Spirit upon Him;
> He will bring forth justice to the nations (Isa 42:1).

---

14. *Anoixēs ton ouronon* (Isaiah 63:19c, LXX); note Gen 7:11; Ps 77.23 (LXX); Isa 5:1; 18:6; 24:18; Ezek 1:1; Zech 14:4; also T. Levi 18:6–8; T. Jud. 24:3—link Spirit with Messiah.

15. The reference *dove*, sometimes used as a symbol of Israel (b. Ber. 53b; b. Š49a; Ct. Rab. 1:15, 2; 2:14, 1; 4:1, 2); also a likely reference to the flood (1 Pet 3:20–21; Gen 8:8–12), making a stronger connection to God's redemptive action in time and space.

"You Will Appear as Fishers" (Mark 1:17)

He said, "Take now your son, your only son, whom you love, Isaac, and go to the land of Moriah, and offer him there as a burnt offering on one of the mountains of which I will tell you" (Gen 22:2).

"I will surely tell of the decree of the Lord:
He said to Me, 'You are My Son,
Today I have begotten You'" (Ps 2:7).

Then you shall say to Pharaoh, "Thus says the LORD, 'Israel is My son, My firstborn'" (Exod 4:22).

Rather than choosing which OT prophecy God is fulfilling, there is value in understanding that all are implied, particularly since all foretell redemptive-historical and typological aspects of God's action in history. Each establishes Jesus' link to OT expectations and typological correspondences regarding Jesus' authority as God's Son-King over the nations (Ps 2:7),[16] his association to the nation-blessing promises given to Abraham (Gen 22:2), the redemptive expectations of Yahweh's Servant of the New Exodus (Isa 42:1), and the undervalued reference to God calling his newly "baptized" Israel, "My Son" (Exod 4:22).[17]

The voice out of the heavens appears in order to affirm publicly (egeneto) that Jesus is God's Son-King, the fulfillment of the Abrahamic promises, and the One who inaugurates the new exodus. Jesus is, indeed, one of God's eschatological agents of the inaugurated kingdom.

Fishing is the outcome of God's inauguration of his kingdom

Each of the first three *ginomai* texts introduces characters in the narrative who have roles that play a part in inaugurating the presence of the kingdom. Perhaps, this is why there is a summary interlude, referring to the gospel and Jesus' mission (1:14–15) which contains both the need for repentance and belief/faith (*The time is fulfilled, and the kingdom of God is*

---

16. It is broadly understood that the foretold future Messiah is related to David (Ps 2; cf. 1QS 9:11; Test. Levi 7; Test. Jud. 21:1ff.). C. Rowland notes that "later the Messianic figure narrows more specifically to be described as a 'descendent of David who would act as the eschatological agent of God' (cf. 2 Esd 12:32; Syr. Bar 29:3; 39:7; 40:1; 70:9; 72:2)" ("Messiah," in *Westminster Dictionary of Christian Theology*, 358–59). Also see Dunn, *Jesus Remembered*, 705–8; Scobie, *Ways of Our God*, 312–13.

17. It should be noted that the reference to God calling Israel "My Son" also leads into the first exodus event.

at hand; repent and believe in the gospel, 1:15) just prior to the last of the *ginomai* texts in the series. These eschatological characters promote (and imitate) that mission. It is no happenstance that Mark bridges the first three eschatological agents (John, the Holy Spirit, Jesus the Messiah-King-Son of God) to the fourth *ginomai* text, the *fisher*-promise (Mark 1:17), by a summary of Jesus' preaching: *God's eschatological agent declares his mission, as well as the substance of the presence of the kingdom and invites followers to join in the mission.* As the first three make public the present marks of eschatological fulfillment, there is a reasonable basis to consider the same intent for the fourth *ginomai* text, namely that Mark 1:17 also refers to another eschatological agent. After setting the character introduction pattern, with its OT expectation, announcing the arrival of the kingdom as the time of fulfillment, Jesus invites followers with the promise that he will make them *appear* as *fishers*—they will *appear* publicly as God's eschatological agents, as have John, the Holy Spirit, and Jesus.

Although there are no direct phrase parallels in the OT, various *fisher* texts are available as potential background for deciphering Jesus' choice of the expression *fishers of men (halieis anthrōpōn)*: Jeremiah 16:16; Ezekiel 19:4–5; 29:4–5; 38:4; Amos 4:2; Habakkuk 1:14–17. *Fishers/hunters* in the OT are presented as God's instruments to accomplish his will, primarily through acts of judgment. Most commentators refer to these OT *fisher* texts, but mostly dismiss them, because they do not fit what appears to them as Mark's stress on positive aspects of God's work in Jesus the Messiah. R. T. France recognizes the OT metaphorical background, noting Jeremiah 16:16; Amos 4:2; Habakkuk 1:14–17, yet does not see such potential judgment in light of the Good News.[18] France sees rescue in the Good News, not hook or catch for judgment. But, he does not exactly explain why. Guelich notes the OT background, as well, but points out that the referent "carries a negative tone of judgment," which he deems unsuitable for Mark's context.[19] Ted Blakley, in his recent dissertation on Mark 4–8, recognizes the negative OT context, but disallows for its relevance in Mark. He writes:

> Yet, in all of these texts, the metaphorical deployment of fishing language and imagery (e.g., fish, fishers, nets, and hooks) occurs in contexts of judgment, which does not correspond to the Marken context with its stress on salvation.[20]

18. France, *Gospel of Mark*, 96.
19. Guelich, *Mark 1–8:26*, 51.
20. Blakley, "Incomprehension or Resistance?," 160.

Others simply conclude that the background of the disciples as fisherman is sufficient for the meaning and metaphorical correspondence.[21]

Viewing the Markan *fishers* as positive, as a rescue, nonetheless, seems to invalidate the fishing metaphorical correspondence, for fish are not rescued—there is nothing positive for *fish-people* in the actual metaphorical correspondence. Furthermore, William Lane reminds us,

> To interpret this phrase only as a play on words appropriate to the situation is to fail to appreciate its biblical background and its relevance to the context, which has focused attention on God's eschatological act in sending Jesus. In the OT prophetic tradition it is God who is the fisher of men. The passages in which the image is developed are distinctively ominous in tone, stressing the divine judgment.[22]

Lane continues by noting the "intimate connection" between the summary verse in 1:15 and the *fisher*-promise in 1:17: The eschatological act of *fishing* is evidence of the presence of the kingdom that Jesus proclaimed.[23] *Fishing* is the outcome of "God's decisive action."[24]

Lane's observations are more aligned with both the OT referents and in how Mark actually has set up his introduction. Furthermore, it makes sense that, as the first three *ginomai* texts introduce God's eschatological agents used to inaugurate the kingdom, so also does the fourth introduce similar characters: the followers/disciples who will be made *fishers*. This can be observed by how Mark introduces *the invitation-call/promise* and then how Jesus commissions his followers as an extension of his mission in Mark 3 (first and then expanded in Mark 6):

---

21. Guelich, *Mark 1–8:26*, 51; note Taylor, *Gospel According to St. Mark*, on this text.
22. Lane, *Gospel of Mark*, 68; also see Rudman, " 'Fishers of Men' in the Synoptic Gospels," 106–18.
23. Lane, *Gospel of Mark*, 68.
24. Ibid., 68; also see 1QH vv. 7–8.

Mark 1:17—Invitation/fisher-promise	Mark 3:13–16—Summons/creating fishers
And Jesus said to them, "Come (after) me . . ." (1:17a, b).^A	And [He] summoned those whom He Himself wanted, and they came to Him (3:13b).
And <u>I will make/create</u> (*kai poiēsō*) you to become fishers of men (1:17c).	And <u>He makes/creates</u> (*kai epoiēsen*) twelve . . . (3:14a; note 3:16a *kai epoiēsen tous dōdeka*).

A. Author's translation of Mark 1:17 and Mark 3:13–16 throughout unless otherwise noted.

There is an obvious parallel—promise-fulfillment—crafted into Mark's narrative. In Mark 1, amid the introduction of eschatological characters that play a role in the "gospel of Jesus Christ," we have the invitation to follow Jesus as characters to carry out the mission of Jesus (1:14). This invitation is also cast as a promise, "I will make [*poiēsō*] you to become fishers of men." This invitation is, then, met with fulfillment in Mark's summons in 3:13–19 when he "creates [*epoiēsen*] twelve . . ." (v. 14a). Jesus' fisher-promise of 1:17 is fulfilled in the Mark 3 commission of the twelve. It then follows that the content of the commission is the nature of being a *fisher*. Fishers are those who are "with him" and those who are sent to preach and cast out demons.[25]

> *fishers* = those who are with Jesus (i.e., followers/disciples)
>   who are sent to herald [the gospel of God, cf. 1:14–15]
>   and
>   who are sent to have authority to cast out demons

The initial narrative call or invitation to *follow after* Jesus comes immediately after the summary of Jesus' message and mission (1:14–15). The first call is, as is the whole of the introduction, an inaugural act that points to the "enactment of God's dominion."[26]

---

25. For an expansion and fuller analysis on the meaning of the Mark 3 commission see chapter 6, "Significance *Before* Application."

26. Blakley, "Incomprehension or Resistance?," 158; note Henderson, ". . . 'Jesus' recruitment of the fishers constitutes an inaugural—and thus momentous—step in his enactment of God's dominion'" (*Christology and Discipleship*, 49–50).

"You Will Appear as Fishers" (Mark 1:17)

Although Blakley only sees a weak connection to OT *fishers*, he is correct in observing that the "appointment of the Twelve in Mark 3:13–19 is the logical progression of Jesus' promise in 1:16–20, as indicated by the verbal and thematic features shared by these two episodes."[27] Jesus promises to make (*poieō*) those who "come after" him to be *fishers*. Mark draws a correspondence between the call-promise in Mark 1:17 and the naming and commissioning in Mark 3:13–19. The narrative reveals that the Mark 3 commission is the inaugurated fulfillment of the *fisher*-promise. This is why Jesus' word in Mark 1:17 is future, a promise. So it follows that Mark 1:17 is further explained (defined) by the role and responsibilities given to the "followers" in the commission pericope in Mark 3 (and later expanded in Mark 6). The ones invited to follow in the initial call (the fourth *ginomai* text, 1:16–20) head the list of the Mark 3 commissioning of the twelve in the fulfillment of the promise to be *made* (*poiēsō*, 1:17/*epoiēsen*, 3:14, 16) *fishers*. None of the other Gospel writers use *poieō* (*make/create*) to characterize the calling/naming of the twelve, making it more likely that Mark wants the reader/listener to make this narrative connection between the promise to be made *fishers* and the fulfillment in commissioning and naming of the twelve. The meaning of *fishers* in Mark 1 finds its content in the Mark 3 commission of the twelve, namely, *fishers* are those who are *with Jesus* and who, then, will be sent out *to preach* and *to have authority to cast out demons*. This is what it means to be "*made to become fishers of men.*"

THE SELF-EVIDENT MEANING: OT FISHER CONTEXTS SHAPE THE NATURE OF EVANGELISM

As with the earlier *ginomai* texts (1:4, 9, 11), the Mark 1:17 *fisher*-promise also yields evidence of an antecedent OT background that fits the Mark's context. Acknowledging Mark's OT and eschatological pattern in the first set of character introductions, the *fisher*-promise should inform and shape the church's understanding of both the nature of discipleship and of evangelism.

---

27. Blakley, "Incomprehension or Resistance?," 163; "Jesus' promise to make Simon and Andrew fishers of people (1:17) introduces a narrative thread of logical progression that works its way through the narrative, from the callings of James and John (1:19–20) and Levi (2:14), through the appointment of the twelve, to the commissioning and sending out of the Twelve, first to Jews (6:7–13) and then to Gentiles (6:45)" (Blakley, 167).

Many who comment on Mark 1:17 acknowledge the seminal and exhaustingly detailed study by Wilhelm H. Wuellner, *The Meaning of "Fishers of Men"* published in 1967. His study examines the *fisher/hunter* and other related metaphors throughout ancient biblical and non-biblical literature. Although most acknowledge that the *fisher* imagery, as presented and surveyed by Wuellner, is used widely and carries a range of metaphorical meaning, there are analogous meanings that are particularly relevant to Mark's Gospel narrative. The *fisher* metaphor carries a Greco-Roman pedagogical meaning that is associated with educators, philosophers, wise men, and is explained within a "learning-teaching" context.[28] A philosophical teacher-student relationship as *fisher*-pupil/disciple metaphor also can be found in Ancient Near Eastern, Jewish, Christian, Rabbinic, and Greco-Roman traditions, and, as well, it occurs in cultic, prophetic, didactic, social, and cultural contexts—all of which can carry both positive and negative connotations. Additionally, Wuellner shows the *fisher* metaphor's association with the establishment of justice, which is identified in a range of uses from the Egyptian *Book of the Dead*, OT prophetic traditions, as well Lucian's essay "The Fisherman."[29] Any suggestion, therefore, that the metaphorical correspondence is a simple word-play with the follower's occupation as fisherman seems rather narrow and even improbable given its wide and pervasive use in ancient biblical and non-biblical literature.

Though many define the *fishers* metaphor as a positive one, the meaning of the promise can only be deduced from the context. Those finding the OT with its negative connotations an unsuitable referent, do so on the basis that such a background does not fit Mark's context and is incongruous to the Good News, should note it is precisely that particular *fisher* metaphor—packed with the content of God's action in sending *fishers* as described in the OT—that corresponds to the introduction crafted by Mark and the Gospel narrative he develops. Even Blakley comments that "Jeremiah 16:16, which offers the closest parallel to Mark, occurs in a context in which YHWH announces judgment for Judah's idolatry."[30] Yet, it is precisely the issue of idolatry which begs the stern language from Jesus against the scribes in Mark 3 (in the Beelzebul conflict) and, as well, against those who do not have *ears to hear* the gospel as indicated in the harsh use of the Isaiah 6 idolatry-taunt in Mark 4:10–12. The issue of idolatry is present in

---

28. Wuellner, *Fishers of Men*, 70–71.
29. Henderson, *Christology and Discipleship*, 59.
30. Blakley, "Incomprehension or Resistance?," 160.

"You Will Appear as Fishers" (Mark 1:17)

Mark's narrative world.[31] In fact, idolatry is embedded into the contexts of the three blended OT texts that provide Mark's underlying foundation and programmatic summary of the gospel (Mark 1:2–3; Isa 40:3; Exod 23:20; Mal 3:1).[32] How Mark has framed his introduction and crafted his narrative, then, begs the reader/listener to draw significance from the OT *fisher* referents.

The fisher (con)texts: Jer 16, Amos 4, Hab 1, Ezek 29, 38, Isa 37

The OT *fisher* concept carries a connotation of God's judgment—*fishers* are God's agents of judgment, given the authority to carry out God's will to judge injustice and to establish his sovereignty and rule over the realm of humankind. What is overlooked by most commenting on the Markan *fisher* text is that the concentration of judgment throughout these texts (Jer 16:16; Amos 4:1–2; note Hab 1:14–15; Ezek 29:4–5; 38:4; Isa 37:29) draws the reader/listener back to covenantal obedience, avoiding idolatry, *and* identification with the economically vulnerable.

The closest and, perhaps, the primary referent for Mark is the Jeremiah *fisher* text where the prophet announces:

> "Behold, I am going to send for many fishermen," declares the Lord, "and they will fish for them; and afterwards I will send for many hunters, and they will hunt them from every mountain and every hill and from the clefts of the rocks" (Jer 16:16).

The obvious reason for God's *fisher*-agents of judgment was the people had become idolatrous:

> "Then you are to say to them, 'It is because your forefathers have forsaken Me,' declares the LORD, 'and have followed other gods and served them and bowed down to them; but Me they have forsaken and have not kept My law. You too have done evil, even more than your forefathers; for behold, you are each one walking according to the stubbornness of his own evil heart,[33] without listening to Me. So I will hurl you out of this land into the land which you have not known'" (Jer 16:11–13).

---

31. See chapter 5, "Idolatry and Poverty," for Mark's use of OT texts referring to idolatry.

32. See chapter 2, "Wasted Evangelism."

33. *Stubbornness* = reference to being an idolater; see Beale, *We Become What We Worship*, 124–25.

The flow of thought in Jeremiah, where the prophet is the initial *agent of judgment* (Jer 15–19), contains numerous references to idolatry (including *God vs. the gods* tautologies) as a cause/effect for God's judgment:

> "I will first doubly repay[34] their iniquity and their sin, because they have polluted My land; they have filled My inheritance with the carcasses of their detestable idols and with their abominations."
> O Lord, my strength and my stronghold,
> And my refuge in the day of distress,
> To You the nations will come
> From the ends of the earth and say,
> "Our fathers have inherited nothing but falsehood,
> Futility and things of no profit."
> Can man make gods for himself?
> Yet they are not gods!
> "Therefore behold, I am going to make them know—
> This time I will make them know
> My power and My might;
> And they shall know that My name is the Lord" (Jer 16:18–21).[35]

> "Yet they did not listen or incline their ears, but stiffened their necks in order not to listen or take correction" (Jer 17:23).[36]

> "For My people have forgotten Me,
> They burn incense to worthless gods
> And they have stumbled from their ways,
> From the ancient paths,
> To walk in bypaths,
> Not on a highway" (Jer 18:15).

In the midst of the references to idolatry are reminders—direct and indirect—of the covenant stipulations concerning the poor. In Jeremiah 16–18, those who refuse to provide and advocate for the economically vulnerable will become subject to *sword* and *famine*, becoming *childless*, that is *widows* and *orphans* (Exod 22:24; cf. Ps 109):

---

34. Interestingly, the "doubly repay" reference is also found in Isaiah 40:2, further linking the programmatic summary in Mark's opening verses to the eschatological nature of the *fisher*-promise.

35. See Jer 17:2.

36. Reference to *not listening ears* draws similarities to Isaiah 6 idol-taunt and *stiffened their necks* pulls the listener back to the original golden-cow-worship in Exodus (See Beale, *We Become What We Worship*, 82).

"You Will Appear as Fishers" (Mark 1:17)

"They will die of deadly diseases, they will not be lamented or buried; they will be as dung on the surface of the ground and come to an end by sword and famine, and their carcasses will become food for the birds of the sky and for the beasts of the earth" (Jer 16:4).

Therefore, give their children over to famine[37]
And deliver them up to the power of the sword;
And let their wives become childless and widowed.
Let their men also be smitten to death,
Their young men struck down by the sword in battle (Jer 18:21).

These consequences are reminiscent of covenant expectations and threats:

You shall not wrong a stranger or oppress him, for you were strangers in the land of Egypt. You shall not afflict any widow or orphan. If you afflict him at all, and if he does cry out to Me, I will surely hear his cry; and My anger will be kindled, and I will kill you with the sword, and your wives shall become widows and your children fatherless (Exod 22:21–24).[38]

Cursed is he who distorts the justice due an alien, orphan, and widow. And all the people shall say, "Amen" (Deut 27:19).

Your carcasses will be food to all birds of the sky and to the beasts of the earth, and there will be no one to frighten them away. The Lord will smite you with the boils of Egypt and with tumors and with the scab and with the itch, from which you cannot be healed. The Lord will smite you with madness and with blindness and with bewilderment of heart (Deut 28:26–28).[39]

The identification of *fishers* as a means of judgment is also found in Amos 4:1–2, narrowing the focus of judgment specifically to those oppressing the economically vulnerable:

Hear this word, you cows of Bashan who are on the mountain of Samaria,
Who oppress the poor, who crush the needy,

---

37. Note the curse of famine, Deut 32:24.

38. See Exod 23:9; Lev 19:33–34; 25:35; Deut 1:16; 10:18–19; 15:9; 27:19; 24:17–18; Job 34:28; 35:9; Pss 10:14, 17–18; 68:5; 109:2–9; Prov 23:10–11; Jer 7:6–7; Zech 7:10.

39. Note *cursed* for serving other gods (Deut 28:14); also, the curses are reminiscent of plagues on Egypt's gods.

> Who say to your husbands, "Bring now, that we may drink!"
> The Lord God has sworn by His holiness,
> "Behold, the days are coming upon you
> When they will take you away with meat hooks,
> And the last of you with fish hooks" (Amos 4:1–2).

The reference here draws upon the cause of God's judgment, namely affluent ladies of the Northern Kingdom who are oppressing the poor. The mention of *cows of Bashan* could be a pun related to idolatry (*cow* draws us back to the original idol-calves, Exod 32) and pinpoints the idolatry to wanton wealth accumulation without concern for its effect (as implied in the exuberant, sarcastic comment "to bring on the drinks!"), specifically implying covenant breaking in oppressing/defrauding the poor.

Amos 4:1–2 is part of a thread that links covenantal unfaithfulness and misshapen values of wealth accumulation at the expense of the poor:

> Thus says the Lord,
> "For three transgressions of Israel and for four
> I will not revoke its punishment,
> Because they sell the righteous for money
> And the needy for a pair of sandals.
> These who pant after the very dust of the earth on the head of the helpless
> Also turn aside the way of the humble;
> And a man and his father resort to the same girl
> In order to profane My holy name" (Amos 2:6–7).

> Therefore because you impose heavy rent on the poor
> And exact a tribute of grain from them,
> Though you have built houses of well-hewn stone,
> Yet you will not live in them;
> You have planted pleasant vineyards, yet you will not drink their wine.
> For I know your transgressions are many and your sins are great,
> You who distress the righteous and accept bribes
> And turn aside the poor in the gate (Amos 5:11–12).[40]

---

40. Note Amos 5:10. The *poor in the gate* refers, not to the poor who "hang" at the city gate, but the role of the leadership who are "at the city gate" who were responsible for legislatively applying the covenant stipulations, the place where the poor were to go for presenting their case. The Amos context implies that *the poor* were not getting their justice by the municipal leadership/elders and the injustice was related to the economic well-being of those whose land was not returned as the Sabbath laws commanded, but were subject to *heavy rent*, and thus continuous/prolonged poverty.

> Hear this, you who trample the needy, to do away with the humble
> of the land, saying,
> "When will the new moon be over,
> So that we may sell grain,
> And the sabbath, that we may open the wheat market,
> To make the bushel smaller and the shekel bigger,
> And to cheat with dishonest scales,
> So as to buy the helpless for money
> And the needy for a pair of sandals,
> And that we may sell the refuse of the wheat?" (Amos 8:4–6).

This thread points to those who have security and power and yet prevent the economically vulnerable to escape out of prolonged poverty, disregarding justice for the economically vulnerable "at the gate." The call to follow Jesus implies a *fisher*-discipleship and evangelism that are associated with the covenant expectations toward the poor and the consequences of idolatrous patterns of social life.

Similar language is used in Habakkuk 1 and Ezekiel 29, where the imagery of *fishing* is a tool of judgment. This, too, has an apologetic nature: Ultimately this judgment activity of God will reveal that he alone is Lord (Jer 16:21) and, through this revelation, God will make himself *known in the sight of many nations* (Ezek 38:23). In Habakkuk, it is through the *fishing* activity that the ungodly, the unrighteous, and those who oppose God are gathered together for judgment (Hab 1:14–15). The judgment passages that utilize *fishing* imagery also promise a future remnant (through God's *fisher*-agents of judgment) that returns/restores the outcomes of covenant stipulations, offering a reasonable correspondence to the remnant theme developed throughout Mark's narrative.

THE INAUGURATED KINGDOM AND ITS AGENTS OF JUDGMENT: IMPLICATIONS

As Mark has set up the eschatological framework to introduce pivotal characters in his Gospel, the reference to the fishing metaphor links Jesus' *followers* to prophetic threads that present "God's apocalyptic rectifications of the world," which are carried out through Israel and other various *authorized* agents that involve both redemption and accompanying judgment.[41] The above survey of OT material and threads indicates that within

---

41. Note Wuellner, *Fishers of Men*, 123.

the promise-fulfillment/expectation-consummation pattern there is an underlying eschatological framework that includes judgment regarding the issues of poverty that effect the economically vulnerable. It is not whether we like that connection or not, but what significance it has for Christian discipleship and potential evangelistic outcomes?

The pattern set by Mark in his character introductions through the four *ginomai* texts help to give an eschatological connotation to Jesus' *fisher*-promise in Mark 1:17. This view is strengthened in that the call to follow appears immediately after the summary announcement concerning the gospel of God (Mark 1:14–15). This is then followed by "the launch" of Jesus' Galilean ministry (Mark 1:21–3:12),[42] which aligns the disciples' initial call and the description of their *fisher* character role "with Jesus' own mission."[43] Jesus' invitation to *come after Me* (1:17b) and the *fisher*-promise connect the *fisher* role to the in-breaking of God's rule. Everything about Mark's introduction points to the OT and its *fisher* contexts, identifying "Jesus' imperative as a call to eschatological holy war."[44]

When Jesus invited followers, he promised to make them *fishers of men*. There is a direct correlation between the promise in 1:17 and the commission in 3:13–15, specifically marked by the repeated use of *poieō* (*create/make*), often translated *appointed*, *ordained*, *chose*, which can mask the reference back to the *fisher*-promise. There should be little doubt, therefore, that, as Jesus makes the *fisher*-promise (1:17), the narrative links the OT *fisher* metaphor to the role followers are to play in inaugurating the kingdom (i.e., expanding the influence of the gospel). The OT background offers a reasonable place to discover the meaning—OT *fishers* were God's authorized agents to demonstrate his rule, challenge idolatry, and to ameliorate injustice. *Fishers* were used, not in a narrow sense of judgment, but in its full definition, namely, as God's active agents against oppressors and their systems that oppress. *Fishers* were utilized to demonstrate God's sovereignty as he moved over the realms of humankind to bring about his purposes, gathering people for judgment in order to establish his ends (in both punishment and restoration). Considering the wider context, it is fair, therefore, to expand and offer the following exegetical idea for the presentation of the Mark 1:17 *fisher*-promise:

---

42. At the end of this "launch" segment, Mark closes, ironically, with a demon recognizing that Jesus was indeed "the Son of God," drawing the reader's attention back to 1:1, *Jesus Christ, the Son of God*, the subject of the story.

43. Henderson, *Christology and Discipleship*, 48.

44. Ibid., 56.

"You Will Appear as Fishers" (Mark 1:17)

> *Come after Me and I will make you appear in history as God's agents of judgment who actively pursue the outcomes that reflect the inauguration of My kingdom.*

As the commission in Mark 3 indicates, this is exactly what happens and God appoints his followers to be his eschatological agents, agents of judgment that are to establish his kingdom among humanity. To narrow the *fisher*-promise to just verbal witnessing truncates it and misses the broader implications of the inauguration of the rule and reign of God. The OT explains the content of God's rule is both salvific (as in bringing people to Christ) and in calling the realms of humankind to reflect the justice of God's kingdom. The *fisher*-promise is not to draw *followers* to a narrow activity of simply "witnessing," but defines them and gives them eschatological significance for activities that are consistent with Mark's thematic and programmatic understanding of the nature and content of the gospel-kingdom that is inaugurated with the appearance of Jesus, the Messiah-Son of God, and the coming of the Spirit.

Suzanne Henderson begins her book on *Discipleship* pointing out that in Mark's Gospel, more than the others, Jesus is always and everywhere in the company of his disciples.[45] Invited and then commissioned by Jesus, the disciples "repeatedly bear witness to activities that characterize his early mission." They are "more than mere bystanders," benefiting from Jesus' private counsel and teaching; they actively participate in demonstrating that God's dominion has broken into the realms of humankind, through proclamation, confronting the demonic, and in healing.[46]

Becoming *fishers* is not the call, but the outcome of the call to be followers. The significance of the *fisher* text in Mark is suited for making application relevant to the implications of the OT judgment texts, which include promise of exile and societal destruction (i.e., curse) and promise of remnant and social restoration in the likeness of God's design (i.e., blessing and salvation). The *fisher* metaphor is appropriate, not just narrowly for individual, private salvation, but more broadly for applications, activities, and outcomes of social action and justice, as well.

---

45. Henderson (*Christology and Discipleship*, 3) referencing Trocmé, *Foundation of the Gospel According to Mark*, 142.

46. Henderson, *Christology and Discipleship*, 3; also note, "The gospel's opening call to discipleship (Mark. 1:16–20) will serve as a critical launching point for examining the intended function of 'following Jesus' in the second gospel" (Henderson, 32–33).

4

A Prelude to Judgment (Mark 3:20–35)
The Beelzebul Episode and Its Significance for Evangelistic Social Action

"We live in enemy-occupied territory, not neutral ground. As long as no effort is made to proclaim the gospel throughout the city, the devil may even come to church and make a substantial contribution. But when signs of community appear in a deteriorating neighborhood, the beast is roused. His bulldozer engines roar."

— Rev. Henry K. Yordon (1926–2005), "My visions of a New Jerusalem"

He who shuts his ear to the cry of the poor
Will also cry himself and not be answered.

—Proverbs 21:13

"If you can't be a good example, then you'll just have to serve as a horrible warning."

—Catherine Aird

A Prelude to Judgment (Mark 3:20–35)

And He came home, and the crowd gathered again, to such an extent that they could not even eat a meal. When His own people heard *of this*, they went out to take custody of Him; for they were saying, "He has lost His senses." The scribes who came down from Jerusalem were saying, "He is possessed by Beelzebul," and "He casts out the demons by the ruler of the demons." And He called them to Himself and began speaking to them in parables, "How can Satan cast out Satan? If a kingdom is divided against itself, that kingdom cannot stand. If a house is divided against itself, that house will not be able to stand. If Satan has risen up against himself and is divided, he cannot stand, but he is finished! But no one can enter the strong man's house and plunder his property unless he first binds the strong man, and then he will plunder his house.

"Truly I say to you, all sins shall be forgiven the sons of men, and whatever blasphemies they utter; but whoever blasphemes against the Holy Spirit never has forgiveness, but is guilty of an eternal sin" —because they were saying, "He has an unclean spirit."

Then His mother and His brothers arrived, and standing outside they sent *word* to Him and called Him. A crowd was sitting around Him, and they said to Him, "Behold, Your mother and Your brothers are outside looking for You." Answering them, He said, "Who are My mother and My brothers?" Looking about at those who were sitting around Him, He said, "Behold My mother and My brothers! For whoever does the will of God, he is My brother and sister and mother"(Mark 3:20–35).

Some Bible stories seem to elicit more questions than offer answers. The Beelzebul episode depicted in the Gospel of Mark (3:20–35) is one of these stories. The fear of having "blasphemed the Holy Spirit" has plagued conscientious Christians throughout church history. The harshness of the warning that such offense is *unpardonable* worries many well intentioned believers. More often than not, a pastoral answer comes to reassure doubting Christians that they are not candidates to have committed the unpardonable sin, that is, if they are concerned about it. In other words, those concerned about blaspheming the Holy Spirit are not in danger of committing the unpardonable sin. As such, the meaning of the text is resolved—it has no bearing for the Christian and now can safely be ignored, passed over. It applies to someone else. Application trumps interpretation. The problem of a difficult Bible passage is solved: the text is for others who are *not bothered* about blaspheming the Holy Spirit.

To lessen the difficulty the Beelzebul controversy creates, the text is too often narrowed down to the individual, relegated to the vagueness of introspection, and subjected to a privatized application (or ignored at the personal level "since it doesn't apply to me"). Granted, applying Scripture at the personal level is a needed discipline, but there are times when interpretation is confused with application. Personal application is often leveraged to lift out an interpretation of a text. This is a flawed, backward method for determining a text's meaning. Thus, the value of the warning against blaspheming the Holy Spirit is often eclipsed by pastoral counsel and by privatized application rather than seeking the significance of the Beelzebul episode through its role in Mark's Gospel and by his narrative choices. Whatever the meaning of this tension-filled text, it should further develop the content of *the gospel of Jesus Christ, the Son of God* (Mark 1:1) and it should form the church community by *this* gospel.

The intent of this chapter is to move away from privatized application and demonstrate that the Mark 3 Beelzebul episode (Mark 3:20–35) continues the programmatic content already established in the Gospel, and, thus, to show that the episode's contextual significance should include social action outcomes as a component of the church's task of evangelism. Such a direction on this line of application (i.e., social action outcomes) is admittedly, not at first apparent. However, in supporting this thesis, the study will develop the following areas: establish a framework to *re*hear the text; identify narrative clues that give the episode its contextual significance; establish the programmatic connection to Mark's underlying OT foundation; and, finally, examine how the significance of the blasphemy of the Holy Spirit-warning encourages the church to include social action as a component of its evangelistic activities.

REHEARING THE BEELZEBUL EPISODE

Before starting a discussion on this most difficult and perplexing text (Mark 3:20–35), it is good to ask, *How should we listen to this text?* We all hear biblical texts and, especially, Bible stories with some level of noise (e.g., preconceived notions, personal religious experience, political and social awareness, etc.). So, determining upfront what is needed to listen well seems rather reasonable and fair. As mentioned, many seem to focus pastorally on the text, or through *a priori* application to determine the personal meaning

A Prelude to Judgment (Mark 3:20–35)

of blasphemy *against the Holy Spirit*.[1] There is good reason to move beyond the narrow, privatized readings and to listen at the social level for God's voice through this thorny episode. For even at the end of the Gospel, Pilate, Caesar's surrogate over the province of Judaea, recognized a social reason for the Jewish leadership's desire to destroy Jesus: *For he was aware that the chief priests had handed Him over because of envy* (Mark 15:10).

Preventing a narrow, privatized application through a sociological imagination

A social perspective or framework is often avoided by conservative Christians as a means to explain the work of God in the world and, as well, as a means to understand humankind's interactions with each other—the good, the bad, and the mysterious. Christians can lack what C. W. Mills called a "sociological imagination,"[2] which can limit hearing the intent of a biblical text or story. Such a lack can deter from hearing social-centered texts of Scripture, such as Mark's Beelzebul episode. In other words, a consequence of the conservative Christian community's aversion to sociological models for understanding the world can cause one to overlook or ignore the sociological significance of biblical texts, particularly narrative texts crafted with specific social locations and social contexts that instruct (and, in this case, warn) its readers/listeners. The lack of a sociological imagination in the interpretative process can block the observation of valid social constructs and, as well, prohibit hearing the discourse voice between the author and audience that might help to unlock a text's meaning, particularly when the setting of the text is inherently and obviously social. A sociological imagination can provide the ability to see how social groups interact and influence each other. In the case of the Mark 3 Beelzebul episode, the power of a sociological imagination will connect us to the social value of the controversy story and, as a result, help provide a potential range for applying the significance of the story.[3]

---

1. See Cole's *Engaging with the Holy Spirit* for a review of the typical range of interpretative options and choices for application.

2. Perkin, *Looking Both Ways*, 130; also, Leon-Guerrero, *Social Problems*, 2; see Mills, *The Sociological Imagination*.

3. Employing a sociological imagination in the interpretative process is similar to what Kuruvilla calls "the two rules" needed for developing the world "in front of the text" that culminates "in application for the reader" (*Text to Praxis*, 72): 1) the *Rule of Plot* that "prepares the interpreter of biblical narrative to attend to the structured sequence of

Like the subsequent parable of the Sower who sows the seed/word (Mark 4:1–8, 14–20), the Beelzebul episode comes to us, not as a syllogistic argument, but as a carefully placed episode within a larger story. A sociological imagination helps us listen to the *biography* in the Beelzebul episode as it relates to the whole Gospel narrative, offering context to understand properly why the characters in the episode act and think as they do, and then to connect that biography to our own story to explain why we act and think as we do.[4] We should not ignore *the social* aspect that is embedded into the very fabric of the text, which offers clues to Mark's meaning and its significance for us who stand before this rather difficult, bothersome text.

Shaming the readers/listeners into listening well

Commentators have noted a social convention of shame/honor has been integrated into Mark's Beelzebul episode and its wider context. In the first century, a person's honor rating was everything, allowing a person a higher public trust, more righteous status, and more powerful social standing.[5] What is at stake was the honor of the Jerusalem scribes (3:22), of Jesus' family (v. 31), of Jesus' associates (v. 21), and of Jesus. The scribes sought to devalue Jesus' honor through shaming him publically. The question is, however, *what is Mark attempting to do to his readers/listeners?* The social convention of shame/honor fits Mark's narrative elsewhere, being implied or claimed in numerous texts and episodes throughout his Gospel.[6] However, it is the reader/listener who is being addressed. Mark seems to harness the same cultural convention, directing it toward his audience, since hearers are also being *shamed* into obedience, for they, too, are warned that blasphemy *against the Holy Spirit* is unpardonable (*whoever blasphemes,*

---

events emplotted in the text, in order to apprehend the world projected by that text" (73) and 2) the *Rule of Interaction* that "directs the interpreter of biblical narrative to attend to the interpersonal transactions of the characters as represented therein, in order to apprehend the world projected by the text" (75).

4. "Without a sociological imagination, which links biography to history, our efforts to understand properly who we are—that is, why we act and think as we do—are substantially handicapped" (Perkins, *Looking Both Ways*, 134).

5. May, "Mark 3:20–35," 83–87.

6. May cites 1:40; 5:22; 10:17; 15:19; 6:4; 6:14–29; 7:9–13; 10:35–45; 3:28; 8:12; 9:1,41; 10:15, 29; 11:23; 12:43; 13:30; 14:9, 18, 25, 30. I include *the widow vs. the duplicitous scribes* episode (12:38–44), the interaction between the religious leaders and Jesus during the trial scenes (14:53–65), and the episode of Peter's denial (14:66–72).

3:29a). This was not simply a problem for the scribes who will "destroy" Jesus (Mark 3:6; 11:18). Ultimately, it is the Christian community's problem, as well, for they, as well, must determine Jesus' honor rating and demonstrate loyalty by doing *the will of God* as his true family (Mark 3:35).

Biblically, *shame* is not psychology; it hints at a state of affairs or politics,[7] indicating the status of one's covenant relationship with Yahweh, the Creator-God of the Bible. *Shame* is the way back to creation as it should be under God's rule, a restoration of life and community under God's covenant. The use of shame in the OT can be seen through texts such as penitential prayers that indicate repentance, creating a personal, group, or national "narrative repair" of a sad state of affairs or of an open rebellion against God, indicating that the ones shamed have discovered that they are too closely identified with the destructive patterns of those opposed to God's reign and covenant. This shame is intended to provoke a return to creation as it should be, or to covenantal obedience that honors God and his rulership (i.e., his kingdom).[8]

We assume the scribes actually believed Jesus to be demon-possessed and in league with Satan and not simply using a public relations ploy (which actually seems as likely) to guarantee a malevolent outcome.[9] The text only tells us they accused Jesus of such (and people never make false allegations to malign others in order to lower their public honor and status—right?). We are left to determine motive from the context. Mark gives us hints that the Jewish leadership were afraid of Jesus because *the whole crowd was astonished at His teaching* (11:18) and through Pilate's assertion that religious leaders had brought Jesus to trial out of envy (15:10). Mark's Beelzebul episode is a culmination of several public, confrontational interactions between Jesus and Jewish leadership (2:1—3:6). The shame/honor significance is then further sustained through the interaction Jesus has with his own disciples and followers, specifically at those points in the narrative

---

7. Smith-Christopher, *Biblical Theology of Exile*, 120–21.

8. Ibid., 120: ". . . statements of shame serve an important function, though not in the contemporary sense of 'spiritually cleansing,' nor are they associated with some psychological view of necessary penitence. To miss the social significance of a litany of shame is to miss much of the integrative and transformative function of these prayers. In these prayers, 'our shame' is associated with *too closely identifying with a past that was destructive* [his emphasis]."

9. The scribes' accusations concerning Jesus and Beelzebul is a ploy to accomplish what is proposed earlier, namely to "destroy" Jesus (Mark 3:6). This is affirmed by the same basic accusation of blasphemy at the trial scenes, which lead to Jesus' actual "destruction" (Mark 14–15).

where they are perilously close to falling under the same judgment as the Jewish leadership (Mark 6:51–52; 8:16–21; also note 8:34–38; 16:14).

NARRATIVE CLUES TO UNDERSTAND THE ROLE OF THE BEELZEBUL CONTROVERSY

The Beelzebul controversy is the culmination of a contiguous thread of conflict stories between Jesus and Jewish leadership (2:1—3:6) and is set within a Markan intercalation (3:20–35), typically referred to as a "sandwich."[10] Mark often inserts "an event or narrative" between lines or accounts in order to heighten "the tension" or to draw attention to a "significant parallel or contrast."[11] A closer examination of the Mark 3 sandwich[12] and its relationship to the Mark 2–3 conflict-thread and the wider narrative offer clues to understand the significance of the Beelzebul controversy, Mark's first sandwich.[13]

The Mark 3 sandwich—A1-B-A2 (3:20–35)

The Mark 3 sandwich is crafted with corresponding outer components (A1, A2) and a middle section (B) comprised of what is often referred to as the "Beelzebul controversy."[14] Most focus on "family" (A1, A2) and the Beelzebul episode (B) to frame this sandwich, which is generally described in the following manner:

> A1 Family (vv. 20–21)
>
> > B Beelzebul Controversy (vv. 22–30)
>
> A2 Family (vv. 31–35)

---

10. Edwards, "Markan Sandwiches," 193–216; also Witherington, *Gospel of Mark*, 153.

11. Lane, *Gospel of Mark*, 137; Witherington, *Gospel of Mark*, 153.

12. The "Mark 3 sandwich" refers to Mark 3:20–35 and throughout this chapter.

13. Markan sandwiches: 3:20–35; 4:1–20; 5:21–43; 6:7–30; 11:12–21; 14:1–11; 14:17–31; 14:53–72; 15:40—16:8.

14. The "Beelzebul controversy" component of the Mark 3 sandwich is found in vv. 3:22–30. When reference is made to the Beelzebul Episode, the full sandwich is implied (3:20–35).

A Prelude to Judgment (Mark 3:20–35)

However, there are other indicators suggesting a different frame, offering clues to the significance of the blasphemy warning and its potential range for application.

Although most acknowledge there is some ambiguity, whether it is Jesus' "family" (3:21) that approaches him in the first component (A1), most recognize the analogous content in the outer components (A1, A2). Some take the phrase "His own people" (NASB) in A1 to be Jesus' family because the sandwich determines such, for "family" is clearly referenced in A2. The shock of hearing that Jesus' family members were in direct conflict with Jesus, as were the scribes (B), has astounded commentators. This so-called family conflict is "so lacking in reverence both for Jesus and for his family that it is not surprising to see alternatives proposed" in variant readings for this text.[15] However, the correspondence in the outer A components offer a different direction, focusing rather on the imprecise identity of the characters.

In 3:21, Mark simply indicates that *the ones beside him went out to take custody of him*.[16] The referent for the phrase *the ones beside him* is ambiguous, leaving room for disagreements among commentators and Bible translations. The identity of *the ones beside him* could be understood as "associates, kin, or followers as well as friends or family."[17] Translations offer a range, but mostly attempt to identify Jesus' family as the referent (e.g., ESV, Good News, NIV, Phillips, TNIV). The NASB attempts Mark's vagueness by translating the phrase as *his own people* and the KJV and ASV offer *his friends*. Guelich remarks strongly, "Mark 3:31 makes clear that Jesus' 'family' is the subject of 3:21."[18] The "family" parallel only *seems* apparent because "family" in the later component (A2) is clear; however, the family is identified for comparison to those who are *truly* Jesus' family (vv. 34–35). The Greek, *hoi par' autou* (v. 21), is vague and perhaps intentionally so. The phrase simply means *the ones beside him* (or *the ones near Him*) and, as Edwards points out, "appears to be a calculated ambiguity."[19] Although "family" can be included in *the ones beside him*, it seems Mark intentionally

---

15. France, *Gospel of Mark*, 165; Witherington, *Gospel of Mark*, 154.

16. The ambiguous *hoi par' autou* (3:21a) causes the debate. It may be woodenly translated as "the ones beside him" (and is used throughout the remainder of this chapter unless otherwise indicated).

17. Edwards, *Gospel According to Mark*, 118.

18. Guelich, *Mark 1–8:26*, 172; France, *Gospel of Mark*, 167; Witherington, *Gospel of Mark*, 154n28.

19. Edwards, *Gospel According to Mark*, 118.

leaves the group unidentified, suggesting that whoever is taking the action toward Jesus in the first slice "is not entirely clear."[20] Furthermore, in A1 the ambiguous nature of *the ones beside him* who *went out(side)* (*exēlthon*, v. 21b) could be juxtaposed with the ambiguous nature of those who are *around him* (*tous peri auton*, v. 34a) inside the house in A2.

There is, however, another indicator in the text that is clear, offering a more likely parallel in the outer A components. Although the reference to a *crowd* has a vague quality to it, the reference to *crowd* in the outer A components is, indeed, clear (vv. 20, 32). Herein lies a key to deciphering the sandwich: The *crowd* that had gathered in A1 are, in the concluding component (A2), identified as being "inside" (*around* [*peri*]) Jesus, who implies they are his true family as long as they *do the will of God* (v. 35). Besides, the scene set in A1 seems to suggest that *the ones beside him* were inside, but went outside (*exēlthon*) to take custody of Jesus (3:21); whereas in A2, his family is stated as already being *outside* the house (*echō*, vv. 31, 32) and Jesus inside. If the latter outer component (A2) is used to clarify or interpret the first, it is not "the family" to which our attention is drawn, but to the *crowd*. The bookends of the sandwich are the *crowd* who gathered at the onset and then are *inside* the house in the end.[21]

As noted in A1, the *crowd* and *the ones beside him* are ambiguous; yet, the scene in the first slice is clearly of those who were *inside* and then are *outside*. In A1 a *crowd* gathers at another Jesus-event, apparently causing congestion at the house (for there was no room to even *eat a meal*, v. 20a); then, in A2 the *crowd is inside* (vv. 32). In A1, *the ones beside him* are inside, but *went out(side)* (*echēlthon*) to take custody of Jesus (v. 21); meanwhile, in component A2 Jesus' maternal family is clearly identified as being *outside* (*echō*, vv. 31, 32), while a *crowd* is clearly inside *sitting around him* (*ekathēto peri auton*, v. 32). Jesus' true family is identified as inside, *sitting around him* (v. 34), and finally, at the close of the sandwich, those who do God's will are *inside* (v. 35). Mark's choice of words, juxtapositions, locations, and the two outer scenes (vv. 20–21; vv. 31–35) suggests that A1 and A2 are about *outsiders* and *insiders*.

Mark frames the Beelzebul controversy by sandwiching the episode between "*outsider-insider* matters" rather than "*family* matters." Framing it this way relieves the interpreter from straining the ambiguous nature of

---

20. Ibid.; also, Kee, *Miracle in the Early Christian World*, 162.
21. Edwards, *Gospel According to Mark*, 117.

A Prelude to Judgment (Mark 3:20-35)

the Greek and allows the ambiguity of the players and their *outsider-insider* status in the scenes to speak.[22]

The focus in the B component is not on "Beelzebul," but rather on the contest between the strongman and the Stronger Man. This corresponds to the outer slices: there are those who attempt to *take custody* of Jesus (A1, v. 21) and those who *seek* to control him (A2, v. 32); whereas, in the middle component (B), Jesus-the Stronger Man *binds* the strongman-Satan (v. 27) and "frees his captives to become followers of the strong Son of God,"[23] turning *outsiders* into *insiders*. The focus in the B component on *the strongman vs. the Stronger Man* follows Mark's narrative elsewhere. This fits the introductory and programmatic content of Mark's Gospel first initiated in the desert confrontation between Satan-the strongman and Jesus-the Stronger Man (1:7) and, then, confirmed through multiple exorcisms (1:21-27, 32; 5:1-20; 6:7, 13; 7:26-30; 9:14-29, 38-41; also note 8:33; 16:9), a demonstration that Jesus-the Stronger Man overtaking Satan-the strongman's dominion/house (3:23-27).[24]

The parables Jesus employs in the Mark 3 sandwich (vv. 23-27) are not so much to answer the false accusations of the scribes that Jesus has a demon and is in cahoots with Satan (v. 22), but to render judgment on those who are *outside* (Mark 4:11-12). The parables mirror Jesus' ministry activity: decisive actions that demonstrate that the strongman's house/dominion will not stand and that a Stronger Man has arrived to deliver those made captive by the strongman. The scribes come to the battle with false accusations to shame Jesus; armed with parables of judgment, Jesus presents the Good News that Satan-the strongman's house/kingdom will fall and that the Stronger Man is now conquering enemy territory.[25] The scribes stand *outside*; those benefiting from the Stronger Man's action against Satan are freed to be *insiders*. Thus, the Mark 3 sandwich is better, contextually, framed in the following manner:

---

22. Juel, *Master of Surprise*, 72.

23. Edwards, *Gospel According to Mark*, 117.

24. See Watts's *Isaiah's New Exodus*, 146-52; also Watts, referring to R. Leivestad (*Christ the Conqueror*), underscores that "each exorcism" was "an instance of binding and plundering" (*Isaiah's New Exodus*, 146n47).

25. As the first result of sown "wasted seed" (Mark 4:1-8, 13-20) and of the mustard-bush invading the garden (4:3-32), the Mark 5 "casting" episode ironically depicts Satan's army destroying itself (as Jesus foretold, 3:24-26): the demonic-legion entered the herd of pigs and threw themselves off a bank into the watery grave (5:10-13).

> A1 Outsider-insider (vv. 20–21)
>
> B Strongman vs. Stronger Man (vv. 22–30)
>
> A2 Outsider-insider (vv. 31–35)

Framed this way, the Mark 3 sandwich *is* the gospel. This should not surprise the reader/listener, for the overall purpose of the sandwich technique is to underscore "major motifs" in Mark's Gospel.[26] Blasphemy *against the Holy Spirit*, then, is tantamount to a warning against being on the *outside* rather than the *inside* of the kingdom and, thus, of course, *unpardonable* (3:31–35; 4:10–12).

Thread of accusation and plotting

The social setting implied by the sandwich invites us to consider the confrontations between Jesus and Jewish leadership, that is, the thread of accusation and eventual plotting that precedes our text. Mark 2:1—3:6 is wholly built on a thread of five uninterrupted confrontation stories (2:1–12; 2:13–17; 2:18–22; 2:23–28; 3:1–6) and concludes with the religious and political leaders plotting *how they might destroy* Jesus (3:6).[27] Thus, both the particulars of 3:20–35 and the larger narrative thread offer clues for understanding the *outsider-insider—strongman vs. Stronger Man* sandwich.

Mark 1:21–28.

The prelude to the confrontation episodes and the inaugural ministry-event launched at the onset of the Galilean mission, Mark 1:21–28, depicts a clash between Jesus and an *unclean spirit*[28] that he *casts out*, the very activity that is turned against him, giving rise to the Beelzebul accusations (3:22). The scene informs us that Jesus teaches as *having authority, and not*

---

26. Edwards, "Markan Sandwiches."

27. Including the Mark 3 sandwich, of the sixty-three verses found in chapters 2–3, fifty verses (or 79 percent) are given to conflict stories, taking up overwhelming space given to this leg of the Galilean mission. Note Edwards, "Markan Sandwiches"; Lane, *Gospel of Mark*, 137; Witherington, *Gospel of Mark*, 153.

28. The phrase "unclean spirit" is used significantly in Mark (1:23, 26, 27; 3:11, 30; 5:2, 8, 13; 7:25; 9:25); the apostles are given authority over "unclean spirits" (6:7); also an underlying social location—the public place where Jesus' authority is revealed and the place of demonic casting happened in a sacred social location (a synagogue) and during a sacred time (the Sabbath).

A Prelude to Judgment (Mark 3:20–35)

as the scribes (v. 22), setting up the forthcoming conflict-thread (2:1—3:6) that focuses on Jesus' authority in stark contrast to Jewish leadership. Four important elements in this inaugural ministry-event are programmatic for the following conflict-thread and for hearing (better) the Mark 3 sandwich.

First, Jesus' authority is contrasted with that of the scribes (1:22). The actual teaching is not revealed, which focuses the reader/listener on the issue of Jesus' authority verses the scribes' (v. 22) and not upon the content of the teaching.[29] Second, the affirmation of Jesus' authority is juxtaposed immediately with his first confrontation with a demon (1:23–26). The synagogue attendees witness the rebuke (v. 25) and recognized the casting out of *the unclean spirit* (v. 26) as a new teaching (v. 27), namely Jesus commands Satan's minions and they obey (v. 27). As they were *amazed* (*ekplēssō*) at his teaching (v. 22), so they were *amazed* (*thambō*) at the casting out of the demon (v. 27).[30] The link is made clear by identifying the miracle of exorcism as a *new teaching with authority* (v. 27b). Jesus' authority was on public display in the action of casting out the demon, which is the content of the teaching that was contrasted publically with the authority of the scribes.

Although Joel Marcus finds it unclear if the *kai* (*even*) in 1:27 includes the ordering of *the unclean spirit* to obey,[31] the question (*What is this?*) that follows the miracle implies one singular reference (*touto, this*), signifying an intentional seamless thought between teaching and miracle. Additionally, the closest connection to the crowd's amazement is Jesus rebuking the unclean spirit (v. 26). The new teaching underscores the eschatological significance that Jesus has begun taking over Satan's domain, a campaign which was inaugurated at the desert confrontation (1:12–13) and announced in Jesus' mission summary (1:14–15).[32] This is affirmed by Jesus conferring his own authority on his "sent ones" to preach and to cast out demons (3:14–15; 6:7–12).

Third, the *unclean spirit* knows this was an eschatological battle with Jesus. This is understood when the demon cites Jesus' name (*the Holy One*

---

29. The content is presumed from Mark 1:14–15: *Now after John had been taken into custody, Jesus came into Galilee, preaching the gospel of God, and saying, "The time is fulfilled, and the kingdom of God is at hand; repent and believe in the gospel."* This is the *word* (i.e., *teaching*) sown by the Master Farmer (Mark 4:1–10, 13–20). It is *the word* Jesus speaks to the gathered/the crowd in the first conflict episode (2:2).

30. Note other *amazed/astonished/awed* texts in Mark: 6:2; 7:37; 10:24, 26, 32; 11:18.

31. Marcus, *Mark 1–8*, 189.

32. Note Guelich, *Mark 1–8:26*, 58–59; also, see chapter 3, "You Will Appear as Fishers," for an analysis of this text.

of God, 1:24c), indicating an attempt to have "mastery over" him.[33] Also, the terminology used, *I know who you are* (1:24; cf. 3:11), suggests a battle context, for this was a common OT formula "within the context of combat or judgment."[34] Fourth, like the Markan *outsider-insider* sandwich, people sought control over Jesus. Later, after *the news* about Jesus *spread everywhere* throughout *the district of Galilee* (v. 28), the disciples informed Jesus that *everyone is looking* (*zēteō*) for him (v. 37). Mark uses *zēteō* (*seek*, translated *looking* in the NASB) exclusively as a negative term. There is no reason to suggest otherwise here. Edwards rightly points out that *seeking* "connotes an attempt to determine and control rather than to submit and follow."[35] This is significant, for the "seeking to control" comes on the heels of a demonstration of Jesus' power over Satan's realm, which is paralleled in the Mark 3 *outsider-insider* sandwich, in which some *went out*(side) (*exēlthon*, 3:21b) to attempt to take custody of Jesus (3:21) and Jesus' family members, who were *outside* (3:31, 32), *seek* (*zēteō*, *looking* NASB) him (3:32).

Any interpretation of the blasphemy *against the Holy Spirit* in Mark 3 must take into consideration this inaugural ministry-event, since there are obvious associations to the *outsider-insider—strongman vs. Stronger Man* sandwich. The inaugural ministry-event sets the stage, offering a programmatic framework for the following confrontations between Jesus and Jewish leaders. Howard Kee insightfully points out that the defeat of an unclean spirit is "the first of Jesus' actions to be reported" and, thus, "is paradigmatic for the Gospel as a whole."[36] Mark 1:21–28 is the "mission" of Jesus, which is characterized by both Jesus' "word and deed" (i.e., teaching and casting/miracles) that are publically affirmed and contrasted with Jewish leadership.

---

33. Edwards, *Gospel According to Mark*, 57; Marcus, *Mark 1–8*, 193.

34. Lane (*Mark*, 73) notes use in the LXX: Judg 11:12; 2 Sam 16:10; 19:22; 1 Kgs 17:18; 2 Kgs 3:13; 2 Chr 35:21; Isa 3:15; 22:1; Jer 2:18; Hos 14:9; also Watts, *New Exodus*, 154.

35. Edwards, *Gospel According to Mark*, 67.

36. Kee, *Miracle in the Early Christian World*, 161; also Iwe, *Jesus in the Synagogue of Capernaum*, 323.

A Prelude to Judgment (Mark 3:20–35)

Mark 2:1–12.

The first conflict scene of the thread is a return to the same locale as the inaugural ministry-event (1:29),[37] signifying a continuation of Mark's programmatic themes. Mark indicates there was "no longer room, not even near the door" (2:2b), implying Jesus' growing public appeal, an intentional link with the *outsider-Stronger Man* sandwich, where the crowd also has no room *even for a meal* (3:20). Also, the gathered heard Jesus *speaking the word* (v. 1b) that already has been identified as *having authority, and not as the scribes* (1:22). They witnessed the healing of the man lowered through the roof (v. 4) and were privy to the scribes' protest concerning the authority to forgive sins (vv. 6–12). The gathered *were all amazed and were glorifying God, saying, "We have never seen anything like this"* (v. 12), immediately heightening the contrast to the scribes—an open, public shaming of the scribes in contrast to their rebuke.

There is an interesting link to the *outsider* sandwich found in Mark's use of *existēmi* (*amazed*, 2:12; *lost his senses*, 3:21). In 2:12, Mark used *existēmi* (*amazed*) in a positive way to describe the crowd's reaction to the teaching-healing event. In Mark 3:21, it was used in a pejorative manner to indicate Jesus was *beside Himself* (KJV), *lost His senses* (NASB), or *out of His mind* (ESV, NIV).[38] Mark's choice of *existēmi* in the Outsider-Stronger Man sandwich seems intentional. John uses *mainomai*, which clearly means *gone mad* or *insane*, for what appears to be the same accusation that Jesus has a demon (John 10:20; cf. Acts 26:24). Mark ties these two episodes together with parallel issues: people's reactions to Jesus, the scribes' public disapproval of Jesus, and issues of blasphemy and forgiveness (2:5–11; 3:28–29). Mark's use of *existēmi* links the public's awareness of Jesus' teaching and miracles to the conflict with Jewish established authority (Mark 2:6; 3:23–27). R. T. France points out that the "effect of Jesus' words is immediate and public" and is a public display of Jesus' authority "not only to heal physical illness but also *a fortiori* to forgive sins."[39] In Mark 2:1–12, as

---

37. Guelich, *Mark 1–8:26*, 84; note, Mark uses *again* (*palin*) "to refer to a previous place or event" (Guelich, 84); note 2:13; 3:1, 20; 4:1; 5:21; 7:31; 8:1; 10:1, 10, 32; 11:27; Edwards, *Gospel According to Mark*, 98; France, *Gospel of Mark*, 149.

38. See also 2:12; 5:42; 6:51 (*amazed, insane, beside one self,* or literally, *he has stood outside*); *gone mad,* GNT; *crazy,* CEV; see Marcus, *Mark 1–8,* 271.

39. France, *Gospel of Mark,* 129; note 2 Cor 5:13–15, where Paul utilizes a similar "spiritual" logic and rationale for evaluating his own apostleship, using *existēmi*, the term used of Jesus' mental state in the Mark 3 Beelzebul sandwich, to describe sarcastically his

soon as forgiveness of sins is mentioned, "the story abruptly shifts from the paralytic to the scribes,"[40] placing Jesus publically at odds with Jewish leadership. This suggests that the Mark 3 sandwich reflects the result of social embarrassment over the public shaming of Jewish authorities by Jesus. It puts *his own people* (3:21) in a precarious social place! This reinforces the shame/honor paradigm embedded in the Mark 3 sandwich.

The scribes' inner disposition is made known to the reader/listener, offering insight into Mark's intentions behind the Beelzebul episode. In 2:6–8, Mark uses *dialogizomai (reasoning*, v. 8) to indicate the scribes' judgment of Jesus, a word "almost always used in a negative sense"[41] in the NT. Mark uses this same word consistently in a similar way to describe the inner inclination of those who do not understand or who resist Jesus' plans and will (Mark 8:16–18; 9:33–34; note 11:31). Ironically in Mark 8:16–18, the disciples themselves *reason (dialogizomai)* as to why there is "no bread," which drew Jesus' rebuke regarding their inability to *perceive* and *understand*, eliciting from Jesus a harsh question, *Do you have a hardened heart?* (8:17). This recalls Jesus' analysis of the Jewish leadership (3:5) and the idolatry-taunt used in the parable rationale (4:10–12). Later, Jesus asked his disciples, again, about their "reasoning" (*dialogizomai*) over who was the greatest (9:33–34), a deliberate contrast to the pattern of discipleship set by Jesus himself (*If anyone wants to be first, he shall be last of all and servant of all*, 9:35). This is important, for the significance of both 2:1–12 and 3:20–35 are ultimately for those who stand before the text. The readers/listeners are being shamed (i.e., offered a "narrative repair") into obedience.

There is an ironic association between "blasphemy" and "forgiveness" found, first in this inaugural confrontation, then in the Mark 3 sandwich. Here, rather than healing the man—which is why they came and dug through the roof!—Jesus declared, before the watching public, the lame man's sins forgiven. The scribes scornfully asked, *Why does this man speak that way? He is blaspheming; who can forgive sins but God alone?* (2:7). The focus quickly turns away from the healing to Jesus' authority as the Son of Man's *to forgive sins* (v. 10). If the issue of Jesus' authority is the basis of the conflict with Jewish leaders, this was a provocative reference for Jesus to make—for it further clarifies the implications of the open, public hostility between the two competing authorities. Darrell Bock asserts that the

---

own mental capacity in regards to his apostleship.

40. Edwards, *Gospel According to Mark*, 77.

41. Marcus, *Mark 1–8*, 216.

A Prelude to Judgment (Mark 3:20-35)

"offense appears to revolve around the fact that forgiveness comes outside any cultic requirements in a mere declaration, an approach that points to Jesus' own authority."[42] In both 2:1-12 and 3:22-30, Jesus met his accusers with a reference to "forgiveness." In 2:7 and, later, in 3:29, Mark set up what Bock refers to as a "battle of the blasphemies" with each competing authority accusing the other of ultimate offence—no forgiveness for the blaspheming leaders (3:29-30) and death for the blaspheming Jesus (14:64; also 3:6; 11:18).

The juxtaposition of *blasphemy* and the *Son of Man* culminates in the final blasphemy battle at Jesus' trial (Mark 14:53-65). Before the high priest, the chief priests, the elders and the scribes, Jesus was accused of blasphemy after he referred to himself as the Son of Man (Mark 14:62-64). The significance is that Jesus was establishing his authority as outside the temple system and apart from its rebellious, hard-hearted guardians. Of course, God can only forgive sins,[43] but the Jewish temple-leadership understood they had an intermediary role: the temple system and its guardians were the respected, accepted authority to mediate God's forgiveness.[44] Jesus' teaching and deeds challenged this authority: not only did Jesus teach with authority (*exousia*), *not as the scribes* (1:22), he had authority to command demons (1:27; also 3:15; 6:7) and authority to forgive (2:10)—all established outside the recognized temple leadership.[45]

There is an ironic twist in this conflict that offers an interpretive clue for the Mark 3 sandwich: the confrontation brings out the nature of the conflict between Jesus and Jewish leadership, linking "blasphemy" and "forgiveness" with Jesus' authority. And, it is not just Jesus' authority that is challenged, but his authority publically recognized in contrast to Jewish leadership's, publically displaying an authority to work outside the

---

42. Bock, "Blasphemy and the Jewish Examination of Jesus," 53-114.

43. Marcus, *Mark 1-8*, 222; Watts, *Isaiah's New Exodus*, 175; Marcus notes Exod 34:6-7, Isa 43:25, and 44:22.

44. Bock, "Blasphemy and the Jewish Examination of Jesus."

45. Jesus' "Son of man" reference at the trial draws a similar accusation of blasphemy. Bock points out that the leadership understood the implication, namely they might be judging him now, but "he will eventually rule or judge them later." The charge of blasphemy and the verdict of death was the leaders' natural response for the "Son of Man" inference was understood as a violation of Exod 22:28, which includes warnings against both blaspheming Yahweh (i.e., Jesus' claiming divine representation) and blaspheming the leaders of Israel (Jesus as the Son of Man returning to judge) (see Bock, "Blasphemy").

established temple system, openly "shaming" Jewish leadership, and publically raising his honor rating.

Mark 2:13–17.

Immediately following the first direct skirmish (2:1–12), the next episode further expands the public nature of the conflict and hostility. As Jesus set out, "all the people" ("a large crowd," NIV) gathered and he *was teaching them* (2:13), linking the second episode programmatically to the 1:21–28 foundational episode. This is no passing observation, for amid the issue of hostility between Jesus and Jewish leadership is the relationship Jesus had with the *crowd*, namely Jesus and his teaching is in direct public contrast to that of the established temple authorities.[46] This public conflict is sharpened by a pointed, almost passing, reference to Jesus' call to follow him to Levi, the tax collector, who was sitting in a tax booth. This is not incidental, for the picture is that of a crowd of people hanging on Jesus' words (2:13) and a local tax collector publically responding to his invitation to be a follower—an *outsider* becoming an *insider* (*And he got up and followed Him*, v. 14c).[47] This is significant because the *Jesus vs. the scribes* conflict is sharpened by the immediate scene where Jesus joined this new *outsider*-tax-collector-turned-*insider* at his house, accompanied by *many tax collectors and sinners* (v. 15). The *scribes of the Pharisees* (v. 16a) note that Jesus is having table fellowship with the likes of uneducated and impure *sinners* and *tax collectors*—again, the issue of *outsiders*-turning-*insiders*.

The *scribes of the Pharisees* presented a hostile inquiry (*Why is He eating and drinking with tax collectors and sinners?*, 2:16), which arises out of what Marcus suggests is "spiritual shortsightedness." Jesus *saw* (*eiden*) Levi as a "potential disciple," yet the Jewish leaders *see* (*idontes*) the tax collector and his house guests only as sinners.[48] Although Jewish, *tax collectors* were "despised as a class"[49] by Jewish leaders, considered outsiders in their social standing. Additionally, *sinners* lacked observance to legal require-

---

46. Mark 1:21–22; 6:2, 34; 7:7; 10:1–2; 11:17; 12:35; note also 8:31; 9:31; 12:14; 14:49.

47. *Follow* (*akoloutheō*) used only of disciples, never of those who oppose Jesus (making followers = insiders); see Edwards, 81; also chapter 3, "You Will Appears as *Fishers*."

48. Marcus, *Mark 1–8*, 230; also reflecting the continued problem in the faith community in Rome, namely welcoming "outsiders" into its fellowship (see Rom 14:1–12); see my "Romans 1:1–5 and the Occasion of the Letter," 25–40.

49. France, *Gospel of Mark*, 133; see Matt 5:46; 18:17; 21:31–32.

A Prelude to Judgment (Mark 3:20–35)

ments, placing them, as well, outside the pure company of temple leaders.[50] At the house party, amid table-fellowship, Jesus was brought into contact with unclean persons who were considered *outsiders*—but, for Jesus, they were potentially *insiders*, the issue that frames the Mark 3 sandwich.

This plays an important part for the up-coming Beelzebul controversy and the full Mark 3 sandwich at two levels. First, the obvious *insider-outsider* frame is reversed in the Beelzebul sandwich. Although Jesus was the one being accused of the ultimate impurity (i.e., possessed of Beelzebul, *the ultimate outsider*), it was the religious elite who were *outsiders* and at risk of being eternally outside (3:29; 4:10–12). In the Mark 3 conflict the scribes claimed that something unclean (i.e., Beelzebul) had possessed Jesus, publically declaring Jesus essentially an outsider; thus, attempting to lower his honor rating through an explicit, public "shameful" accusation.[51] The question in 2:16 (*"Why is He eating and drinking with tax collectors and sinners?"*) was intended to underscore similar public shame; Levi, nonetheless, was called to follow Jesus and became an *insider*. Compounding the issue of Jesus' authority was his willingness to associate publically with those who appear to be shameful and religiously *outsiders*; not only does Jesus have the authority to forgive sinners, but he also associated with them as potential *insiders*. This is an outcome of the battle to bind the strongman, as well as the sign of victory of the Stronger Man to free the *outsider*-captives to be *insider*-followers.

Mark 2:18–22.

The scene opens with a declaration that John's disciples and the Pharisees practiced fasting and a nameless group that asked why Jesus' disciples do not. This sets the narrative effect for the third conflict.[52] The questioners implied a comparison between the pious disciples of John and the Pharisees and the impious disciples of Jesus. Mark harnesses the occasion to heighten the public conflict that includes a comparison between the old/current religious patterns and the inaugurated kingdom (another version of the *outsider-insider* framework). The following parables of the bridegroom and

---

50. Ibid., 133.
51. May, "Mark 3:20–35."
52. Edwards, *Gospel According to Mark*, 54–55. It is unclear who comes to Jesus, but the overall Markan context suggests that it is probably the scribes, rather than John and the Pharisees (Marcus, *Mark 1–8*, 233).

the old/new wineskins suggest such a comparison of the old and new age.[53] Although these parables speak to a developing Christology, the scene as a whole and the parables individually sustain the issue of Jesus' authority and the inadequacy (or end) of the authorities who were the guardians of the current temple system.[54] In explaining why Jesus' disciples did not fast, Jesus utilized a wedding to underscore that his disciples were celebrating the inauguration of God's kingdom—these are *insiders*. Although fasting was a sign of public piety,[55] everyone should have been celebrating, not fasting, while Jesus, the Bridegroom, is here. The emphasis on a Bridegroom reinforced the issue of Jesus' divine authority, for in the OT it was Yahweh who is the Bridegroom of Israel,[56] furthering the implications of the previous Son of Man reference (Mark 2:10; note 2:28).

The ultimate "destruction" of Jesus is foreshadowed amid the celebration, for there is prediction of a future without the Bridegroom, suggestive of other teaching in Mark's Gospel on suffering at the hands of Jewish leaders and the climax of the conflict-thread, namely Jesus' destruction (Mark 3:6). There is irony indicative of the end of the Bridegroom and the end of the old wineskins. The new wine of God's kingdom *destroys/bursts* (*apollymi*) the old wine skins of the present temple-cult system, implying its eventual judgment and ruin (Mark 13:1–2). Ironically, in the final conflict scene (Mark 3:1–6), the Pharisees and the political rulers plot to *destroy* (*apollymi*) Jesus (3:6). Later, Mark indicates that the scribes and chief priests sought *to destroy* (*apollymi*) Jesus *for they were afraid of Him, for the whole crowd was astonished at His teaching* (11:18). The conflict narratives revolve around the ultimate battle of authorities—each side a public shaming, each side's end to be one of destruction.

The end of the old wine skin/current religious system (*a worse tear* [*schism*] *results*, 2:21) also recalls the Spirit's *opening* (*schizomenous*) the heavens (1:10; 15:38) at the announcement that God's Son-King had arrived.[57] This maintains the association of the Spirit to the arrival of the

---

53. See France, *Gospel of Mark*, 137.

54. Note the cursing of the fig-tree (Mark 11:12–14, 20–21) and the ultimate judgment on the temple system in Mark 13 (i.e., the destruction of the temple itself).

55. See chapter 1, "Widows in Our Courts," for the meaning of the outward appearances; also Edwards, *Gospel According to Mark*, 89; Marcus, *Mark 1–8*, 238–39.

56. France, *Gospel of Mark*, 139; note Isa 61:10: 62:4–5; Hos 2:14–20.

57. Marcus, *Mark 1–8*, 238.

kingdom and the end of the current temple-system, and thus an end (judgment) of Jewish leadership who stand as *outsiders*.

The Bridegroom and wineskin parables, along with the accompanying conflict, further develop the themes of Jesus' authority, judgment on the present authorities, and the initiation of God not only working outside "the approved" system, but even for its ruin.[58] This conflict offers a backstory to the blasphemy *against the Holy Spirit*: the accusations are part of the thread indicating a strategy to destroy Jesus because the Jewish leadership was aware that Jesus' presence and association with *the crowd* was inaugurating actions that could destroy them (i.e., God's judgment).

Mark 2:23–28.

This conflict episode centers on violations of Sabbath-keeping, presenting an occasion that links Jesus' authority as the Son of Man to forgive with his authority over the Sabbath.[59] Jesus appeals to Scripture (*Have you never read*, 2:25a), continuing Mark's continued emphasis on Jesus' teaching in contrast to the scribes' (1:21–22). The reference to David plays a twin role: first, a greater authority than even David had arrived on the scene; second, like David, Jesus works outside the established Jewish leadership to accomplish his mission (with his own band of supporters and, like David, his own conflict with established power).[60] The accusation of Sabbath breaking also underscores the plan to destroy Jesus, for violating the observance of Sabbath was punishable by death (Exod 31:14–15; 35:2; also note Num 15:32–36; Jub. 50:8, 13). The fourth confrontation continues to push the reader/listener to recognize that Jesus was establishing his credentials outside the current religious authorities and temple system, setting up the pretext with which to "destroy" him (Mark 3:6; 11:18; 14:63–64).

Mark 3:1–6.

The last of the five conflict episodes (3:1–6) and the first (2:1–12) have a number of "striking parallels" that suggest an intentional framing by Mark: both contain a healing miracle, near identical introductory phrases (*kai*

---

58. Bock, "Blasphemy and the Jewish Examination of Jesus."
59. France, *Gospel of Mark*, 147–48.
60. Marcus, *Mark 1–8*, 244; note 1 Sam 21.

eiselthōn/esēlthen palin eis), and are located in Capernaum.⁶¹ Mark intentionally ties the thread to Jesus' first public ministry-event (the conflict-thread's programmatic foundation) in 1:21–28 by locating the fifth conflict with Jewish leadership in a synagogue and on the Sabbath (1:21; 3:1–2). Underlying the obvious intensification of hostility, the last episode continues the open shaming behind the conflict, for Jesus silenced his opponents (3:4c), a form of publically humiliating the opposition.⁶²

In the last conflict episode Jewish leaders have moved from identifying Jesus as a threat to their authority to "watching closely," intentionally scrutinizing his every move "to see if he would heal" again in order to incriminate him as a lawbreaker deserving destruction (3:6).⁶³ Mary Ann Tolbert notes that Jesus' opposition "from first to last" never waivers.⁶⁴ Nonetheless, throughout the conflict stories there has been "a steady intensification" of the conflict between Jesus and Jewish leaders.⁶⁵ The first confrontation (2:1–12) opens and closes with positive, responsive crowds; whereas, the final episode (3:1–6) opens with malicious intent and closes with a plot to destroy Jesus.⁶⁶ The first conflict begins with an accusation of blasphemy against Jesus; the last conflict episode culminates with a malevolent, pro-active temple establishment—Jesus' opposition—conspiring together with the political establishment to *destroy* Jesus (3:6).⁶⁷

Mark ties the last conflict episode to the ultimate, judicial condition of the Jewish leadership, namely their hardness of heart. The *hardness of heart* (v. 5) is linked to the Isaiah 6 idolatry-taunt Jesus directs toward *outsiders* (Mark 4:11–12) and is closely tied to a stock NT expression referring to Israel's inability or failure to recognize Jesus as their Messiah (John 12:40; Rom 11:7, 25; 2 Cor 3:14; Eph 4:18).⁶⁸ This is significant on two fronts: first,

---

61. Ibid., 213.

62. Ibid., 248; also note Mark 11:33; 12:34.

63. *They were watching* (*paretēroun*), an imperfect verb, gives the sense of "hanging in suspense" (Edwards, *Gospel According to Mark*, 98); the NIV translates it as "they watched him closely" (Luke 6:7; 14:1; 20:20; Acts 9:24); the LXX uses *paretēroun* to indicate sinners lying in wait for the righteous to kill them (Ps 36[37]:12) (Marcus, *Mark 1–8*, 248).

64. Keegan, "The Parable of the Sower," 501–18; Tolbert, *Sowing the Gospel*, 139–40.

65. Edwards, *Gospel According to Mark*, 86.

66. Marcus, *Mark 1–8*, 250–51; the plotting continues throughout the Gospel (3:6; 11:18; 12:12; 14:1, 10–11).

67. Edwards, *Gospel According to Mark*, 101–2; Lane, *Gospel of Mark*, 125; note Matt 12:14; Luke 6:11.

68. France, *Gospel of Mark*, 151; the references are also indicative of the same Isaiah

A Prelude to Judgment (Mark 3:20–35)

it indicates the continued exiled condition of Jesus' opponents, offering a foundation for the warning against blaspheming the Holy Spirit; second, the last conflict draws Mark's audience close in order to hear the warnings, for they, too, can fall under "the hardness of heart" category as continued listening to Mark's Gospel indicates (Mark 6:52; 8:17; note also 16:14; Eph 4:18).[69]

The Blasphemy against the Holy Spirit/hardness of heart parallel

The final narrative clue to decipher the intent of the Mark 3 sandwich and the warning against blaspheming the Holy Spirit is the analogy drawn between blasphemy *against the Holy Spirit* (Mark 3:29) and Jesus' parable rationale (Mark 4:10–12). The grid below shows that the blasphemy/no forgiveness-warning and Jesus' parable rationale line up to support a measure of mutual (contextual, narrative) meaning.

Mark 3:29	Mark 4:12 (Isa 6:9–10)
Judicial promise-threat: "... but whoever blasphemes against the Holy Spirit <u>never has forgiveness</u>, but is guilty of an eternal sin"	Judicial promise-threat: "... so that while seeing, they may see and not perceive, and, while hearing, they may not understand, <u>otherwise they might return and be forgiven</u>."
Outsider-insider framing of the Mark 3 sandwich	"And He was saying to them, 'To you [insiders] has been given the mystery of the kingdom of God, but <u>those who are outside</u> get everything in parables'..." (4:11).
Prologue to Mark 3 sandwich: conflict with Israelite leadership (Mark 2–3)	Prologue to the Isa 6 idolatry-taunt: conflict with Israelite leadership (Isa 1–5)

There are too many intentional similarities to be ignored.[70] There is the obviously similar judicial outcome: no forgiveness (3:29; 4:12). For Mark, blasphemy *against the Holy Spirit* is analogous to the judgment of the Isaiah 6 idolatry-taunt in the parable rationale. Both texts are set within an

---

6 idolatry-taunt.

69. A theme Paul picks up in addressing the church in Rome (Romans 9–11), which ironically he later draws upon a Satan/Beelzebul-eschatological theme similar to Mark's (note Romans 13:11–14; 16:20).

70. Watts, *Isaiah's New Exodus*, 196–97.

outsider-insider framework. Clearly, in Mark 4, *outsiders* are given parables because they are under judgment and will not be forgiven. This is precisely what is depicted in the Mark 3 *outsider-insider* sandwich. This is significant, for in chapter 3 the scribes' accusations (v. 22) are met with parable (vv. 23–27), indicating they are, indeed, *outsiders*. Those inside receive the mysteries of the kingdom (4:11a); those who do *the will of God* are *insiders* (3:34–35). And, both texts rely on antecedent conflict with disobedient, rebellious Jewish leadership (Mark 2–3; Isa 1–5).

The Beelzebul confrontation strategically follows the five conflict stories in Mark 2–3 and is set just prior to the Mark 4 parables. The Mark 3 sandwich amplifies the conflict between Jesus and Jewish leadership (v. 22), who are the keepers of the Israelite world (the religious and social order) and guardians of the temple system.[71] Jesus' parables of judgment (3:23–27) are directed at the opposition's rejection of his authority and their erroneous description of his kingdom activity.[72] The Isaiah 6 idolatry-taunt (vv. 9–10) is used in a similar manner in the parable rationale (Mark 4:10–12) and is "exactly in keeping with the original Isaianic context of a Jerusalem leadership" that had rejected the wisdom, covenant stipulations, and authority of Yahweh in favor of "its own idolatrous categories."[73] In the prelude to the original idolatry-taunt, Isaiah uses a parable of judgment (the parable of the vineyard, Isa 5:1–2), directing the judicial threat (Isa 6:9–10) toward Jerusalem leadership.[74] There is also an "authority" issue in the Isaiah context, namely against Yahweh's kingship and covenant expectations. Meanwhile in Mark's Beelzebul episode, the scribes are depicted as those *who came down from Jerusalem* (3:22), which, as Watts points out, implicates "the national centre."[75] Most likely the judgment announced in Mark 4:10–12 is directed at the Jewish leadership that had rejected Jesus and had begun plotting his destruction (Mark 3:6)—foreshadowed and "parabled" in the Mark 3 sandwich.

Mark's Beelzebul controversy links the rebellious Jewish leadership to its continued judgment of exile as the use of the Isaiah 6 idolatry-taunt in chapter 4 makes clear. The Mark 3 Beelzebul false accusations eventually

---

71. The confrontations continue afterward throughout Mark: 7:1–5; 8:31; 9:11, 14; 10:33; 11:18, 27; 12:13, 28, 32, 35–38; 14:1, 43, 53–65; 15:1, 31.

72. Watts, *Isaiah's New Exodus*, 156.

73. Ibid., 154.

74. See chapter 2, "Wasted Evangelism."

75. Watts, *Isaiah's New Exodus*, 195.

A Prelude to Judgment (Mark 3:20–35)

find their climax at the trial scene (14:53–65) where Jesus is ultimately condemned for blasphemy and handed over for destruction (i.e., death). Although all need to heed the warning, the blasphemy *against the Holy Spirit* finds its significance, not in a general sense as the ultimate rejection of Jesus as Savior (as is popularly interpreted), but specifically toward the Jerusalem leadership for their rejection of God's kingdom, through which Jesus-the Stronger Man has come to plunder the kingdoms of Satan-the strongman, *the prince of demons* (Mark 3:22–27; John 12:31; Eph 2:2; 6:12; Col 1:13; Rev 11:15; 12:10–12).

THE PROGRAMMATIC CONNECTION AND PRELUDE TO JUDGMENT

The Mark 3 sandwich specifically warns against blaspheming the Holy Spirit (3:29). But why the Holy Spirit? Why not blasphemy against God or against Jesus? It seems reasonable that blasphemy against God would result in ultimate, eternal judgment. There are texts that indicate such (Exod 22:28; Lev 24:15–16; note also 1 Kgs 21:10–14; Isa 65:7) and this is the charge that ultimately "destroys" Jesus (*You have heard the blasphemy; how does it seem to you?"And they all condemned Him to be deserving of death*, 14:64; note 3:6).[76] And, the conflict-thread (2:1–3:6) establishes that Jesus, as the Son of Man, has the authority to forgive sins, thus showing consistency with the broader narrative.[77] So, why the Holy Spirit? An answer lies in the programmatic foundation of Mark's Gospel introduction (1:2–3).

The Beelzebul episode has been linked to a number of OT texts (e.g., Isa 49:24–26; 53:12; Ps 68:18) that focus on Jesus as the Stronger Man taking captive the captives of the defeated strongman-Satan. Watts, in *Isaiah's New Exodus in Mark*, ties the Beelzebul controversy to Isaiah's Divine Warrior, furthering the Stronger Man imagery and, as well, showing the episode's redemptive link to the New Exodus.[78] Yet, there is an overlooked association that needs to be explored between the Mark 3 sandwich and

---

76. Exodus 22:28 (*You shall not curse God, nor curse a ruler of your people*) is relevant for the Mark 3 text, for it blends the two charges against Jesus that condemn him to destruction/death: "blasphemy" (*curse*) against God and "blasphemy" (*curse*) against the Jewish leaders (see Mark 14:53–65); additionally, there is a narrative connection, projecting the Mark 3 blasphemy warning to the trial seen (see Bock, "Blasphemy").

77. See Mark 2:1–12; Matt 9:2–8; Luke 5:18–26; also Luke 7:47–50; 12:10; Mark 3:28–29; Matt 12:31–32.

78. Watts, *Isaiah's New Exodus*, 144–52.

Wasted Evangelism

Mark's programmatic OT foundation at the opening of his Gospel (1:2–3). This is significant, for the programmatic content of the gospel is embedded with OT ties to covenant stipulations that include how God's people are to relate to the economically vulnerable and to issues of justice.[79]

The Spirit and programmatic link to the gospel's foundation

Mention of the Spirit is somewhat limited in Mark and is focused primarily in the introductory sequence of the narrative (Mark 1:8, 10–11, 12). Perhaps the brevity in the narrative holds a key. The role of the Spirit in Mark is intensively and intimately related to the programmatic content of the gospel. In rapid succession, Mark gives the impression that the foundation (i.e., *the beginning*, 1:1) of *the gospel of Jesus Christ* is marked by the presence of the Spirit. The dawning of the promised redemptive era is revealed in the appearance of a Messiah-King who is the bearer-baptizer of the Spirit (vv. 7–11). The binding of the Mark 3 strongman happens through a Stronger Man with whom the Spirit is associated (Mark 1:8; 3:27). The Mark 3 sandwich intentionally links Jesus, the Spirit-endowed "Mightier One" (*ho ischyroteros*, Stronger One, 1:7–8) to the Stronger Man (*ton ischyron*, 3:27) who comes to plunder Satan's kingdom-house (3:24, 27).[80] The Spirit comes upon Jesus (1:8) and instigates the initial contest between Satan-the strongman and Jesus-the Stronger Man, literally casting Jesus into the desert-contest (1:12–13). The Spirit is intimately associated with the new redemptive era that has dawned in the arrival of the Messiah-Son of God (1:1), the inaugurated "new exodus."

At the onset, without much knowledge of the OT, readers/listeners can sense that the "essence" of Mark's Gospel story is connected to ancient promises and expectations. Mark's Gospel is linked to a "tapestry" of three OT passages (1:2–3; Exod 23:20; Mal 3:1; Isa 40:3). Of primary interest is the Exodus 23:20 component, a first exodus reference located in what is a final warning immediately before the seal of the covenant (24:1–18):[81]

> "Behold, I am going to send an angel before you to guard you along the way and to bring you into the place which I have prepared. Be on your guard before him and obey his voice; do not be rebellious toward him, for he will not pardon your transgression, since My

79. See chapter 2, "Wasted Evangelism."
80. France, *Gospel of Mark*, 174; Watts, *Isaiah's New Exodus*, 146.
81. Watts, *New Exodus*, 65.

A Prelude to Judgment (Mark 3:20-35)

name is in him. But if you truly obey his voice and do all that I say, then I will be an enemy to your enemies and an adversary to your adversaries. For My angel will go before you and bring you in to the land of the Amorites, the Hittites, the Perizzites, the Canaanites, the Hivites and the Jebusites; and I will completely destroy them" (Exod 23:20-23).

Amid the promises is a warning, elements of which are associated with the Mark 3 sandwich. We hear that *the Angel* goes before them and Israel is warned to *obey his voice* and *not be rebellious toward him, for <u>he will not pardon your transgression</u>, since My name is in him* (Exod 23:20-21). This is followed by warnings against idolatry (vv. 32-33; cf. Isa 6:9-10; Mark 4:12),[82] also an element (as discussed above) associated with the Mark 3 sandwich and its narrative relationship to the idolatry-taunt in Mark 4. The programmatic link is made even stronger through the role of the Spirit, who is associated with the Exodus 23 Angel. Elsewhere, the OT makes the connection between the Angel of the exodus and God's Spirit (e.g., *As for the promise which I made you when you came out of Egypt, My Spirit is abiding in your midst; do not fear!*, Hag 2:5; *You gave Your good Spirit to instruct them, your manna You did not withhold from their mouth, and You gave them water for their thirst*, Neh 9:20; note Num 11:17).[83]

The parallel is very apparent and almost completely overlooked as a key to deciphering the intent behind the warning against blaspheming the Holy Spirit. At Israel's founding moment, the newly formed people of Yahweh were identified by the presence of the Spirit and given promises and warnings. They were to obey the voice of the Spirit and warned not to rebel against him for he would *not pardon* their *transgressions* (23:21). It is not a stretch to note the parallel framework in Mark's narrative: first, there is the deliberate programmatic link of the gospel and the inauguration of the kingdom of God to the first exodus (Mark 1:1-3; Exod 23:20); second, the commissioning of the twelve immediately precedes the Mark 3 sandwich (3:13-19), an obvious allusion to the creation of God's new Israel (i.e., his new community); third, a warning and threat related to the Spirit (3:29;

---

82. There is a biblical dynamic link between demons and idolatry, linking Jesus' exorcisms and the charge of idolatry against the leaders of Israel (Lev 17:7; Deut 32:17; Ps 106:37; 1 Cor 10:20; also note *Jub.* 1:11; 11:4-6; *1 En.* 19:1; 99:7).

83. Note the association of the Spirit with the wider first Exodus story: The cloud and pillar of fire—Exod 13:21-22; 14:24; 33:9-10; Num 9:15; 14:14; Deut 1:33; Neh 9:12; Pss 78:14; 99:7; 105:39; Isa 4:4-6; 63:9-11; 1 Cor 10:1; and, as well, references to the exodus Angel—Exod 3:2; 14:19; 23:23; 32:34; 33:2; note Judg 2:1-4.

Exod 23:20–23); and fourth, the new community is defined by obedience to God's will (Mark 3:35).

The reason given for why the exodus Angel could not pardon seems basically tautological—the Angel *will not pardon* because the Angel cannot pardon (only God can forgive). This appears to be dividing hairs and nuances; for, if it did not matter that the Angel could not forgive, why even tell them? The warning and threat must, out of necessity, carry some divine weight.

Previously, the newly delivered people of Israel were given a similar warning to obey Yahweh's voice, but it was presented as a positive promise: *Now then, if you will indeed obey My voice and keep My covenant, then you shall be My own possession among all the peoples, for all the earth is Mine* (Exod 19:5). Another parallel can be heard in Deuteronomy 30, which seems to suggest less of a distinction between Yahweh and his Angel:

> See, I have set before you today life and prosperity, and death and adversity; in that I command you today to love the Lord your God, to walk in His ways and to keep His commandments and His statutes and His judgments, that you may live and multiply, and that the Lord your God may bless you in the land where you are entering to possess it. But if your heart turns away and you will not obey, but are drawn away and worship other gods and serve them, I declare to you today that you shall surely perish. You will not prolong your days in the land where you are crossing the Jordan to enter and possess it. I call heaven and earth to witness against you today, that I have set before you life and death, the blessing and the curse. So choose life in order that you may live, you and your descendants, by loving the Lord your God, by <u>obeying His voice</u>, and by holding fast to Him; for this is your life and the length of your days, that you may live in the land which the Lord swore to your fathers, to Abraham, Isaac, and Jacob, to give them (30:15–20).

The calls to life and death, blessing and curse parallel the Exodus 23:20 context of choosing obedience and, as a result, receiving the blessing of God's presence and God's promise to be an enemy to their enemies; whereas, disobedience results in the opposite (note Exod 23:22–23, 27–30). In Deuteronomy 30, "obeying his Voice" is directly related to *loving the Lord their God* (v. 20),[84] which carries the intent of obedience.

---

84. Paul uses Deut 30 in two texts (Rom 2:28–29; 10:6–8) that define the community of God and the mode of faith.

A Prelude to Judgment (Mark 3:20–35)

Later, Joshua will recall the same Exodus 23 and Deuteronomy 30 covenant promise and warning, particularly the same warning to obey the Lord's voice and the threat of "no forgiveness" for those not heeding the warning:

> Then Joshua said to the people, "You will not be able to serve the Lord, for He is a holy God. He is a jealous God; <u>He will not forgive</u>[85] <u>your transgression or your sins</u>. If you forsake the Lord and serve foreign gods, then He will turn and do you harm and consume you after He has done good to you." The people said to Joshua, "No, but we will serve the Lord." Joshua said to the people, "You are witnesses against yourselves that you have chosen for yourselves the Lord, to serve Him." And they said, "We are witnesses." "Now, therefore, put away the foreign gods which are in your midst, and incline your hearts to the Lord, the God of Israel." The people said to Joshua, "We will serve the Lord our God and we will obey His voice" (Josh 24:19–24; also see Judg 2:1–4, 20).

The Exodus association with the Spirit and Israel's rebellion against God is picked up by Isaiah as his preaching prepared a future remnant for the promised new Exodus (63:9–11). There is a clear Exodus motif, connecting the first exodus, the exodus Angel, the Spirit, and rebellion against the Angel's voice (cf. Exod 23:21–22):

> In all their affliction He was afflicted,
> And the angel of His presence saved them;
> In His love and in His mercy He redeemed them,
> And He lifted them and carried them all the days of old.
> But they rebelled
> And grieved His Holy Spirit;
> Therefore He turned Himself to become their enemy,
> He fought against them.
> Then His people remembered the days of old, of Moses
> Where is He who brought them up out of the sea
> with the shepherds of His flock?
> Where is He who put His Holy Spirit in the
> midst of them (Isa 63:9–11).

There is an OT antecedent rationale, based on a thread stemming from the Exodus 23:20 component of Mark's programmatic gospel summary, for the Holy Spirit to be the object of unforgivable blasphemy. There

---

85. This is specifically a reference back to Exod 23:21–22, for the same word, *nasa'* (LXX, *forgive*) is utilized.

are analogous contexts: as the first exodus was marked by the Spirit and obedience was to be a mark of God's newly created people, so, also at the inauguration of God's kingdom, the new exodus, and the creation of Jesus' true family are marked by the Spirit and obedience. *Blasphemy against the Holy Spirit is rejecting God's new Exodus, the inaugurated kingdom, and rebelling against God's present voice* (that is, not the doing of his will) (Mark 3:35).

The Beelzebul episode is prelude to the parable rationale (4:10–12)

The Mark 3 sandwich and its middle Beelzebul episode are the narrative transition for the pending *Sower* parable (Mark 4:1–8), offering a justification for what some consider a "problematic use" of Isaiah 6 by Jesus in the parable rationale (4:12; Isa 6:9–10).[86] The meaning for the idolatry-taunt in Mark 4 is, nonetheless, "virtually identical to the original meaning in Isaiah."[87] Israel's current leadership, who have hard hearts (Mark 3:5), have rejected God's word and the inauguration of the kingdom (i.e., the promised new Exodus)—to their own ruin and destruction (Mark 4:10–12; also 2:21–22; 7:6; 10:5; 12:10–12; 13:1–2, 24–27; 14:62). The Jewish leadership is in jeopardy of remaining in exile, unpardoned, and ultimately *outside* of God's kingdom; therefore, they receive parables of judgment (3:22–25; 4:1–8).[88]

Although the whole nation falls under God's judgment in the Isaiah 1–6 context, specifically the leaders are the ones God holds accountable for provoking rebellion (Isa 1:10, 23), despising the word of the Holy One (Isa 5:24; note 1:4), and abandoning social responsibilities toward the poor (Isa 1:17, 23; 3:14–15).[89] This situation is analogous to the incessant confrontations Jesus had with the Jerusalem temple-leadership in Mark's narrative (Mark 2:1—3:6; 3:22–30). The Jewish leadership of Isaiah's time had stumbled and rebelled against God's *presence* (Isa 3:8) and had called

---

86. Watts, *Isaiah's New Exodus*, 153, 194–96; Beale, "Isaiah VI 9–13," 257–78; also Beale, *We Become What We Worship*, 51–52.

87. McComiskey, "Exile and the Purpose of Jesus' Parables," 59–85.

88. See Keegan ("Parable of the Sower") and McComiskey ("Exile and the Purpose of Jesus' Parables") for an explanation of the parable of the Sower and its rationale and relationship to the Jewish leadership's reaction to and rejection of Jesus and the kingdom.

89. The *whole head is sick* and *the whole heart is faint* are most likely references to Israel's leadership (1:5); also, the temple leadership is implied in the case against the sacrilege of worship (1:10–15).

A Prelude to Judgment (Mark 3:20–35)

evil good, and good evil, substituting *darkness for light and light for darkness* (5:20)—analogous to the Beelzebul accusations (Mark 3:22). The warning against blaspheming the Holy Spirit (as already shown above) is analogous to the conditions and threat contained in Jesus' parable rationale (4:10–12); the promise-threat is directed at those who are *outside* (i.e., their continued condition of exile) and, thus, who will not be forgiven (as it was for the leadership in Isaiah's time).[90] The Mark 3 sandwich is a prelude to judgment for those rejecting the authority of Jesus, the Messiah-King (1:1), and rebelling against his voice, that is, the implications of the inaugurated kingdom (1:15)—the new Exodus (e.g., Isa 63:9–11)—which is the word (i.e., his teaching and deeds) sown by the Sower.

Following on the heels of the Beelzebul confrontation (Mark 3:22–35), the judgment reflected in the parables (3:23–29; 4:1–8) and implied by the Isaiah 6 referent (4:12) is appropriate for Israel's unprepared leadership in Jesus' day.[91] As with the leaders in Isaiah's time, there will be no forgiveness for the temple-leadership who rejects Jesus and his kingdom-word (Isa 2:9; Mark 3:29; 4:12).[92] An OT hermeneutic is at play in the Mark 3 sandwich, indicating the continued judgment of exile[93] (being *outside* the kingdom) for the rebellious leaders who shame, rather than honor Jesus, God's Messiah-King.

IMPLICATIONS: SOCIAL ACTION OUTCOMES

The Mark 3 sandwich provides a penultimate warning as a result of the public conflict between Jesus and Jewish leadership,[94] which gave rise to

---

90. McComiskey, "Exile and the Purpose of Jesus' Parables."

91. Watts, *New Exodus*, 183, 218–19.

92. Note *no healing*, Isa 3:7; Mark 4:12. *No forgiveness* and *no healing* might be interchangeable. The concept of *forgiveness* and *healing* are parallel in Isa 53. In Isa 1–5 there is promise of *no forgiveness* (2:9) and *I will not be your healer* (3:7). This might explain why some readings of Isa 6:10 have lack of *forgiveness* and some lack of *healing*. Perhaps this is why in Mark's Gospel Jesus and his critics link healing and forgiveness (see Mark 2:1–12).

93. Keegan, "The Parable of the Sower"; McComiskey, "Exile and the Purpose of Jesus' Parables"; also for Israel's condition of exile at the time of Jesus, see Wright, *Jesus and the Victory of God*, xvii–xviii, 126–27, 203–4, 236–39; also Wright, *People of God*, 268–72, 299–301; Evans, "Aspects of Exile and Restoration," 299–328; and, Wright, "Continuing Exile" (paper, November 2010).

94. Keegan ("The Parable of the Sower") refers to Kingsbury, *Conflict in Mark*, 69; also Tolbert, *Sowing the Gospel*, 233.

the Beelzebul episode's place as a prelude to the Isaiah 6 judgment used in the parable rationale (4:10–12); *outsiders* continue under the judgment of exile and are, thus, not forgiven (3:28–29; 4:12). This meaning, nonetheless, must now be translated into significance for those who stand before the *outsider-insider—strongman vs. Stronger Man—outsider-insider* sandwich. Belief in Jesus as God's Messiah-King is the needed remedy for this *outsider*-exiled-no forgiveness condition; however, repentance (1:15a) and doing God's will (3:35) are also necessary elements of being truly *insider*-family members (3:34–35). In the absence of a fully developed theory of application, some reasonable guide is needed to move us from meaning to significance and application. More specifically, in light of this study's goal, *how does the significance of the Mark 3 sandwich encourage the church to consider social action as a component of its evangelistic activities?*

In view of the Mark 3 *strongman vs. Stronger Man* parables (3:23–27), the warning against blaspheming the Holy Spirit is *the gospel* (3:28–29), admonishing, first, the Jewish leaders, and, then, whoever hears these words to repent and believe in the inauguration of the kingdom (1:15), that is, to move from exile to remnant/restoration/kingdom, or from *outside* to *inside*. Blasphemy *against the Holy Spirit* is an indication of one's hard heart, that is, the reality of being under the judicial sentence implied by the Isaiah 6 idolatry-taunt; thus, remaining in exile, the biblical state of *outside*. For the disciples, as the fuller narrative indicates, the significance is that they, too, need to guard against having their own hard heart,[95] a dangerous indicator reflective of disbelief and behavior contrary to the sphere of God's kingdom. Additionally, the outer slices (A1, A2) of the sandwich push this warning beyond the obvious Jewish leaders with whom Jesus had conflict to all who *appear* on the *inside*, for they, too, must do the will of God in order to be truly *inside*, that is, part of Jesus' new family (3:34–35). The outcome of blasphemy *against the Holy Spirit* is "no forgiveness." Doing God's will (3:35) is indicative of repentance and believing in the gospel of the kingdom (1:14–15). We are, however, left to decipher the outcomes relevant to the text.

Range of obedience includes social action

An obedient response to the Mark 3 sandwich is to do the *will of God* (v. 35); but, what is genuinely the *will of God* within the range and referents

95. Mark 6:51–52; 8:16–21; also note 8:34–38; 9:33–34; 11:31; 16:14.

A Prelude to Judgment (Mark 3:20–35)

underlying the *Outsider-Insider—Stronger Man* sandwich? The activities of doing the will of God need to correspond in-kind to the text. In other words, there needs to be a reasonable association between the meaning of the text and its compliance. This correspondence is found in the OT foundation for the gospel (Mark 1:2–3) and the Isaiah 6 context that lay behind the Beelzebul episode.

First, the warning in Exodus 23:20, an element of Mark's OT foundation, is to obey the voice of the Angel, pointing back to the land-stipulations that introduce the vulnerable trio, *the widow, orphan*, and *alien/stranger*,[96] and their relationship to the fabric of society. The covenant-keeping community was commanded *You shall not wrong a stranger or oppress him* (22:21a) and *You shall not afflict any widow or orphan* (v. 22). There were statutes regarding how credit and money-lending related to the poor (*If you lend money . . . to the poor among you, you are not to act as a creditor to him . . . If you ever take your neighbor's cloak as a pledge, you are to return it to him before the sun sets*, vv. 25–26). They were not to *pervert the justice due to your needy brother in his dispute* (23:6), or *oppress a stranger* (23:9a). Also, the basis for the seventh year Sabbath rest of farm-fields was so *the needy of your people may eat* (23:11).[97]

The relationship between the covenant community and its disobedience to Exodus land-stipulations was clearly an underlying basis for the judgment of exile. This can be seen in the Malachi 3:1 component of Mark's programmatic OT reference for the gospel (1:2–3). The unprepared leadership (Mal 3:1–2) were judged for ignoring the Exodus land-stipulations regarding the economically vulnerable (*Then I will draw near to you for judgment; and I will be a swift witness . . . against those who oppress the wage earner in his wages, the widow and the orphan, and those who turn aside the alien and do not fear Me . . .*" (Mal 3:5). The remedy for the exiled condition (i.e., the biblical state of being *outside*) is to restore Yahweh's statutes, that is, the land-stipulations (3:7) that directly link the covenant community to the economically vulnerable (3:5).

---

96. The *widow, orphan*, and *alien/stranger* trio is a frequent reference throughout the OT, particularly in contexts that concern God's covenant with his people or a reaffirmation of that covenant: Exod 22:21, Deut 10:18–19; 14:29; 16:11, 14; 24:17, 19–21; 26:12–13; 27:19; Jer 7:6; 22:3; Zech 7:9–10; Mal 3:5; also note Lev 19:34; Ps 94:6; Isa 1:17, 23; 10:2; Hos 14:3.

97. For more on land-stipulations and the poor: Exod 23:10–12; Lev 19:9–10; 23:22; Deut 14:29; 15:7–11; 24:19–22; 26:12–13.

As a prelude to judgment (i.e., continued exile) implied by the Isaiah 6 idolatry-taunt (Mark 4:12), obedient outcomes for the Mark 3 sandwich should correspond to the nature and reason for the judgment being applied. The Isaiah 6 judgment is a consequence "of the nation's covenantal disobedience."[98] The original idolatry-taunt (Isa 6:9–10) relies on Isaiah 1–5 for its own rationale for the judgment of exile. Amid a call to restore *justice* and *righteousness* (Isa 1:17, 21, 26, 27; 3:10; 5:7, 16), there are charges related to the economically vulnerable: *Defend the orphan, Plead for the widow* (1:17); *They do not defend the orphan, Nor does the widow's plea come before them* (1:23); *The plunder of the poor is in your houses . . . And grinding the face of the poor* (3:14–15). The mention of the *orphan* and the *widow* is an obvious reflection on Exodus covenant stipulations (Exod 21–23). Additionally, the Isaiah 6 judgment is associated with Israelite leadership's sin of idolatry (Isa 1:29–31; 2:6–9; 2:12–13; 2:18, 20), also an element of the prelude to judgment in the Mark 3 sandwich.

Later, the prophet Zechariah links social action outcomes to God's covenant restoration from the judgment of exile (Zech 7:8–14), binding together listening to the word of the Lord, the role of the Spirit, idolatry, and exodus land-stipulations. Zechariah declares *the word of the Lord* (7:4) to the exiles. The Israelite leadership made no attempt to show contrition because they had not linked their idolatrous hard hearts to their misplaced social relationships. Those who were in exile are called to *Dispense true justice and practice kindness and compassion each to his brother* and *not oppress the widow or the orphan, the stranger or the poor* (7:9–10). Yet, like the Jewish leaders who confronted Jesus and make accusation in the Beelzebul episode, the exiled leaders' hearts were hard (*their hearts like flint*, 7:12a). They had turned a deaf ear to God's *law* and the *words* provided *by His Spirit through the former prophets* (7:12). The Zechariah 7 pronouncements regarding judgment and restoration find analogous reiteration and realization in the Mark 3 sandwich.

As these OT backgrounds and referents indicate, there is a link between the Beelzebul episode and disobedience to the land-stipulations that were in place on behalf of the economically vulnerable. It should not surprise Mark's readers/listeners that just prior to the pronouncement of ultimate judgment on the temple (i.e., its destruction, Mark 13:1–2) there is

---

98. Beale, "Isaiah VI 9–13"; also McComiskey, "Exile and the Purpose of Jesus' Parables." Note Pss 115:1–8; 135:15–18; Isa 46:7; Jer 10:5.

a contrast between duplicitous scribes and a poor widow (12:38–44).[99] It is reasonable, therefore, to conclude that social action outcomes—protection, care, and advocacy for the economically vulnerable—should be components of a church's evangelistic activities. As "no forgiveness" is the outcome of blasphemy *against the Holy Spirit*, social action outcomes should be the results of doing God's will (Mark 3:35); thus, church leaders should ensure that social action is included in a church's evangelistic activities.

Conditions, indicators, and outcome relevant to the outsider-insider sandwich

Condition	Indicators/Activities	Outcomes/Results
Hard heart/disobedient Outsider/exiled/ outside-the-kingdom	Blasphemy against the Holy Spirit	No forgiveness
Repentance/believing Insider/restored/ forgiven/in-the-kingdom	Doing God's will	Can be social action

POSTSCRIPT—SHAMING CHURCH LEADERS, JESUS' PUBLIC HONOR, AND SOCIAL ACTION

Church leaders cannot escape the narrative fact that the Beelzebul episode, the conflict-thread (2:1—3:6), and the Sower parable (4:1–20) seem specifically directed at them. For church leaders, a posture of shame reminds them of the illusive nature of status, the dangerous allure of power, and the recurring failure of faulty structures to guard the gospel and the church from the destructive influences and seductive cultural patterns that oppose God's reign over all spheres of humankind. It should not surprise us that the shaming of the Beelzebul episode connects church leaders to the church's responsibility toward the economically vulnerable. Caring, protecting, and advocating for the poor gives away power; and, public association with those living with the effects of poverty risks lowering one's church community status. However, maintaining power and its enabling structures so that one's social standing and status remain in place (even among, more particularly, the Christian community) at the expense of the weakest and most vulnerable among us is synonymous with *blasphemy against the Holy*

---

99. See chapter 1, "Widows in Our Courts."

Spirit—breaking covenant, risking *outside* status and, thus, the condition of eternally never being forgiven.

The biography of *Jesus vs. Jewish leaders* is linked to the biography of the disciples, who, like *the ones beside* Jesus (3:21; note 6:1–6) and like Jesus' earthly family (3:31–32), are at risk of being *outside* (6:51–52; 8:16–21; 8:33–38; cf. 9:33–34; 16:14), if they, too, are not doers of God's will (3:33–35). This linking is particularly relevant to church leaders, as they stand before the Mark 3 *outsider-insider* sandwich, for the Beelzebul episode ought to shame them in those areas that are too closely identified with that which opposes God's rule and kingdom (Mark 1:15; 3:25). Mark's Beelzebul episode functions similar to OT penitential prayers, allowing the reader/listener to enter a life narrative that reflects an appropriate shame for allowing those destructive forces and influences to distract from obedience to God's word and work in the world. And like OT penitential prayers, a disposition of shame humbles the readers/listeners before their "disobedience to the Mosaic ideals" that often reflects "mistreatment of the poor and the weak,"[100] and gives them a way home that maps a spiritual disposition for restoring a fractured obedience to God.

Interestingly, after confessing that Jesus is the Messiah, Peter is soon rebuked as a surrogate of Satan's interests: *"Get behind me, Satan!" he said. "You do not have in mind the concerns of God, but merely human concerns"* (Mark 8:33b, NIV). Significant to the reader/listener is the immediate juxtaposition of the Peter-Satan rebuke and Jesus' admonishment that true followers must deny themselves (the opposite of power, an emptying of power) and take up their cross (v. 34).[101] Church leaders who intentionally incorporate social action in a church's evangelistic activities fulfill the obedience implications of the Beelzebul episode and, thus, raise Jesus' honor rating in the public sphere. Without such a public disposition, church leaders, following the convention of shame/honor that has been integrated in Mark's narrative, are further warned that *"whoever is ashamed of me and of my words in this adulterous and sinful generation, of him will the Son of Man also be ashamed when he comes in the glory of his Father with the holy angels"* (Mark 8:38).

---

100. Smith-Christopher, *Biblical Theology of Exile*, 121.

101. Note Mark 1:17 appeals to followers (*opisō*) who will become *fishers* and Mark 8:34 appeals to those who wish to follow (*opisō*) Jesus, broadening the significance beyond the foundational twelve (3:14); also see Anderson, *Destroying Our Private Cities*, 95–96.

5

Idolatry and Poverty
Social Action as Christian Apologetics

"There are more idols than realities in the world; that is my 'evil eye' for this world; that is also my 'evil ear.'"

—Friedrich Nietzsche, *Twilight of the Idols*

"The privilege of churches . . . can shroud the gospel in such middle- and upper-class consumer-oriented style and content that salvation subtly becomes more about providing a warm blanket of cultural safety than about stepping out into the bracing winds of spiritual sacrifice. Such patterns in a church's life can easily, if unintentionally, lead to a focus on consolidating and extending power instead of identifying with the powerless. The former is a lot more like a comfortable bed to sleep in than the latter. No wonder we don't want to wake up, let alone get up and get going in the work of justice."

—Mark Labberton, *The Dangerous Act of Worship*

"The meaning of earthly existence is not, as we have grown used to thinking, in prosperity, but in the development of the soul."

—Aleksandr Solzhenitsyn

Wasted Evangelism

How should non-poor evangelical Christians think Christianly about being a believer in a capitalistic, free market economic society where there are almost 40 million people living in poverty, where eighteen percent of children live with the effects of poverty, and, where forty-two percent of children born in the bottom income quintile will remain in that quintile as adults?[1] At the risk of setting up too many straw men, typically, answers to this question tend to revolve around *individual accountability vs. corporate responsibility* and/or *the individual vs. the state*. Issues of poverty are almost automatically, by default, arranged in *private vs. public* dichotomies, arguments, and responsibilities, which sets up a defective social construction of reality for the Christian.

Most Christians, conservative and liberal, agree that the poor are to be cared for, but the range, methodologies, and degree, as well as government involvement are areas of disagreement. Some Christians give the impression they do not have other than a political affiliation or economic preference as a framework to engage the issue of poverty. Furthermore, the banal posture of many non-poor Christians to the poor can lead to the "bystander effect" (i.e., the diffusion of responsibility), leaving many Christians out of any active role in assisting those affected by poverty or addressing the causes of poverty.

Regarding the issue of poverty in America, there is a lot at-stake for many people, Christians included: Constitutional rights, entitlements, property rights, taxes, freedom, upward mobility. Sides often cast opposing socio-economic approaches to solving issues of poverty as a threat to society or a cause for continued poverty. For most on the political right, the free market system with minimal interference from the government and private charity is what will ameliorate poverty; those on the political left stress public responsibility and that government is to deconstruct "unjust" structures and utilize its power to distribute resources more equitably. While most non-poor Christians understand there is a general Biblical call to help the poor, they, too, are often divided left and right, *public vs. private*. The Christian is then faced with the choice of leaning toward one as biblical, while labeling the other as unbiblical.

---

1. Approximately 13% currently live at or below the Federal poverty level (US Census Bureau, 2009 estimate; also the Bureau of Labor Statistics, US Department of Labor); see Mark Rank, *One Nation Underprivileged*; Isaacs et al., "Economic Mobility of Families Across Generations."; Acs and Zimmerman, "U.S. Intragenerational Mobility From 1984–2004."

Idolatry and Poverty

Christian discussions about poverty and the *private vs. public* approaches that claim to reduce the conditions of poverty often involve the OT. Interestingly, in Mark's Gospel, not only does he utilize the OT to develop the content of the gospel, he also draws from OT texts and contexts where idolatry and the poor are juxtaposed. It seems we do have a biblical paradigm for discussing poverty that actually focuses application down to, not what the government or charitable individuals think or do, but how the Christian and the Christian community define themselves and how they are associated with the poor. In the following, I will explore this idolatry-poverty juxtaposition and will seek to apply its significance to how non-poor Christians ought to think about the issue of poverty.

IDOLATRY: A BIBLICAL PARADIGM FOR THINKING ABOUT POVERTY

Christian responses to poverty often draw from the Sermon on the Mount (Matt 5–7; Luke 6), further substantiated by other NT teaching (e.g., Acts 2–4; Jas 1–2). Although important, this tends to be applied more to church-life and to the private sphere rather than developing a response to those living with the effects of poverty. Others turn to the Pentateuch and the Prophets, and, rightly so, for such biblical material is rich in addressing the issues of poverty. The results, however, can tend toward justification for political alignment and socio-economic policies (right/left, conservative/liberal). Christians across the spectrum wrestle with how the Pentateuch and the prophets apply in the (post)modern world. Many question the contemporary relevance of such documents of antiquity addressed to an ancient nation whose social-political location is the Ancient Near East. Nonetheless, there is a way to decipher the significance of OT ethical texts, namely to draw significance from their incorporation into the gospel itself.

Mark draws upon a fascinating range of OT contexts throughout his narrative that juxtapose idolatry and the economically vulnerable. Although Mark's use of the OT is extensive beyond these particular texts, he embeds his Gospel with OT contexts related to the economically vulnerable, whether Law, land-stipulation, or prophetic announcement, which also contain, within the context or flow of thought, mention of idolatry.

Gospel of Mark	OT references to the economically vulnerable and to idolatry
Mark 1:2–3	Exod 23; Mal 3; Isa 40
Mark 1:17	Jer 16; Amos 4
Mark 3–4	Isa 1–6; Zech 7
Mark 4:32	Dan 4; Ezek 17
Mark 7:6–7	Isa 29; Exod 20, 21; Lev 20; Deut 5
Mark 10:4	Deut 24
Mark 10:19	Exod 20; Deut 5
Mark 11:12–21	Jer 7–8
Mark 12:1	Isa 5
Mark 12:31	Lev 19
Mark 12:41–44	Exod 22; Lev 19, 23; Deut 14, 24; Mal 3; Isa 1, 10
Mark 13:1–2	Mal 3
Mark 13:2	Jer 7
Mark 14:7	Deut 15
Mark 15:33	Amos 8

Mark begins his narrative utilizing an OT composite of three texts which juxtapose idolatry and the economically vulnerable (Exod 23, Mal 3, Isa 40). Then afterward, Jesus calls for followers with the promise they will *become fishers of men* (Mark 1:17),[2] drawing upon OT contexts (Jer 16; Amos 4) that reference idolatry and the poor. Mark embeds Isaiah 1–6 into the fabric of the Beelzebul episode and the Sower parables (3:20—4:20), culminating in his use of the Isaiah idolatry-taunt (Isa 6:9–10; Mark 4:11–12). Isaiah 1–6 builds a case against Israel for its idolatry and the disregard for the economically vulnerable. Then, Mark reaches back to Daniel 4 and Ezekiel 17 to explain the presence and nature of the kingdom (Mark 4:30–32), both provide contexts regarding idolatry and the poor (see also Ezek 18). As Jesus makes his *way* to Jerusalem (Mark 10–12), Mark draws on Jeremiah 7–8, which also contains language and references to idolatry and the economically vulnerable (see Jer 2–5). The *widow vs. duplicitous*

---

2. See chapter 3, "You Will Appear as *Fishers*," for a fuller discussion on the Mark 1:17 *fisher of men* text.

scribes story (Mark 12:38–44) that bridges the *way* to Jerusalem and the eschatological discourse (Mark 13) is formed by references to Exodus 20, Leviticus 19, Deuteronomy 15 and 24, Jeremiah 7, and such texts as Isaiah 10, Zechariah 7, and Malachi 3, all of which contain the twin references to idolatry and the economically vulnerable.[3]

For Christians, the fact that Pentateuchal material and prophetic pronouncements form some background to our view of social justice, whether right or left, conservative or liberal, should provoke our interest, for these very texts also form our understanding of the gospel. The gospel is associated programmatically with the issue of idolatry *and* with those affected by poverty, which ought to (re)form our understanding of Christian discipleship and evangelism.

At an apologetic level: the poor, the ANE, and Image-bearers

Although few doubt the Christian call to serve the poor, the Bible, however, is not the first set of ancient documents to promote the protection and care for the poor, nor did Jews and Christians invent our concepts of justice. The world of the Ancient Near East (ANE) was very familiar with the care and protection to be given the poor, particularly by its deities, monarchs, and sovereigns.[4] The concept and practice was pre-Israelite and pre-dated Israelite propheticism.[5] Israel was indeed unique in excluding the worship of other gods besides Yahweh, but much of the ethical content associated with the biblical God can be found elsewhere in the ancient world.[6] As for the caring and protecting of the poor, there was little *new under the religious and socio-economic sun*. From the beginning of recorded history, people, societies, and governing structures (whether Empires or "at the city gate") have all struggled with *how to assist the poor*.[7] The Pentateuchal texts compare, even regarding the poor, to Sumerian and Akkadian Laws of

---

3. See chapter 1, "Widows in Our Courts," for a fuller discussion on the Mark 12:38–44 text regarding the duplicitous scribes and the poor widow.

4. Fensham, "Widow, Orphan, and the Poor," 129–39; Meadors, *Idolatry and the Hardening of the Heart*, 5; Rodd, *Glimpses Of A Strange Land*, 168–69.

5. Wright, "What Happened Every Seven Years," 129–38; Fensham, "Widow, Orphan, and the Poor."

6. Halpem et al., *Traditions in Transformation*, 55.

7. Mason, "Biblical Teaching and Assisting the Poor," 295.

Babylon.[8] Protection for the unfortunate, the poor, and indigent was "common policy" in the ANE and was not "unfamiliar to the Western Semites." What is of particular interest is that the defense of the poor was "seen as a virtue of gods, kings, and judges," essentially a policy of virtue that proved the piety and character of a ruler, monarch, or god.[9]

In light of antecedent ANE concerns for the poor, the uniqueness for the Israelite is that everything narrows down to *one God* who is alone righteous, who brings about justice for the poor. *Thus, enter the strong warnings against having other deities before Yahweh and the prohibitions against any form of idolatry (political allegiance or cult) that would challenge the place of Yahweh as the one true God.* Idolatry alone was the ultimate expression of unfaithfulness to God, fully deserving divine judgment. The Genesis creation account is set within a *God vs. the gods* polemic. The ten-plagues against Egypt and the Pharaoh were executed to demonstrate Yahweh's place as the true God. Later in 1 and 2 Kings, Israelite kings are portrayed as either good or bad "purely on religious grounds," whether "they destroyed or introduced idols." There is a polemic thread running through the OT that idols and the gods or monarchs they reflect are "powerless" (Ps 115; 135), unable to perform virtuous acts, and there is no profit in trusting them (Hab 2:18–19).[10] The OT presents the God of the Exodus as the one true God who ultimately cares for and protects the poor.

<u>Yahweh's Care, Protection, and Vindication of Economically Vulnerable</u>

"You shall not afflict any widow or orphan. If you afflict him at all, and if he does cry out to Me, I will surely hear his cry; and My anger will be kindled, and I will kill you with the sword, and your wives shall become widows and your children fatherless"(Exod 22:22–24).

"He executes justice for the orphan and the widow, and shows His love for the alien by giving him food and clothing" (Deut 10:18).

A father of the fatherless and a judge for the widows,
Is God in His holy habitation (Ps 68:5).

---

8. Cassuto, *Book of Exodus*, 258–64; also see Mendenhall's *Law and Covenant in Israel* for backgrounds.

9. Fensham, "Widow, Orphan and the Poor."

10. Rosner, "Concept of Idolatry," 21–30.

> The Lord protects the strangers;
> He supports the fatherless and the widow,
> But He thwarts the way of the wicked (Ps 146:9).

> "Beware that there is no base thought in your heart, saying, 'The seventh year, the year of remission, is near,' and your eye is hostile toward your poor brother, and you give him nothing; then he may cry to the Lord against you, and it will be a sin in you" (Deut 15:9).

> So that they caused the cry of the poor to come to Him,
> And that He might hear the cry of the afflicted (Job 34:28).

> You have seen it, for You have beheld mischief and vexation to take it into Your hand
> The unfortunate commits himself to You;
> You have been the helper of the orphan (Ps 10:14).

> To vindicate the orphan and the oppressed,
> So that man who is of the earth will no longer cause terror (Ps 10:18).

Deuteronomy 10 contains one of the clearest passages that portray the God of the OT as the Chief Advocate and Defender of the economically vulnerable. This text also very clearly links God's righteous virtue in providing for the poor to idolatry.

> "Now, Israel, what does the Lord your God require from you, but to fear the Lord your God, to walk in all His ways and love Him, and to serve the Lord your God with all your heart and with all your soul, and to keep the Lord's commandments and His statutes which I am commanding you today for your good? Behold, to the Lord your God belong heaven and the highest heavens, the earth and all that is in it. Yet on your fathers did the Lord set His affection to love them, and He chose their descendants after them, even you above all peoples, as it is this day. So circumcise your heart, and stiffen your neck no longer. For the Lord your God is the God of gods and the Lord of lords, the great, the mighty, and the awesome God who does not show partiality nor take a bribe. He executes justice for the orphan and the widow, and shows His love for the alien by giving him food and clothing" (Deut 10:12–18).

As Israel was encamped on the border of the land of promise, this was an appeal to renew fidelity to the original "Book of the Covenant" land-management stipulations.[11] The command to reflect God's righteousness is heard in admonitions to "fear the Lord," "walk in all his ways," *to love* and *serve* Him, and *keep his commands* (v. 12). An Exodus covenant-memory is placed before them and, then, comparison to other gods is made. Despite claims by other ANE deities and their earthy image-bearers, the God of the Exodus is the one true God, who owns all of creation (. . . *to the Lord your God belong heaven and the highest heavens, the earth and all that is in it*, v. 14). He is *the God of gods* and *Lord of lords*, who cannot be bribed nor does he show *partiality* (v. 17). To bring about such "impartiality," God shows partiality by doing justice for the economically vulnerable, showing them love by granting the basic necessities of life.

Peoples of the ANE all had social regulations that were part of royal legislation and subject to the state's administration of justice.[12] *Thus, enter the biblical concentration on land-management stipulations related to the economically vulnerable.* This is where the significance resides: The protection and advocacy for the poor were polemical, part of an apologetic for God against the false gods and their image-bearers. The prohibition against idolatry not only was to maintain a distinction between Creator and creation,[13] the distinction was to be actualized through maintaining virtues of righteousness, in particular virtues associated with caring for the poor.

The prohibition against images and idols has a slight twist to it, namely, there is a religious logic at play: It was understood that a pagan deity was present in its image[14] and the human monarchs or sovereigns were considered to be image-bearers of their deity. For example, in an inscription concerning the temple for the god Amun, the god calls king Amenhotep, "My son . . . My living image."[15] ANE monarchs were considered "sons" of their gods, representing the image of their god through how they ruled.[16] This is paralleled, first, in Genesis where Adam is the image of God

---

11. Childs, *Book of Exodus*, 451.

12. Waldow, "Social Responsibility," 182–204.

13. Beale, *We Become What We Worship*, 18; Cassuto, *Book of Exodus*, 236–37.

14. Rosner, "Concept of idolatry"; also note: *gods of silver* and *gods of gold*, Exod 20:23; *god of gold*, Exod 32:31; *molten gods*, Lev 19:4; *put away the gods which your fathers served*, Josh 24:14; *every nation still made gods of its own*, 2 Kgs 17:29; see 19:18.

15. Beale, *We Become What We Worship*, 131.

16. Ibid.

(Gen 1:26–27; 5:1; 9:6) and inferred as God's son (Gen 5:7; Luke 3:38). Later in Exodus, Israel is called God's son (Exod 4:22; note Isa 63:16; 64:8; Jer 31:9; Hos 11:1; Matt 2:15; Rom 9:4).[17] This is particularly important in regards to the ethical stipulations where God demonstrates his righteous virtues in protecting and caring for the poor. As God's image-bearer, the work of God's hands, Israel was to reflect *his righteousness* (Isa 60:21; 61:3, 11; 62:1–2; also Isa 42:21; 45:23–24; 59:16–17; 63:1).[18] And, as the present Spirit-image-bearers, so now believers and the church are to reflect such righteousness.[19]

The land and the earth belong to God

The paradigmatic use of OT ethical contexts is also affirmed by the fact that the whole earth belongs to the biblical God, the true owner of *the land*.[20] God's laws were intended to enlighten the nations (Deut 4:5–8), so the OT ethical principles, symbols, and mediating structures should find significance for all cultures.[21] C. J. H. Wright assumes that "if God gave Israel certain specific institutions and laws, they were based on principles which have universal validity." All social contexts should be brought "nearer to conformity with the principles underlying" the OT paradigm, because the same God who is the Redeemer and law-giver of Israel is also the Creator and Ruler of all humanity.[22] The institutions God gave to govern early Israelite society and *the ethical emphases* of these institutions are intended to inform all peoples (Gen 18:18; Isa 2:3; 51:4). The ethical emphases of the Pentateuch find affirmation throughout the Bible (e.g., Luke 16:19–31), along with references to God's covenantal love (Lev 19:18) as fulfillment of the "Law and Prophets" (Matt 19:19; Mark 12:28–31; Luke 10:27; Rom 13:9; Gal 5:14; Jas 2:8).[23] As Israel was to be a light to the nations, "Israel's

---

17. The reference to Jesus as God's Son in Mark 1:11 (. . . *and a voice came out of the heavens: "You are My beloved Son, in You I am well-pleased"*) could be drawn from Exod 4:22, a referent where Israel is referred to as God's Son.

18. Beale, *We Become What We Worship*, 277.

19. E.g., Col 3; Gal 5; Rom 8; 1 Pet 3; Jas 1–2.

20. Wright, "What Happened Every Seven."

21. Note Blomberg, *Neither Poverty nor Riches*, 49; see also Wright, "Biblical Reflections on Land," 153–67.

22. Wright, *An Eye for an Eye*, 162.

23. Mason, "Centralization and Decentralization in Social Arrangements," 3–38.

socio-economic life and institutions, therefore, have a paradigmatic or exemplary function in principle."[24]

The OT affirms God's ownership "as extending over the whole earth and including every living and inanimate thing upon it."[25] Even property under Mosaic Law was not truly private as we are conditioned to think through American mediating structures (e.g., history, the Constitution, the Bill of Rights, local zoning laws, etc.); it was related to family and economic sustainability—a key to understanding the role of the land and the proper view of ownership.[26] The land was a *gift*, and, as such, land-holders were formed by the relationship of Yahweh to the land: Yahweh was the king over Israel, who owned all the land and made distinct demands reflecting his righteousness to those whom he gave it to use. Under Yahweh, each family had their own land: not necessarily individual plots of land, but land associated with the tribe, the family. Israel's ideal was a form of decentralized extended-family ownership as stewardship under Yahweh's absolute ownership.[27] This is important for understanding the relationship of those *in power* with the economically vulnerable: Those *at the gate* are not to centralize power and make decisions that disregard the reason for the distribution of land, particularly family economic stability (one reason for shunning the development of a monarchy in Israel). The people's relationship to the land was to reflect the virtues of God in contrast to surrounding deities and their image-bearers. There was an apologetic to be demonstrated through the people's relationship to the land.

Land-management stipulations regarding the economically vulnerable and the poor are set within a *God vs. the gods* polemic, actually raising justice for the poor to the level of apologetics and evangelism. As for the one true God, if he does not provide for and protect the economically vulnerable, then he is no God at all—at most, just one god among other gods. Furthermore, when the people who are to reflect God's image do not provide a profile and outcomes reflecting such concern and advocacy, not only does this diminish his glory, but also negates the witness and proclamation of his name to outsiders. It should be no surprise, then, that the gospel is defined by OT contexts where poverty and idolatry are at issue. With the

---

24. Wright, *God's People in God's Land*, xviii; also see Stuart, *Exodus*, 442.

25. Wright, *God's People*, 116; Wright refers to Ps. 24:1; 89:11; 95:4–5; Jer. 27; Hag. 2:8; 1 Chr. 29:11.

26. Ibid., 134–36, 141.

27. Sider, *The Scandal of Evangelical Politics*, 118.

inauguration of the kingdom and the church and believers as his image-bearers, there remains the same apologetic concerning God's righteous acts on behalf of the poor. Thus, it seems reasonable that outcomes related to the protection, care, and advocacy of the economically vulnerable can be components of evangelistic activities.

The Gospel of Mark and the Juxtaposition of Idolatry and Poverty

Mark tends to reference the OT at critical points in his narrative and "prefers certain categories of texts for particular concerns."[28] This is very noticeable in how Mark crafts his narrative using OT texts that juxtapose the issue of idolatry and texts that bring to mind Exodus land-management stipulations related to the economically vulnerable and words of judgment for abandoning them. Mark is quite consistent and intentional in this use—and *at critical places* (Mark 1, 3, 4, 7, 10, 11, 12, 13)—thus, making them most likely programmatic for understanding the gospel and, as well, the nature of discipleship and evangelism.

The programmatic summary (Mark 1:1–3)

Mark begins his narrative with a composite OT quotation (Exod 23:20; Mal 3:1; Isa 40:3) that contains juxtaposed references to poverty and idolatry. Mark draws from the concluding summary (Exod 23:20–23) of the "Book of the Covenant" (20:1—23:33), which immediately contains warnings against idolatry (*You shall not worship their gods, nor serve them . . .* , 23:24; *You shall make no covenant with them or with their gods . . .* , 23:32–33). Essentially, the entire "Book of the Covenant" is structured around this theme. Heading the foundational Ten-Words (Exod 20:1–17) are a command to have no other gods before Yahweh (v. 3) and the prohibition of idolatry in any form (vv. 4–5). Even the Ten-Words are bracketed with prohibitions against *forms* of idolatry, for the tenth commandment (*You shall not covet*, 20:17) is associated throughout the OT with idolatry (e.g., Exod 20:23; Deut 7:25; Isa 1:29; 44:9; Ps 115:4).[29] Then, after Israel affirms

---

28. Watts, *Isaiah's New Exodus*, 27.

29. Note Isa 2:7, 20; 13:17; 30:22; 31:7; 40:19; 46:6; Hos 2:8; 8:4; Hab 2:19; 1:18; Zech 6:11; see also Isa 39:2; 60:9; Jer 10:4, 9; Ezek 7:19; 16:13, 17; 28:4; Zech 9:3; and note Acts 20:33; see Chaney, "Coveting Your Neighbor's House," 302–17; Gordon, "Note on the Tenth Commandment," 208–9; Miller, "Property and Possession," 17–50.

hearing Yahweh (Exod 20:18–22), Moses begins to unpack the Ten-Words. Idolatry leads the record (*You shall not make other gods besides Me; gods of silver or gods of gold, you shall not make for yourselves* . . . , Exod 20:23–24).

The first time the economically vulnerable trio (*the widow, orphan,* and *stranger*) are mentioned in Exodus, idolatry frames the pericope (Exod 22:18–20; 23:13).[30] First, Moses presents a trio of commands prohibiting idolatrous behavior,[31] each with a consequence of death: *You shall not allow a sorceress to live* (Exod 22:18); *Whoever lies with an animal shall surely be put to death* (v. 19); *He who sacrifices to any god, other than to the Lord alone, shall be utterly destroyed* (v. 20). This is immediately followed by land-management stipulations concerning the economically vulnerable trio: *You shall not wrong a stranger or oppress him . . . You shall not afflict any widow or orphan* (22:21–22).

As the consequence of idolatry is death, so also is not fulfilling the codes related to the economically vulnerable. They are mirror-retributive in nature: oppressing the poor provokes their outcry to God, bringing about *the sword*, making those who violate these land-management stipulations just like the poor, becoming *widows* and *fatherless* and, thus, economically vulnerable as well (vv. 23–24). Then, there is a set of codes that promote the protection of the vulnerable trio from prolonged and generational poverty (vv. 25–27), strangers are not to be oppressed/defrauded (23:9), and the seventh year rest of the fields, where the natural growth is to be left for the poor (23:12).[32] The segment then closes with a repeated warning against idolatry (*Now concerning everything which I have said to you, be on your guard; and do not mention the name of other gods, nor let them be heard from your mouth*, Exod 23:13). Exodus 23:20–33 reminds and warns that the land-stipulations are to be obeyed, repeating the prohibitions against idolatry (Exod 23:32–33). Idolatry is the antithesis to obeying the "voice" of the angel (v. 21), the referent for Mark's programmatic summary of his Gospel (Mark 1:2–3).

Moving to the Malachi 3 referent (*sending of God's messenger*, Mal 3:1; also Exod 23:20) links John the Baptist as *the messenger* who prepares the way for the Lord (Mark 1:4–8). Overlooked are the contextual concerns

---

30. Note, Exod 23:19, *You are not to boil a young goat in the milk of its mother*, also reflects a prohibition against idolatrous practices.

31. Durham, *Exodus*, 327; Childs, *Book of Exodus*, 478; Stuart, *Exodus*, 511–16.

32. Probably not a cessation of all crops, which would put animals and the poor at risk, but a principle of rotating crops/fields (see Stuart, *Exodus*, 531).

Idolatry and Poverty

regarding the poor that also link the Exodus and Malachi referents. Following Malachi 3:1, the vulnerable trio is encountered (*I will draw near to you for judgment . . . against those who oppress the wage earner in his wages, the widow and the orphan, and those who turn aside the alien*, 3:5). Earlier the issue of idolatry was raised: Israel offered *profane sacrifices* and *polluted offerings* (1:7–12); Judah is rebuked *for profaning the sanctuary of the Lord* and *has married the daughter of a foreign god* (Mal 2:11). Then, in Malachi 3:5, memories are drawn back to the covenant where the vulnerable trio is introduced with the prohibition against *sorcerers* (Mal 3:5; Exod 22:18) and *those who swear falsely* (Mal 3:5; Exod 23:1–3), texts that recall stipulations regarding social relationships, including one's enemy and the needy (Exod 23:1–9; also Exod 20:16; Lev 19:11–17; Jer 5:2, 4; 7:9).

The juxtaposition of idolatry and poverty in Exodus and the memory-judgment context in Malachi bear out the apologetic framework discussed above. Additionally, Mark's constant use of Isaiah also reinforces this framework, which is particularly vivid in Isaiah 40, a component of Mark's programmatic summary. Mark's Isaiah referent itself—*A voice is calling, "Clear the way for the* Lord *in the wilderness; make smooth in the desert a highway for our God"* (Isa 40:3; Mark 1:3)—carries imagery common to Isaiah's world, reflecting the procession of ANE monarchs. Here, Yahweh comes as Victor-king, announcing the *Good News* (v. 9), where *all flesh* will see *the glory of the* Lord (v. 5). Isaiah 40 then compares Yahweh to surrounding idolatrous nations, which *are like a drop from a bucket* (v. 15) and *are as nothing before Him . . . less than nothing and meaningless* (v. 17; note v. 23). Mark's introduction contrasts the gospel to the concept of the imperial cult of Caesar linking it with the apologetic of Isaiah, emphasizing the incomparability of Yahweh, whose sovereign power over creation is boasted of (v. 12) and affirmed to be in need of no-one's counsel regarding justice (vv. 13–14). Yahweh is distinct from the image-bearers made of gold and silver who need to be fashioned by human-hands (vv. 19–20), for he *sits above the circle of the earth* and *stretches out the heavens like a curtain* (v. 22).[33] The Holy One takes on all-comers: *To whom then will you liken Me that I would be his equal?* (v. 25). Isaiah notes the starry hosts (v. 26), each representing idolatrous pagan powers, yet it is Yahweh who *created* them

---

33. See chapter 2, "Wasted Evangelism"; also note the Isaianic references to idolatry are usually in the context of Yahweh's incomparableness to the other powers (42:17; 44:9–10; 45:16, 20; 46:1; 48:5; 57:13; 66:3).

and calls them by name, indicating *his might* and *strength* over the idols of the nations.[34]

Followers will become fishers of men[35]

Mark moves from his programmatic summary of the gospel (1:1–3) and the inaugurated presence of the kingdom (vv. 4–15) to a call for followers: *"Follow Me, and I will make you become fishers of men"* (Mark 1:17). Although Christians differ over the application of *fishers of men*, the OT use of *fishers* and *fishing* yields evidence of an antecedent background that fits the Markan context. The OT concept of *fishing* carries an association with God's act of judgment. Mark draws on this OT thread (Jer 16:16; Amos 4:1–2; also Hab 1:14–15; Ezek 29:4–5; 38:4; Isa 37:29), which also contains an apologetic theme and in the primary contexts refers to idolatry and/or the poor (e.g., Jer 16; Amos 4).

The concentration of judgment throughout these texts draws the reader/listener back to covenantal obedience and to the economically vulnerable. Jeremiah announces that the Lord *will send for many fishermen . . . and they will fish for them* (Jer 16:16). The reason for God's *fisher*-agents, the people had become idolatrous: *It is because your forefathers have forsaken Me . . . and have followed other gods and served them and bowed down to them; but Me they have forsaken and have not kept My law . . . each one walking according to the stubbornness*[36] *of his own evil heart . . . I will hurl you out of this land into the land which you have not known* (Jer 16:11–13). The flow of thought in Jeremiah, where the prophet is the initial "agent" (Jer 15–19), contains numerous references to idolatry (including *God vs. the gods* tauntalogies) as a cause for God's judgment (. . . *they have filled My inheritance with the carcasses of their detestable idols and with their abominations . . . Can man make gods for himself? Yet they are not gods!*, Jer 16:18–20, note17:2; *Yet they did not listen or incline their ears, but stiffened*

---

34. False gods totter, Isa 41:7; misplaced trust in idols, 42:17; compared to idols made by hands, 46:5–7; inability to do anything, 48:5; 44:17–20; wearisome, 44:12–13.

35. See chapter 3, "You Will appear as *Fishers*," for a fuller discussion of the Mark 1:17 *fishers of men* text.

36. *Stubbornness* = reference to being an idolater (see Beale, *We Become What We Worship*).

Idolatry and Poverty

their necks[37] *in order not to listen or take correction*, Jer 17:23; *For My people have forgotten Me, they burn incense to worthless gods*, Jer 18:15a).

Similar language is used in Amos 4, Habakkuk 1, Ezekiel 29, where the imagery of *fishing* is a tool of judgment. This, too, has an apologetic nature: Ultimately, this judgment activity of God will reveal that he alone is the Lord (Jer 16:21) and, through it, the nations like Egypt *will know that I am the Lord God* (Ezek 29:6; also Ezek 38:23). In Habakkuk, it is through the *fishing* activity that the ungodly, the unrighteous, and those who oppose God are gathered together for judgment (Hab 1:14–15). Moreover, the judgment passages utilizing *fishing* imagery also promise a future remnant, a theme evident in Mark's narrative.

In the midst of the references to idolatry are reminders—direct and indirect—of covenant stipulations concerning the poor. In Jeremiah 16–18, those who refuse to provide and advocate for the economically vulnerable will become subject to *sword* and *famine*, becoming *childless*, that is *widows* and *orphans* (Exod 22:24; Ps 109).

> They will die of deadly diseases, they will not be lamented or buried; they will be as dung on the surface of the ground and come to an end by sword and famine, and their carcasses will become food for the birds of the sky and for the beasts of the earth (Jer 16:4).

> Therefore, give their children over to famine
> And deliver them up to the power of the sword;
> And let their wives become childless and widowed
> Let their men also be smitten to death,
> Their young men struck down by the sword in battle (Jer 18:21).[38]

Such consequences are reminiscent of covenant promises and warnings:

> You shall not wrong a stranger or oppress him, for you were strangers in the land of Egypt. You shall not afflict any widow or orphan. If you afflict him at all, and if he does cry out to Me, I will surely hear his cry; and My anger will be kindled, and I will kill you with the sword, and your wives shall become widows and your children fatherless (Exod 22:21–24).

---

37. The reference to *not listen* draws similarities to Isaiah 6 idol-tauntology and *stiffened their necks* pulls the reader/listener back to the original golden-cow-worship in exodus (see Beale, *We Become What We Worship*).

38. Note Deut 32:24, the curse of famine.

> Your carcasses will be food to all birds of the sky and to the beasts of the earth, and there will be no one to frighten them away. The Lord will smite you with the boils of Egypt and with tumors and with the scab and with the itch, from which you cannot be healed. The Lord will smite you with madness and with blindness and with bewilderment of heart (Deut 28:26–28).[39]

In Amos 4:1–2, the focus on judgment specifically addresses the oppression of the economically vulnerable:

> Hear this word, you cows of Bashan who are on the mountain of Samaria,
>
> who oppress the poor, who crush the needy,
> Who say to your husbands, "Bring now, that we may drink!"
> The Lord God has sworn by His holiness,
> "Behold, the days are coming upon you
> When they will take you away with meat hooks,
> And the last of you with fish hooks (Amos 4:1–2).

The reference here draws upon the cause of God's judgment, namely affluent women of the Northern Kingdom are oppressing the poor. The mention of *cows of Bashan* could be a pun related to idolatry (*cow* draws us back to the original idol-calves in Exodus) and pin-points the idolatry to wanton wealth accumulation without concern for its effects (as implied in the exuberant, sarcastic comment "to bring on the drinks!"), specifically implying covenant breaking in oppressing/defrauding the poor.

Amos 4:1–2 is part of a thread that links covenantal unfaithfulness, misshapen values of wealth accumulation, and oppression of the poor:

> Thus says the Lord,
> "For three transgressions of Israel and for four
> I will not revoke its punishment,
> Because they sell the righteous for money
> And the needy for a pair of sandals.
> "These who pant after the very dust of
> the earth on the head of the helpless
> Also turn aside the way of the humble;
> And a man and his father resort to the same girl
> In order to profane My holy name" (Amos 2:6–7).

---

39. Also, *Cursed is he who distorts the justice due an alien, orphan, and widow. And all the people shall say, "Amen"* (Deut 27:19); note in Deut 28:14, there is a curse for serving other gods, reminiscent of the plagues on Egypt's gods.

Idolatry and Poverty

> Therefore because you impose heavy rent on the poor
> And exact a tribute of grain from them,
> Though you have built houses of well-hewn stone,
> Yet you will not live in them;
> You have planted pleasant vineyards, yet
> you will not drink their wine.
> For I know your transgressions are many
> and your sins are great,
> You who distress the righteous and accept bribes
> And turn aside the poor in the gate (Amos 5:11–12).[40]

> Hear this, you who trample the needy, to do away with the humble
> of the land, saying,
> "When will the new moon be over,
> So that we may sell grain,
> And the sabbath, that we may open the wheat market,
> To make the bushel smaller and the shekel bigger,
> And to cheat with dishonest scales,
> So as to buy the helpless for money
> And the needy for a pair of sandals,
> And that we may sell the refuse of the wheat?" (Amos 8:4–6).

This thread points to "haves" (i.e., the landed) who prevent "have nots" (i.e., the land-less) from escaping out of prolonged poverty. The call to follow Jesus implies a discipleship that is associated with covenant expectations toward the poor and the consequences of idolatrous patterns of social life.

The Beelzebul parable and Mark's Isaiah 6 idolatry-taunt[41]

The programmatic themes established in Mark 1 prepare the reader/listener for Jesus' confrontation with *the scribes from Jerusalem* in the Beelzebul episode story (Mark 3:20–35). It seems rather simplistic to narrow

---

40. The *poor in the gate* refers, not to the poor who "hang out" or loiter at the city gate, but to the role of the leadership who are "at the city gate" and responsible for legislatively applying the covenant stipulations. The Amos context implies that *the poor* was not getting their justice by the municipal leadership/elders *at the city gate* and the injustice was related to the economic well-being of those whose land was not returned as the Sabbath laws commanded, but were subject to *heavy rent*, and thus continuous/prolonged poverty.

41. See chapter 4, "A Prelude to Judgment," for an fuller discussion regarding the "Beelzebul controversy."

the Beelzebul[42] parables (vv. 23–27) to the private sphere, namely to those who refuse to accept Jesus as Savior.[43] This misses the text's significance and overlooks Mark's use of antecedent theology.[44] The story is strategically placed at the end of a series of confrontation stories (1:21–28; 2:1–12, 13–17, 18–22, 23–28; 3:1–6; 3:22–30)[45] and functions as a judgment directed against Jesus' political and religious antagonists. The judgment rendered in Mark 3:29 (*whoever blasphemes against the Holy Spirit never has forgiveness, but is guilty of an eternal sin*) is not meant to be applied generally as the "rejection of Jesus as Savior," but the rejection of the implications of the kingdom's presence. The Beelzebul episode (3:20–35) offers a narrative transition for the parable of *the Sower* and a reason for Mark's use of the Isaiah 6 idolatry-taunt,[46] which is the natural consequence of the Beelzebul judgment-parables (3:23–27).[47]

But why blasphemy of the "Holy Spirit" and not blasphemy of God or his Messiah? First, the Beelzebul controversy is set in terms of the kingdom (*If a kingdom is divided against itself, that kingdom cannot stand*, 3:24)[48] with Jesus as the "stronger one" (cf. Isa 40:10) who comes to plunder Satan's *kingdom-house* (3:24, 27). Earlier John the Baptist refers to Jesus as the "mighty one" (*ho ischuroteros*, 1:8; Isa 40:10) who is associated with God's Holy Spirit (1:8; 1:10). Second, there is an association to the first Exodus. The use of *ekbalō* (*cast out*) in the Beelzebul narrative (*by the ruler of de-*

---

42. *Beelzebul* carries the meaning of exalted prince or ruler and is associated with Yahweh's rival deity, Baal, and as well, other foreign gods, often described as demons (Edwards, *Gospel According to Mark*, 120). By the time of Jesus, *Beelzebul* was the "prince of darkness" or Satan, or in a reference to a divided house, *zeboul* can also refer to the house of the god Baal. The reference to *Beelzebul* is also linked to the wider immediate Markan context, for it is also linked to the Canaanite storm god (note Mark 4:35–41).

43. E.g., "Those who refuse Jesus, whom the Holy Spirit reveals, will not find forgiveness."

44. See Watts, *Isaiah's New Exodus*, 195–99.

45. The confrontation continues throughout Mark (7:1, 7:5; 8:31; 9:11, 14; 10:33; 11:18, 27; 12:13, 28, 32, 35–38; 14:1, 43, 53; 15:1, 31), including Pharisees as well (2:16, 18, 24; 3:6); also Mark 1:32; also see Myers, *Binding the Strong Man*, 173; Watts, *Isaiah's New Exodus*, 156.

46. Watts, *Isaiah's New Exodus*, 153.

47. There are similarities between the Beelzebul narrative and the pending Isa 6 judgment in Mark 4 (see Watts, *Isaiah's New Exodus*, 197): There is a contrast between *outsiders* and *insiders* (3:21, 31–35/4:10–11); there is a *kingdom* focus (3:24/4:11); there is warning of unforgiveness (3:29/4:12c).

48. Watts, *Isaiah's New Exodus*, 196.

Idolatry and Poverty

mons He casts out demons, Mark 3:22, 23) connects the exorcism activities of Jesus to what God did to the inhabitants of the land. In the original Exodus story, God *will drive them out [ekbalō] until Israel possesses the land,* delivering *the inhabitants of the land* into their hands so that Israel *will drive them out [ekbalō]* (Exod 23:30–31, LXX).

Third, there is a link between the first Exodus, the Spirit, and "unforgiveness." In Exodus 23, the *angel* of the Lord goes before them to guard them *along the way*. Israel is warned to *obey his voice* and *not be rebellious toward him, for <u>he will not pardon your transgression</u>, since My name is in him* (Exod 23:20–21). This is followed by warnings against idolatry (vv. 32–33; note Isa 6:9–10 and Mark 4:12).[49] Additionally, elsewhere the OT makes the connection between the Angel of Exodus and God's Spirit (Haggai 2:5; Nehemiah 9:20). In Isaiah 63, we have a clear exodus motif connecting the Exodus-Angel, the Spirit, and the rebellion against *his voice* (see Exod 23:21):

> In all their affliction He was afflicted,
> And the angel of His presence saved them;
> In His love and in His mercy He redeemed them,
> And He lifted them and carried them all the days of old.
> But they rebelled
> And grieved His Holy Spirit;
> Therefore He turned Himself to become their enemy,
> He fought against them.
> Then His people remembered the days of old, of Moses.
> Where is He who brought them up out
> of the sea with the shepherds of His flock?
> Where is He who put His Holy Spirit in the
> midst of them (vv. 9–11).[50]

Zechariah 7 also pulls together the exodus, land-management stipulations, the role of the Spirit, and idolatry. Zechariah declares *the word of the Lord* (7:4)[51] to the exiles, for there is no attempt to show contrition, because they had not linked their idolatrous hearts to their misplaced social relationships:

---

49. There is a strong connection between demons and idolatry, which links Jesus ministry of exorcism and the charge of idolatry against the leaders of Israel (Lev 17:7; Deut 32:17; Ps 106:37; 1 Cor 10:20; see *Jub.* 1:11; 11:4–6; *1 En.* 19:1; 99:7).

50. Note v. 12, the reference to Moses dividing the waters (Exod 12–14).

51. Note, *the word* draws the reader/listener back to the Ten-Words (Exod 20:1–17) and forward to the *Word* which is *the seed* in the parable of *the Sower who sows* (Mark 4).

> Then the word of the Lord came to Zechariah saying, "Thus has the Lord of hosts said, 'Dispense true justice and practice kindness and compassion each to his brother; and do not oppress <u>the widow or the orphan, the stranger or the poor</u>; and do not devise evil in your hearts against one another.' But they refused to pay attention and turned a stubborn shoulder and stopped their ears from hearing. <u>They made their hearts like flint</u> so that they could not hear the law and the words which the Lord of hosts had sent by <u>His Spirit</u> through the former prophets; therefore great wrath came from the Lord of hosts. And just as He called and <u>they would not listen</u>, so they called and I would not listen," says the Lord of hosts, "but I scattered them with a storm wind among all the nations whom they have not known. Thus the land is desolated behind them so that no one went back and forth, for they made the pleasant land desolate" (Zech 7:8–14).

All the earmarks of the Beelzebul controversy are contained in Zechariah 7: The judgment of exile is analogous to judgment on idolatry and exile is related to breaking the covenant stipulations regarding the economically vulnerable and the poor.

The Beelzebul parables (Mark 3:23–27) implies the charges that provoked the original idolatry-taunt (Isa 6:9–10), which Mark uses to explain the Sower parable (*while seeing, they may see and not perceive, and while hearing, they may not hear and not understand, otherwise they might return and be forgiven*, Mark 4:11–12; see Isa 6:9–10). Just as the Beelzebul conflict prepares the reader/listener for the Mark 4 idolatry-taunt, Isaiah 1–5 prepared for the original in Isaiah 6; and, as the *Beelzebul* judgment is levied against Jerusalem's leadership, the same is reflected in the original Isaiah context, particularly the charge of idolatry (Isa 1:29–31; 2:6–9; 2:12–13; 2:18, 20). Amid the obvious immoral behavior, there are charges related to land-management and the economically vulnerable—*Defend the orphan, Plead for the widow,* Isa 1:17; *They do not defend the orphan, Nor does the widow's plea come before them,* 1:23; *The plunder of the poor is in your houses . . . And grinding the face of the poor,* 3:14–15. The mention of the vulnerable trio—the *orphan,* the *widow,* and the *alien*—is an obvious reflection of Exodus covenant stipulations (Exod 21–23). The original Isaiah context gives Mark's use significance and implications for the realm of discipleship and evangelism, particularly for social relationships involving the poor.

Idolatry and Poverty

Preparing on 'the way' for the "sudden appearance" at the temple

As Mark prepares his readers/listeners for ultimate judgment on the temple (Mark 13), there is a thread of OT referents and imagery that draws our attention back to covenant expectations. Embedded in this narrative are OT texts that juxtapose the issues of idolatry and poverty. Mark begins this section with a reference to divorce (10:2–9) and ends with the story of a poor widow (12:38–44). The divorce reference reaches back to Deuteronomy 24, which more likely has to do with protecting women, widows, and orphans than a so-called "divorce exemption" for modern American Christians. This makes sense, given that Deuteronomy 24 also contains the gleaning codes designed to sustain the economically vulnerable trio—the *widow*, *orphan*, and *alien* (Deut 24:19–22).

Jeremiah's temple speech (Mark 11:15–18) forms the background to the confrontation in the Court of the Gentiles, where Jesus topples merchant tables and reproves the corrupted leadership that had allowed profane activity to invade the central symbol of Israel's faith (Mark 11:17). In part, Jesus' words are drawn from Jeremiah 7:11. By using this source, Jesus gives them an OT context, directing our attention back to the Exodus prohibitions against idolatry and stipulations regarding the poor:

> Do not trust in deceptive words, saying, "This is the temple of the Lord, the temple of the Lord, the temple of the Lord." For if you truly amend your ways and your deeds, if you truly practice justice between a man and his neighbor, if you <u>do not oppress the alien, the orphan, or the widow</u>, and do not shed innocent blood in this place, nor <u>walk after other gods</u> to your own ruin, then I will let you dwell in this place, in the land that I gave to your fathers forever and ever. Behold, you are trusting in deceptive words to no avail. Will you steal, murder, and commit adultery and swear falsely, and <u>offer sacrifices to Baal and walk after other gods</u> that you have not known, then come and stand before Me in this house, which is called by My name, and say, "We are delivered!"—that you may do all these abominations? Has this house, which is called by My name, become a den of robbers in your sight? Behold, I, even I, have seen it," declares the Lord (Jer 7:4–11).[52]

---

52. Later, *The children gather wood, and the fathers kindle the fire, and the women knead dough to make cakes for the queen of heaven; and they pour out drink offerings to other gods in order to spite Me* (Jer 7:18). Also, the *fig tree* reference (Mark 11) partially derives from Jer 8:13, also having a close association with foreign idolatrous influences ("*I will surely snatch them away*" declares the Lord; "*there will be no grapes on the vine, and*

Similar to Isaiah's charges against Israel (1–5), outward appearances and rituals were all in place, but there was a misplaced trust that God would protect their religiosity despite neglecting covenant expectations toward the economically vulnerable and their disregard for justice (Isaiah 56:1–7).

Mark 12 draws on the Isaiah 1–6 context, particularly the chapter 5 imagery of God's unproductive vineyard (Isa 5:1–2). Just prior to the Isaiah 6 idolatry-taunt, there is Isaiah 5:7–8:

> For the vineyard of the Lord of hosts is the house of Israel
> And the men of Judah His delightful plant.
> Thus He looked for justice, but behold, bloodshed;
> For righteousness, but behold, a cry of distress.
> Woe to those who add house to house and join field to field,
> Until there is no more room,
> So that you have to live alone in the midst of the land![53]

Jesus' words reflect implications drawn from the original Isaiah parable and the contextual implications regarding the poor (Isa 1–5), idolatry (the taunt, Isa 6:9–10), and judgment (i.e., exile).

Mark ends the thread (12:38–44) with the ultimate disregard for covenant land-management expectations: oppression of a widow right there in the temple courts. The widow story carries associations to Exodus 22, Leviticus 19, 23, Deuteronomy 14–15, and Malachi 3—texts that juxtapose idolatry and the poor. Mark focuses on the abuse of a *poor widow*, whose only financial resources are stripped from her just so she can enter into the doomed temple.[54] The *poor widow* story, despite its common (mis)use as an illustration of sacrificial giving (to modern-day temples), is likely a capstone to the thread Mark has woven throughout his narrative, namely that the gospel and the presence of the kingdom are associated with social relationships, particularly toward the economically vulnerable. This is made even more clear as the reader/listener encounters Jesus' *sudden* appearance in the temple (Mark 11:11, 15b, 27; 13:1), where the final judgment is foretold,

---

no figs on the fig tree, and the leaf will wither; and what I have given them will pass away"). Furthermore, the Markan context here includes the *widow* reference and "selling doves" as part of the description of the "buying and selling in the temple" (11:15), which also ties to the maltreatment of the poor through a reference to the Levitical provision given to the impoverished (*But if he cannot afford a lamb, then he shall bring to the Lord . . . two turtledoves or two young pigeons . . .*, Lev 5:7).

53. See Mic 2:1–2.

54. See chapter 1, "Widows in Our Courts."

Idolatry and Poverty

drawing on the Malachi 3 threat, which, as well, juxtaposes idolatry and the neglect of the economically vulnerable (Mal 3:5).[55]

IDOLATRY: A DEFECTIVE SOCIAL CONSTRUCTION OF REALITY

Mark's consistent references to OT material that juxtaposes idolatry and the poor is certainly embedded into the very nature of the gospel, suggesting that the gospel is formative for social arrangements. Mark's highlighting of these OT texts that juxtapose idolatry and expectations regarding the poor, as well, points to an apologetic and evangelistic potential for social action. Still, moving from ancient text *to* significance *to* application can be very difficult, especially as we consider how the application of such texts can include social action outcomes. At the risk of over-generalization, even Christian approaches to poverty tend to align with political views, party affiliations, and social-locations: Politically conservative Christians tend to read capitalism, free markets, and individual charity as biblical solutions to poverty; the politically liberal tend to read more public, state-centered solutions. Although both find some textual support, neither consider the biblical juxtaposition of idolatry and poverty, nor our own human capacity for idolatrous alignments in our own social-locations.

L. T. Johnson reminds us that "idolatry comes naturally to us, not only because of the societal symbols and structures we ingest from them, but also because it is the easiest way for our freedom to dispose itself."[56] Shifting the issue of poverty to the realm of discipleship and apologetics focuses our attention on the social-location of *non*-poor Christians and their relationship to the poor. In light of the gospel framed by Mark, non-poor Christians should be mindful of the idolatries that can form their own social reality, particularly those experiencing everyday life in places where poverty *is not concentrated* (i.e., non-urban life). It is not necessarily how OT ethical texts apply to our modern social-location (although important) that is significant, but how the apologetic nature of the idolatry-poverty juxtaposition relates to those who are to be formed by the gospel, then, how *that* significance dissuades Christians from conforming to any *private vs. public* dichotomous response to poverty.

55. See chapter 2, "Wasted Evangelism," for a fuller discussion regarding the relationship between Mark's Gospel and the Malachi threat (Mal 3:1).

56. Johnson, *Faith's Freedom*, 60.

Idolatry promotes a defective social reality for the non-poor Christian

The OT story-line through narrative, singers, sages, and prophets is, for the most part, a story of the tension between Israel's faith and the presence and pressures of idolatry.[57] P. C. Craigie defines *idolatry* as the "worship of an idol or of a deity represented by an idol."[58] The Bible's range of terms for *idol* and *idolatry* allow the concept to mean both the worship of images and the worship of foreign gods, making both senses possible. The first direct prohibition against idolatry was associated with God's revelation of himself to Israel, his *self-disclosure*, not through images, but words *and* the Sinai redemptive event, constituting a paradigm for God's continued self-disclosure (Exod 20).[59] God chose to make himself known primarily through words rather than any other kind of form; the incomparability of the Lord renders all representative forms inadequate (Deut 4:1–8; Isa 40:18, 25).[60] The severe exclusion of images (i.e., idols, symbols, and signs) or serving other gods was "to maintain a continuing consciousness among the Israelites that their God is different from and incomparable to the pagan gods" (Isa 40:18–26).[61] Although much of OT ethical content is similar to surrounding ANE religions, one of the striking contrasts to Israel's neighbors is not only the prohibition of idolatry, but in how idolatry formed social relationships.

In *Nature and Destiny of Man*, Reinhold Niebuhr observed that idolatry is making the contingent absolute, something relative into "the unconditional principle of meaning."[62] Johnson points out that, when we consider something as ultimate, this is worship, not just what our lips or cultus ritual render, but in the exercise of our freedom in service to that which we consider absolute and unconditional, and thus derive our significance. It is, however, not just an image fashioned with gold and silver that provides the danger of idolatry, for the Bible is clear, such idols are no-things (Isa 41:21–24; 44:10; Ps 115; 135; Acts 14:15; 1 Cor 8:4; 10:19;

---

57. Baldwin, "Idolatry," 503–5.

58. Craigie, "Idolatry," 542–43.

59. See Curtis, "Idol, Idolatry," 379; see Beale's introduction on the concept of idolatry in *We Become What We Worship*, 17–20.

60. Rosner, "Concept of Idolatry."

61. Beale, *We Become What We Worship*, 18–19.

62. Rosner, *Greed as Idolatry*, 176; Niebuhr and Lovin, *The Nature and Destiny of Man*, 1:178.

Gal 4:8).[63] It is idolatrous when anything other than the biblical God is the object of such service and meaning.[64] Johnson reminds us that "important idolatries have always centered on those forces which have enough specious power to be truly counterfeit, and therefore truly be dangerous: sexuality (fertility), riches, and power (or glory)."[65] It is the body of knowledge that accompanies the object and service of worship and, then, the social and cultural habits that follow, developing an everyday "world," with meaning and definitions for relationships (repeated action, mundane habits), that objectifies reality and maintains significance and plausibility (its symbols and corresponding institutions). Our socially constructed world, then, is reality formed by our service of worship and sustained (validated) through the habits and experience of everyday life.

Idolatries are socially constructed and then objectified through routines of daily life, making "the relative absolute, the contingent necessary, and the end-all that which is neither end nor all."[66] The result is a distorted construction of reality for the Christian, whose whole orientation can be in conflict with the reality of the inaugurated presence and outcomes of the kingdom. As far as biblical revelation is concerned, "Idolatry [is] the Big Lie about reality."[67] This is equally true of economic realities and social-locations that form everyday habits of non-poor Christians as it is for those who worship multiple gods or idols. This understanding of the function of idolatry is affirmed by Peter Berger and Thomas Luckmann, who remind us *reality* itself *is socially constructed*.[68] However, to understand fully the non-poor's *everyday reality*, it is simply "not enough to understand the particular symbols or interaction patterns of individual situations." It is how the "overall structure or meaning" within "these particular patterns

---

63. In the latter half of Isaiah, idols are frequently referred to using the term "nothing" or one of its cognates. Similarly, Paul refers to idols as a thing that has no existence (1Cor 8:4–6), literally "an idol has no real existence" (RSV) or as the KJV translates, "an idol is nothing in the world." The Bible does not question the "existence" of idols, nor their significance in representing some*thing*; it is futility to trust in them that is at issue (see Isa. 41:21–24; 44:10).

64. "Idols only exist, in other words, in virtue of service. Since whatever is not God is contingent, that is not the necessary or sufficient cause of its own existence, it cannot give life but can only receive it" (Johnson, *Sharing Possessions*, 46).

65. Johnson, *Sharing Possessions*, 52.

66. Ibid., 53.

67. Johnson, *Faith's Freedom*, 61

68. Berger and Luckman, *Social Construction of Reality*, 1.

and symbols" are experienced. Seeking to apply the gospel that is embedded with texts regarding idolatry and, as well, texts indicative of relationships toward the economically vulnerable, it is important to understand how the social-location experienced by many non-poor Christians was formed and its implications for their participation in the outcomes of this social-location.[69]

Religion once offered an integrating principle that helped provide a "life-world" that was "more or less unified."[70] But, modern life not only provides a less unified everyday life, now religion often aligns itself with the socio-economic forces that help sustain the plausibility of faith, which can then inoculate the non-poor Christian from the idolatrous forces embedded in their social-location. Over time new symbols and signs (lawns, yards, gated communities, commutes and highways, social status, shopping malls, upward mobility, the market, double-entry accounting, etc.)[71] that permeate the social-location the modern non-poor Christian experiences as everyday life *compete* with biblical symbols (e.g., the words of God, the cross, redemptive-historical acts of God in history, etc.). Johnson reminds us, "Prior to any action or pattern of actions we might term 'Christian' is a whole set of perceptions and attitudes, which themselves emerge from a coherent system of symbols, and an orientation toward the world and other humans, which we call Faith."[72] In fact the very habit of experiencing the fragmented, often unintegrated social-locations over and over everyday might feel like freedom bestowed by our socio-economic system, but actually weakens the plausibility of biblical faith to inform our *home world*. Non-poor Christians are in danger of idolatry when finding themselves in need of affirming "this worldly" system and its institutions as God-given in order to be *at home*, plotting their lives on *the societal map* provided by social institutions rather than biblical discipleship in order to relate—comfortably, plausibly, securely—to the overall web of acceptable meanings in society.[73] Because of the plurality of social worlds—work, school, play, third places, highways, commutes, home, shopping, church—in modern society,

---

69. Peter Berger et al., *Homeless Mind*, 63–64.

70. Ibid., 64.

71. For exchanging symbols, particularly suburban *lawns*, see Messia's essay, "Lawns as Artifacts," in *Suburban Sprawl*, 69–84; also Pahl's *Shopping Malls and Other Sacred Spaces*, particularly the chapter "Private Possessions," 103–20; Gardella, *Domestic Religion*, 1–8.

72. Johnson, *Sharing Possessions*, 31.

73. Berger et al., *Homeless Mind*, 76.

"the structures of each particular world are experienced as relatively unstable and unreliable."[74] The separated sectors of our social world are rationalized and relativized, forcing the non-poor Christian to justify religiously *this worldly* system and institutions in order to feel less exposed and vulnerable and more relevant and secure. After decades of political alignment and religious justification, for the most part, the non-poor Christians living in the suburbs now feel *at home*.

A duplicitous, self-righteous double standard in the "burbs"

Often, non-poor Christians respond to the poor as those living in a socially constructed reality that is mostly alienated from those living with the effects of poverty. The non-poor Christian's participation in non-urban life causes a need for continuous reaffirmation of a biblical plausibility for their social-location, which alienates rather than connects them to the economically vulnerable.[75] Without *a sociological imagination*, many non-poor Christians are not fully aware of their own socially constructed exurban reality, nor how it has been formed, which can lead to duplicitous, self-righteous double standards toward the poor.

Often arguments rest, not on biblical grounds, but realities constructed by everyday life outside concentrated areas of poverty, namely the ability of the non-poor who have taken the "opportunities" presented in our socio-economic system to develop wealth and prosperity. *The poor in the cities only need to do the same. Equal opportunity, not equal distribution of wealth is just, they reason.* But this is not a fair picture, for the so-called "opportunity" has had a history and an opportunity that has been largely absent from social-locations with the most concentrated poverty, a consequence that is more akin to the injustice described by the prophets than simply the results of a good Christian work ethic and *the invisible hand* of the market.[76] The exurban[77] non-poor benefit from histories and institutions that have

---

74. Ibid., 77.

75. Lindstrom and Bartling, eds., *Suburban Sprawl*, xii–xiii.

76. For idolizing *the market* see Halteman, " Market System, the Poor, and Economic Theory" in *Toward a Just and Caring Society*, 72–111.

77. I use the terms "exurban" and "suburban" basically interchangeably throughout to mean "non-urban," although they are geographically distinct: strictly suburban means the residential area outside an urban-center; exurban is the region lying beyond the suburbs of a city.

developed in favor of the suburbs and, for the most part, at the expense of central-cities—for decades. The shift from urban to suburban came with an intentional redistribution of efforts and transactions ranging from Federal subsidies to government policies to perceptions of urban and non-urban life.[78] The ability to enjoy prosperity today, especially in upwardly mobile exurbia, is built on socio-economic transactions that have contributed to the current socially constructed reality of many non-poor.

Since the end of WWII suburban development has been "celebrated," while urban decline was often "explained away as inevitable." The "industrial cities' obsolescence" and the flourishing of the suburban way of life, for many, has been "a sign of progress" rather than "a national defect," even necessary for continued economic growth.[79] Young married couples were "confident enough of the future to flee apartments in the cities for homes with mortgages in the suburbs," while at the same time "the industrial cities were undergoing precipitous decline."[80] Urban-centers, along with their infrastructures and economies, were failing and residents who could afford to do so left for the suburbs in great numbers. The industry clusters, particularly manufacturing that supported much of the urban population, closed up and left for "more favorable locations." Jobs left the central cities *en mass* and there was negligible workforce and corresponding educational development supportive of those who could not afford to leave.[81] Urban-municipalities became overly burdened with a dwindling tax-base and an ever-increasing demand for services. The shift toward exurbia was not simply "an inevitable evolution or a historical accident," but "the direct result of a number of policies that conspired powerfully to encourage urban dispersal,"[82] which would create two almost alien segments of society, with two distinctively estranged realities (i.e., habits of everyday life).

78. For a review of the social impact on the shift to exurban sprawl and urban decline see Savage and Lapping, "Sprawl and Its Discontents," *Suburban Sprawl*, 9–14.

79. Beauregard, *When America Became Suburban*, 5; also, Beauregard points out that post-1950s "housing and employment opportunities outside the cities, coupled with recognition of spreading blight, rising minority presence, and the deepening fiscal difficulties of city governments, further inflamed public ambivalence toward living in cities" (*When America Became Suburban*, 23); also see Hayduk, "Race and Suburban Sprawl," *Suburban Sprawl*, 144–148.

80. Beauregard, *When America Became Suburban*, 1–2.

81. Monsma, "Poverty, Civil Society and the Public Policy Impasse," in *Toward a Just and Caring Society*, 48; also see Wilson's *When Work Disappears*.

82. Duany et al., *Suburban Nation*, 8; see also Beauregard, *When America Became Suburban*, 28; Lindstrom, *Suburban Sprawl*, xiv.

Idolatry and Poverty

Furthermore, current upwardly mobile non-poor who live outside central-cities are the beneficiaries of a change in how home ownership was made possible. Even before WWII, Federal regulations began to restructure the home buying process to allow for lower down-payments and longer term-mortgages. The principle of amortizing loans made it possible to borrow on longer lengths of time for more affordable, smaller monthly payments. Later, after WWII, other Federal Housing Authority (FHA) policies helped to structure home ownership to be very attractive and easier to obtain, crafting regulatory guidelines for subdivisions on the outskirts of urban centers, the first fruits of what was to become suburbs. In effect, the government, through legislation and acts of congress (the FHA and Veterans Administration in particular), disproportionately encouraged new home ownership in the suburbs rather than fixing or rehabilitating older structures in urban centers.[83]

The sociological pressures resulting from the end of WWII, the "released pent-up demand for starting families and buying consumer goods," a housing shortage in the central cities, the availability of low-cost mortgages for new homes, the mortgage-interest tax credit, mass production techniques in the housing industry all contributed to a rapid expansion of the suburbs. The shift in regulatory policies for long-term-little-down mortgages, government subsidized development of major highways for access in and out of central-cities, the GI Bill (a government funded education/training program), and other Federal aid to the newer exurban regions made prosperity possible as we know it today.[84] Zoning laws and affluent developers, not just *the invisible hand* of the market, protected the preferences of those with power. Furthermore, advertisers of home-related products, women's magazines, the FHA, and bank officials all sought to make "the sharpest possible contrast between the private, comfortable, safe, and protected environment of the suburbs and the open, competitive, dangerous, and seductive world of the central city."[85]

---

83. "Intentionally or not, the FHA and VA programs discouraged the renovation of existing housing stock, while turning their back on the construction of row houses, mixed-use buildings, and other urban housing types" (Duany et al., *Suburban Nation*, 8).

84. Track housing mirrored the techniques developed by the Armed Forces during WWII, keeping building costs low and making the move away from urban centers more affordable. Highways were almost 90% federally funded (Duany et al., *Suburban Nation*, 8). See Hayduk, "Race and Suburban Sprawl," in *Suburban Sprawl*, 138–70.

85. Beauregard, *When America Became Suburban*, 77–78; Beauregard references Frug in *City Making*, 155.

The *invisible hand* had and continues to get help—sometimes through Federal, State, and municipal efforts; sometimes through creative marketing; sometimes through celebrity-trend makers; sometimes by politically empowered zoning codes.[86] Growth and decline, expansion and contraction, growth in one area at the expense of another area—all unavoidable within a socio-economic system that prizes "progress," supported by desire for upward-mobility (and, too often, greed), promote the ultimate goal of "the Suburban Way of Life." It is an empirical fact, *the system* and its mediating institutions ignored its central-cities and promoted life in the "burbs" as the ultimate goal of prosperity, all for the gods of growth, progress, and the new.[87]

CONCLUSION: SOCIAL ACTION AS CHRISTIAN APOLOGETICS

Simply, affluent suburbanites, despite a claim to a higher work ethic or a more developed sense of responsibility, didn't do it on their own; they had help along the way. On the one hand, the non-poor's social construction of reality, which they now experience as everyday life, allows them to benefit, not just from the market, but also from past actions of government that laid much of the groundwork for continued prosperity. On the other hand, the concentration of poverty in central-cities is not simply about laziness, slothfulness, or even personal sin. (I assume the non-poor who benefit from the current structure and mediating institutions are just as much "sinners" as those living in geographic areas of concentrated poverty.) Indeed, much of what is in place and experienced now as normal arose from various forms of racism and redlining practices, as well as "the concentration of subsidized housing projects [that] destabilized and isolated the poor, while federal home-loan programs, targeting new construction exclusively, encouraged the deterioration and abandonment of urban housing."[88] The fact of poverty and the reality of those affected by it in the central-cities could not have happened any more effectively if it were actually planned and implemented with malice. Without the aid of government policies and sub-

---

86. "While government programs for housing and highway promoted sprawl, the planning profession, worshipping at the altar of zoning, worked to make it the law" (Duany et al., *Suburban Nation*, 9).

87. See Beauregard, *When America Became Suburban*, 9–14.

88. Duany et al., *Suburban Nation*, 154.

sidies, as well as municipally empowered zoning laws and discriminatory business policies, the foundation for exurban wealth in America might not have happened. Rather than lamenting this inequitable state of affairs, participants, including many non-poor believers, have been encouraged to rejoice in the "prudence" of such strategies and the institutions, capitalism and the "mythical" market that sustain them.[89] The modern, non-poor suburban dweller is the heir of such socially constructed forces.

The present model for socio-economic progress and prosperity objectifies the non-poor Christian's reality (i.e., hers or his "home world") through habits and experiences of everyday life that are incorporated into his or her belief system—seemingly validating the plausibility of personal faith. The problem for the non-poor Christian living in such a history and current social-location is that it provides only a partial reality, through its defective social construction. The Bible warns of God's judgment upon those who create or maintain economic structures that benefit some and exclude others, that pave the way to prosperity for some and prolonged, generational poverty for others (Exod 22–23; Lev 19, 24; Deut 15, 24; Jer 4–8, 16–17; 22; Ezek 17–18, 22; Amos 4:1–2; Mic 2:1–2; Zech 7; Isa 5:7–12). Unaware or in denial of their socially constructed world, the non-poor believer often can accept a world that is duplicitous, limiting the historic and current benefits of a socio-economic system to those the "market blessed."[90]

Emil Brunner remarked, "For every civilization, for every period of history, it is true to say, 'show me what kind of gods you have, and I will tell you what kind of humanity you possess.'"[91] For the Christian and Christian community it is: *Show me what kind of association you have with those living with the effects of poverty, and I will tell you what kind of god you worship.* The reality of everyday life is that Suburban life and its enablers—the free market and human acts of power—are often at odds with the gospel, especially a gospel that has been formed by the idolatry-poverty juxtaposition. For the non-poor Christian, this is an idolatrous mode of living and does not offer a biblically defensible apologetic for the God revealed in the gospel of Jesus Christ.

---

89. Beauregard, *When America Became Suburban*, 9.

90. Recall the significance of the Mark 12 *poor widow vs. duplicitous scribes* text (see chapter 1, "Widows in Our Courts").

91. Emil Brunner, *Man in Revolt*, 34.

6

Significance *Before* Application (Mark 3:14–15)

The Mark 3 Commission and Its Implications for Social Action

"It's not enough that we do our best; sometimes we have to do what's required"

—Winston Churchill

"*Orthopraxis* (right action) is thus closely allied with the evidence of orthodoxy (right belief)."

—Andrew Davey, *Urban Christianity and Global Order*

"As followers of Christ, we must take the whole of the gospel seriously: the passages that speak of a call to conversion and also the ones that instruct us to pay attention to the poor, the widows and the oppressed."

—Mae Elise Cannon, *Just Spirituality*

Significance Before Application (Mark 3:14–15)

"You need to be more practical."

These are the dreaded words no preacher or Bible teacher wants to hear, particularly if he or she wants to be considered effective and well-liked in modern, contemporary church circles. I am among the unfortunate who have been admonished and, even, scolded with these words more often than I'd like to admit. Yet, I am not ready to yield to the tyranny of the practical.

As modern Christians, particularly evangelicals, we often measure biblical information (teaching, preaching, sermons, commentary, Bible studies, etc.) by its immediate practical value. The up-side—Christians want to be obedient to Scripture. This is a good thing. The down-side—a preoccupation with the "practical" can too often dissuade us from thinking deeply about the significance of a text, the kind of reflection needed for developing well-thought through application, which ought to be based on an appropriate and authoritative reading (i.e., an exegesis) of the text. The path to application can be too quickly made and too frequently unconnected to the original intention of the biblical author.

This volume has not been "practical." However, I have worked hard throughout the last five chapters to uncover the meaning of the Markan texts under consideration, ending each study with the significance of these texts for church communities, for church leaders, and for those who call themselves Christian. Each chapter unfolded more fully the nature and content of the gospel we are to believe (Mark 1:1, 14–15), seeking to answer the question, *How should my faith, our church, our discipleship, our evangelism be informed and formed by the narrative of Mark's Gospel?*

I mentioned early in this book that chapters 1 through 5 were originally papers presented at meetings of the Evangelical Theological Society between 2006 and 2012.[1] At the conclusion of my paper on the Mark 1:17 "fishers of men" text (chapter 3 in this volume), I made this assertion:

> The *fisher* metaphor is appropriate, not just narrowly for individual, private salvation, but more broadly for applications, activities, and outcomes of social action and justice, as well. (p. 105)

I offered this deduction based on the antecedent OT meaning of the *fisher* concept and on my conclusion that the Mark 3 commission (vv. 13–15)[2]

---

1. This chapter was originally, in part, presented at the annual meeting of the Northeast Region of the Evangelical Theological Society, which met at the Alliance Theological Seminary, Nyack, NY, April 2013.

2. The full text encompasses vv. 13–19, which includes the list of the twelve in vv.

was the inaugural fulfillment of the Mark 1:17 promise that Jesus would create his followers *to become fishers of men*. After I finished presenting the paper, during the Q&A, a very nice gentleman (a pastor I believe) asked a reasonable follow-up question: "Does that mean 'casting out demons' is social action?" Without hesitation I responded, "Yes, it does." As a result of my overly confident off-the-cuff response, I began crafting a longer answer. This chapter, in part, is that longer answer:

> *In light of the promise to be created fishers, what is the significance of the Mark 3 commission for Christians and church communities on this side of the text?*

This final chapter is a far cry from any "how to" regarding specific, practical application. Although there is a measure of exegetical investigation regarding the Mark 3 commission, this chapter, more so, offers a model for deciphering the significance of the text. Here, I will focus on *the process* for developing application that reflects obedience to the text and a legitimate range of potential outcomes, which I posit can be related to social action that addresses the issues of poverty that surround local congregations.

This will be as practical as I get!

THE GOSPEL, DEEP ENOUGH TO INCLUDE GOD'S CONCERN FOR THE POOR

The previous five chapters have been a series of in-depth exegetical arguments, demonstrating that Mark's programmatic content links the gospel and evangelism to social action.[3] Thus, social action falls legitimately within the realm of evangelism. I have endeavored to show that a narrow, proclamation-centered definition of evangelism based exclusively on word-studies and isolated proof-texts does not match the narrative meaning of the gospel, particularly as Mark presents *the gospel of Jesus Christ, the Son of God* (1:1). Clearly a mere verbal- and cognitive-based definition of evangelism solely related to the etymology of the word "evangelize" is

---

16–19; however this study more specifically will focus on vv. 14–15, the Mark 3 commission component.

3. My working definition for biblical social action: *a means to ensure that the blessings and benefits of living in society reach to the poor* (see the Introduction for an extended explanation).

Significance Before Application (Mark 3:14-15)

too narrow and devoid of much of the biblical content that Mark gives his Gospel narrative.

As the previous studies have shown, Mark relies on OT backgrounds and contexts (e.g., 1:2–3) to fill *the gospel of Jesus Christ* (1:1) with defining and programmatic content. Typically, it is accepted that the gospel is defined by incorporating various OT motifs and concepts such as God's dominion, the Exodus, exile, redemption, and even sacrificial propitiation and forgiveness. The previous chapters have shown that the same OT contexts that Mark harnesses to give programmatic definition to the gospel also clearly contain correspondences and direct references regarding socio-economic relationships and community responsibilities toward the economically vulnerable and the poor.[4]

As the five previous studies have demonstrated, social action, therefore, can be evangelism.

In chapter 3, "You Will Appear as *Fishers*," an examination of Mark 1:17, I concluded that the promise to be created "fishers of men" finds its inaugural fulfillment and premiere "application" in the Mark 3 commission; namely, *fishers* are those who are *with Jesus* and who, then, will be sent out *to preach* and *to have authority to cast out the demons*. Through the Markan context and antecedent OT background, I showed that the "*fisher* metaphor is appropriate for applications, activities, and outcomes of social action and justice"(p. 105).[5] This implies that the Mark 3 commission *to preach* (v. 14c) and *to have authority to cast out the demons* (v. 15) can be associated with social action and, thus, can be legitimate obedience to Jesus-Messiah and faithful application of the gospel.

Close examinations of Mark's programmatic understanding of *the gospel of Jesus Christ* (1:1–3), the *fisher*-promise (1:17), the Mark 3 sandwich and Beelzebul episode (3:20–35), the Mark 4 parable of the Sower who Sows, and the account of the *widow vs. duplicitous scribes* in Mark 12 all have shown that the gospel itself is defined broadly and deeply enough to include God's concern for the poor. *Fisher*-followers of Jesus, the Messiah-King (1:1, 17), are commissioned to demonstrate the presence of God's kingdom (3:14–15), which is the gospel of God (1:14–15). As part of the application process (that is, thinking deeply and more thoroughly about

---

4. All the previous studies/chapters in this volume address the wide range of OT texts related to the poor; see chapter 5, "Idolatry and Poverty," specifically for a list of OT texts and contexts Mark utilizes in his Gospel which refer to the economically vulnerable and issues of justice.

5. See chapter 3, "You will Appear as *Fishers*" for the full exegetical argument.

application), the following seeks to show that the significance of "preaching" and "casting" (3:14–15) provides a basis for building social action outcomes into a church's evangelistic activities.

PAY ATTENTION TO SIGNIFICANCE—THINK DEEPLY ABOUT APPLICATION

Walter Kaiser reminds us, "Exegesis is never an end in itself."[6] In *Toward an Exegetical Theology*, he rightly points out that the ultimate purpose of exegesis is "never fully realized until it begins to take into account the problems of transferring what has been learned from the text over to the waiting Church."[7] Obedience to the biblical text is essential to the Christian life and is, as well, defining for the life of the church. This should be the goal of the mindful Christian and what faithful leadership should intentionally foster in a church community (Mark 3:35). This is why developing appropriate, not just "relevant," application is important. Yet, applying the Bible can offer its own set of problems and difficulties. If we move too quickly to application, it is quite possible to miss the obedience implied by the text (any text for that matter) and, as well, the gospel. Before examining the Mark 3 commission, specifically vv. 14–15, it is worth considering the problem of application.

The problem of application

In their book, *How to Read the Bible for All Its Worth*, Gordon Fee and Douglas Stuart point out that many Christians start with "the here and now" and "read into texts meanings that were not originally there." They rightly affirm that Christians "want to know what the Bible means for us," and "legitimately so." However, we cannot make the Bible or the gospel or any text for that matter "mean anything that pleases us and then give the Holy Spirit 'credit' for it."[8] Fee and Stuart hit the mark as it relates to the problem of interpretation: the step of good study and exegesis to decipher the original author's intention is too often skipped or undertaken lightly,

---

6. Kaiser, *Toward an Exegetical Theology*, 149.
7. Ibid.
8. Fee and Stuart, *How to Read the Bible*, 26.

Significance Before *Application (Mark 3:14–15)*

with readers/listeners jumping straight-away to "the here and now." This actually confuses *interpretation* with *application*.

Although Fee and Stuart's point concerns interpretation of the text, the same problem occurs when the "here and now" of contemporary application is read *back into* the text. We cannot make any application we want from any text, give the Holy Spirit credit, and then call it obedience. Application can often be read *into* a text, again, confusing interpretation with application. A fixation on the practical does not inevitably lead to obedience of the biblical text. In view of these present set of studies, application, as evangelism is typically understood, might not necessarily indicate faithfulness to *the gospel of Jesus Christ* (Mark 1:1). This can be a problem with application—that is, *application* is not always *obedience*.

Moving from meaning to significance, then to application

Understanding what the biblical author (in this case, Mark) meant is certainly the first step necessary for seeking faithful obedience to *the gospel of Jesus Christ* (1:1). The previous five chapters have sought to do just that. Yet, bridging the gap from the *then* to the *now* demands thoughtful attention. In order to think more deeply and thoroughly about application, three basic steps are essential to the process:

1) Meaning—what the original author meant

2) Significance—what the text's meaning signifies or denotes to the reader/listener

3) Obedience (i.e., application)—what we do to be obedient to the text

Meaning is that which is represented by the text, that is, what the biblical author intended by the words, syntactical and contextual relationships, and use of antecedent biblical material and contexts. *Significance* establishes the relationship between the original meaning and the person, persons, place, or situation (or "anything imaginable") on this side of the text.[9] The meaning of the text does not change, but its significance to those on this side of the text (who, when, where, etc.) does change and can be relevant in different ways.[10] *Application*, on the other hand, is the least rigid of the three elements for determining faithfulness to the gospel and can take multiple

---

9. Hirsch, *Validity in Interpretation*, 8.
10. Ibid., 255.

forms to reflect obedience. Still, application needs to flow from *significance* and be an appropriate action that reflects the obedience implied by the text (e.g., the Mark 3 commission) or biblical concept (e.g., the gospel).

For example, the *meaning* of the Mark 3 commission is determined by exegesis (an analysis of the text and surrounding narrative). The *significance* of that meaning is deciphered by the text's relationship and its implications to those on this side the text. In other words the reader/listener should ask, *What is the significance of the Mark 3 commission to me, to my church, and to the community where I live?* Application, then, is the appropriate and analogous actions, behaviors, and/or attitudes that produce or indicate faithful obedience to the text. If Mark intended his audience to understand that those who follow after Jesus will be created *fishers of men* who have a role in inaugurating the kingdom that has arrived in the appearance of God's Messiah-King (1:1, 14–15, 17),[11] then it is important to discern the significance of the commission components *to preach* and *to have authority to cast out the demons* (3:14–15) for today's readers/listeners. Application, then, requires a determination of what appropriate and analogous actions correspond to *that* significance.

Authority for application: narrative intention and antecedent authority

The process from exegesis to application is characteristically discussed within the context of sermon preparation or homiletics.[12] Typically there is detailed discussion regarding the need to discover the "significance of a text," that is the time and cultural gaps between the Bible's historical and cultural settings and *the now* of the reader/listener. This process is labeled under various titles: contextualization (Osborne), transferring the message (Greidanus), fusion of horizons (Gadamer; Thiselton), and principlization (Kaiser; Virkler).[13] Developing the significance of a text, however, is not simply about seeking the universal truth *behind* the text and its historical context, or attempting to link the ancient cultural value or historical situ-

---

11. See chapter 3, "You will Appear as *Fishers*," for the background of this interpretation.

12. See Greidanus, *Modern Preacher*, 157; and, Osborne, *Hermeneutical Spiral*, 318.

13. Osborne, *Hermeneutical Spiral*; Greidanus, *Modern Preacher*; Gadamer, *Truth and Method*; Thiselton, *Two Horizons*; Kaiser, *Toward an Exegetical Theology*; Virkler, *Hermeneutics*.

ation to something similar in the contemporary so it may be "applied." It should also establish the relationship of the text's meaning to those in front of the text. Put another way, we need to decipher *the significance* of the biblical author's original meaning to the contemporary reader/listener and church community *before* determining application.

Also, simply attaching an "application" to a text, or even a text to an "application," is not enough; application should be built on reasonable authority.[14] It must produce analogous and relevant obedience reflective of the text. Obedience (i.e., application) ought to correspond in-kind to Mark's narrative. There needs to be a reasonable association between Mark's understanding of the gospel *and* faithful obedience to that gospel. When application is detached and/or dissimilar from his narrative (in this case the Mark 3 commission and his overall Gospel narrative), then there is no authority for *that* application. In fact, it might not be obedience at all. Application on the contemporary side of the text should find support by analogous associations and applications made by the original author. When application is based on the consequence or result of a text's meaning, then it carries the weight of biblical authority, which leads to relevant faithful obedience.[15]

Abraham Kuruvilla offers a helpful set of principles for developing the significance and range of potential application from a biblical narrative such as Mark's Gospel. Kuruvilla proposed what he calls "the two rules" for establishing the significance of the text to the readers/listeners, that is, their relationship to the text:1) the *Rule of Plot* "prepares the interpreter of biblical narrative to attend to the structured sequence of events emplotted in the text, in order to apprehend the world projected by that text" and 2) the *Rule of Interaction* that "directs the interpreter of biblical narrative to attend to the interpersonal transactions of the characters as represented therein, in order to apprehend the world projected by the text."[16] Thus, our move here toward application will seek its underlying authority from Mark's surrounding plot and the role and responsibilities of the characters in the story

---

14. Kaiser, "Inner Biblical Exegesis," 33–46.

15. Ibid.

16. Kuruvilla, *Text to Praxis*, 73. The word "emplot" or "emplotted" is not found in the *Oxford English Dictionary* or in any dictionary to my knowledge. Kuruvilla, in the context of his "two rules," refers to "a plot" as "a sequence of causally related events" (*Text to Praxis*, 73), therefore I take the word and use it here and throughout the chapter to mean *em-plotted*, or to embed material into a plot; more specifically to assemble together historical events and place them strategically into a narrative in order to create a plot (i.e., a storyline).

(i.e., the *fisher*-followers who are sent forth *to preach and to have authority to cast out the demons*, 3:14c–15).

FIRST, REREAD THE MARK 3 COMMISSION AND ITS COMPONENTS—TO PREACH AND TO CAST

In order to obey the Mark 3 commission and, thus, show faithfulness to *the gospel of God* (1:14), we need to think more deeply about the significance of the Mark 3 commission and its application; then, we should seek activities and measurable outcomes that indicate obedience and faithfulness to the gospel. To do this it is necessary to *re*read the Mark 3 commission more effectively. This will be accomplished by seeking to understand the narrative relationship between the two commissioning components—*to preach* (v. 14c) and *to have authority to cast out the demons* (v. 15)—within the "sequence of events emplotted" in Mark's Gospel.[17]

The Mark 3 commission and the fisher-promise—the inaugural connection

In chapter 3, "You Will Appear as *Fishers*," I demonstrated that the Mark 1:17 *fisher*-promise finds its inaugural fulfillment in the Mark 3 creation and commission of the *twelve* (vv. 13–15). Some of those observations and connections bear repeating as we begin to *re*read the Mark 3 commission. The link between the *fisher*-promise and the commission can be seen in how Mark introduces the promise (1:17) and, then, how he presents the creation of the *twelve* (3:13–15):

Mark 1:17—Fisher-follower promise	Mark 3:13–15—Creating fishers
And Jesus said to them, "Come follow (after) me . . ." (1:17a, b).ᴬ	. . . and [He] summoned those whom He Himself wanted, and they came to Him (3:13b).
And I will create (*kai poiēsō*) you to become fishers of men (1:17c).	And He creates (*kai epoiēsen*) twelve . . . (3:14a; note 3:16a *kai epoiēsen tous dōdeka*).

A. The author's translation of Mark 1:17 and Mark 3:13–15.

17. Ibid.

Significance Before Application (Mark 3:14–15)

An obvious promise-fulfillment (*I will create/He creates*) is crafted into Mark's narrative regarding the call and creation of the *fishers*. In Mark 1, the eschatological characters (i.e., Jesus, John the Baptist, the Spirit, and *fisher*-followers)[18] that play a role in inaugurating *the gospel of Jesus Christ* are introduced (vv. 4–17). After the mission summary (1:14–15), there is an invitation to become followers (1:17) that includes a promise: *"I will make [poiēsō] you to become fishers of men."* This promise, then, is fulfilled when Jesus *creates* (*epoiēsen*) the *twelve* in the Mark 3 commission episode (3:14a).

There is a narrative relationship between the call and promise in 1:17 and the summons and commission in 3:13–15, specifically discernible by the repeated use of *poieō* (*create/make*), which is often translated *appointed, ordained, chose* that can mask the reference back to the *fisher*-promise. The other synoptic Gospel writers did not use *poieō* (*make/create*) to characterize the establishment of the *twelve*, making it more likely that Mark wanted his readers/listeners to make the narrative connection between the *fisher*-promise (1:17) and its inaugural fulfillment in the commissioning of the *twelve* (3:14–15). The *fisher* metaphor and the role of the created *twelve* indicate that *fisher*-followers are to be inaugurators of the kingdom (1:17; 3:13–15; 6:7–13)—that is, presenting its demands (1:14–15), expanding (sowing/harvesting) the gospel (4:1–5:43), and imitating Jesus' ministry (Mark 1:21—6:13). It follows, then, that the content of the commission (vv. 14c–15) is the nature and activity of the created *fisher*-followers: those who are *with Him* (v. 14b) are also sent forth *to preach* and *to have authority to cast out the demons* (v. 15).

At this point, and in light of the Mark 1:17 *fisher*-promise discussed in chapter 3 ("You Will Appear as *Fishers*"), the following interpretive summary (I) gives a sense of the meaning of the Mark 3 commission:

<u>Interpretive Summary I</u>

As inaugurators of the kingdom, *fisher*-followers are created so they would be with Jesus and so that they would be sent forth to preach and to have authority to cast out demons.[19]

---

18. See chapter 3, "You Will Appear as *Fishers*," for an elaboration of these characters (from Mark's introduction) as inaugurators of the kingdom.

19. After each section I present an interpretative summary of the Mark 3 commission in order to show the development of the text's significance to the reader/listener; as the study expands, the interpretative summary develops.

Rereading the Mark 3 commission text

Three main verbs related to Jesus govern the establishment of the *twelve* whom he commissioned: *he went up* (*avabainei*, v. 13a), *he summoned* (*proskaleitai*, v. 13b), and *he created* (*epoiēsen*, v 14a). The force and combination of all three verbal expressions stress Jesus' authority, which aligns with Mark's narrative plotline.[20] Additionally, these actions focus on his unique authority for establishing God's kingdom through a ministry outside of Jewish temple leadership (i.e., a new Moses and a new exodus) and for the creation of a people (a new twelve, 3:13–19; a new family, 3:33–35), who are to reflect the kingdom-outcomes associated with his appearance. These elements have been the emphasis of the plot (i.e., the "sequence of events emplotted in the text") so far, indicating that Mark continues to follow his established programmatic content that defines the nature of the gospel. The Mark 3 commission (vv.14–15) for the created *twelve* not only forms (and informs) their *fisher*-ministry (i.e., the application that will reflect their faithful obedience to the gospel), it also provides a paradigm for all *fisher*-followers; namely, those who believe in the gospel (1:14–15) and follow after Jesus (1:17) are those who demonstrate (through actions and outcomes) the inauguration of God's kingdom.

A typical reading of Mark 3:14–15 understands that the *twelve* are commissioned for two distinct tasks: "to preach" *and* "to cast out demons." This heightens the tendency to view the "to preach" component as solely the verbal proclamation of the Good News that Jesus died for our sins. Although a very important component of the Good News, this aspect of the gospel is appropriated from other NT documents and texts and, then, "applied" here. As a result, for many "preaching" *is* "evangelism" that is applied as various verbal- and cognitive-based activities (e.g., preaching, teaching, witnessing, etc.) about the personal, redemptive implications of Jesus' death on the cross with someone's conversion as the hopeful outcome. When the text is viewed in this way, application is separated into two distinct components that disconnect the Mark 3 commission from the narrative plot. A reading that separates the two components without syntactical or narrative consideration can limit the inferred evangelistic significance for those standing on this side of Mark's Gospel story, which, then, can result in narrow, misdirected, and, even, non-authoritative application. However,

---

20. See chapter 4, "A Prelude to Judgment," for a discussion regarding the centrality of Jesus' authority in the Mark 1:21—3:6 conflict thread, which is an integral part of Mark's plotline.

Significance Before *Application (Mark 3:14–15)*

the Mark 3 commission suggests, not two distinct tasks, but interrelated aspects that are associated with the sequence of events emplotted in Mark's narrative. A re-examination of the commission text (specifically vv. 14–15) will show another potential reading that better aligns with Mark's narrative, the programmatic nature of the gospel, and Jesus' kingdom-inaugurating ministry.

A syntactical analysis[21] of Mark 3:14–15 can aid in reading the text more effectively:

> And
> he [Jesus] created twelve (*epoiēsen dōdeka*),
>   so that (*hina*)
>   they would be with him
>   and (*kai*, conjunction)
>   so that (*hina*)
>   he would send them forth
>   to preach (*kēpyssein*)
>   namely (that is) (*kai*, epexegetical)
>   to have authority to cast out (*echein exousian ekballein*)
>   the demons.

This display of syntactical relationships helps to visualize how Mark crafted the commission together, offering a potentially different, yet legitimate, reading of the commission. My translation below reflects the syntactical relationship between the two components *to preach* and *to have authority to cast*.

> And he [Jesus] created twelve, so that they would be with him and so that he would send them forth to preach, namely (that is) to have authority to cast out the demons [author's translation].[22]

In contrast to the typically understood cognitive-based definition for evangelism, this reading of the commission, which the text allows, suggests a different direction regarding its significance for *fisher*-followers on this side of the text. As a result, it opens a wider range for potentially relevant and

---

21. A syntactical analysis helps to show how the parts of grammar relate to each other, indicating the relationships of subjects, main verbs, direct and indirect objects, and subordinate and explanatory clauses. The syntactical analysis here informs and reflects the author's translation of the text. See Kaiser, *Toward an Exegetical Theology* (pp. 87–104) for an explanation of the syntactical analysis as a component of exegesis.

22. The following references to Mark 3:14–15 reflect my translation.

appropriate evangelistic activities and outcomes that should be adopted by the church.

After "summoning" *those whom He Himself wanted* (v. 13b), Jesus *created twelve* (v. 14a) *so that* they (i.e., the created *twelve*) *would be with Him* (v. 14b) and *so that he would send them forth* with a commission (v. 14c–15). The two *hina* (*so that*) clauses indicate two resulting purposes that align with Mark's narrative.[23] The first *hina* clause (*so that they would be with him,* v. 14b) suggests an intentional relationship between Jesus and the created *twelve*. Certainly being "with Him" has many implications and means more than just "tagging along with Jesus." While "being with Jesus" is set in motion at the initial calls in Mark's first chapter (see vv. 16–20), the results are given content (definition) throughout the narrative before Jesus actually grants the *twelve* the *authority to cast* in 6:7. At the narrative level being "with Him" (3:14b) means that the created *fisher*-followers are *insiders* who do "the will of God" (3:35), who receive direct teaching and insight concerning the kingdom (4:10–11), and who witness his divine power (4:35–41) and the inaugural increase of God's kingdom (5:1—6:6). Additionally, the twelve *fisher*-followers, who were created to be *with Him* (3:14b), experienced the spread of the seed/word/gospel, not solely through verbal- and cognitive-based activities (e.g., Jesus' preaching, teaching, parables), but primarily through Jesus' deeds (e.g., casting, healing, and other miracles).[24]

The created *twelve* are also "sent forth" *to preach* (v. 14c) and *to have authority to cast* (v. 15). It should be noted there is no object (i.e., the content) for the "preaching" component (v. 14c). This provokes many to supply "the gospel" for what is preached. It is fair, perhaps, to suggest supplying the unwritten "Good News," but it is unnecessary. An assumption is made of the text, namely that the "and" (*kai*) between the two infinitive clauses functions as a simple conjunction, inferring, then, two distinct tasks: preaching *and* casting. This, too, is not necessary. Also, note that the commission component after the "and" (*kai*) is actually, not "to cast out the demons," but <u>to have authority</u> to cast out the demons (v. 15).

The syntactical analysis displayed above indicates that the conjunction "and" (*kai*) should be understood epexegetically, that is, offering a

---

23. *Hina* (*so that*) may express purpose, result, or content depending on the context. In a few cases it may even express other (related) relationships such as an imperative or a generic-specific relationship. I have chosen "resulting purpose" intentionally to indicate a fine line between the two. Jesus *creates twelve* for a purpose that results in "being with him" and "being sent forth." See Arndt and Gingrich, *Greek-English Lexicon*, 376–78.

24. See Mark 1:21—6:6.

fuller explanation and the content of *to preach*. I have, therefore, rendered the "and" (*kai*) as "namely (that is)": *so that he would send them* [the created *twelve*] *forth to preach*, namely (that is) *to have authority to cast out the demons*. In other words, the content of the "preaching" is the *authority to cast out the demons*.

The narrative significance of "to preach"

As displayed in the previous section, not only is it grammatically and syntactically allowable to view the *authority to cast* (3:15) as the content of the commission *to preach* (14c), this reading also makes contextual sense of Mark's narrative. The Mark 3 commission is both preceded and followed by episodes and summaries describing Jesus casting out demons or unclean spirits (1:23–27, 32–34, 39; 3:11; 5:2–13; 6:13; 7:25–30; 9:25–29, 38; note 3:22–27). Jesus' first public ministry, launched at the onset of the Galilean mission, depicts him teaching in a synagogue and opposing an *unclean spirit* that he rebukes and casts out (Mark 1:21–28)—a pattern foreshadowing the Mark 3 commission. Those who witnessed the event recognized the casting out of *the unclean spirit* (1:26) as a *new teaching* (v. 27); namely, Jesus, *with authority*, commands Satan's minions and they obey (v. 27). The question that follows the casting (*What is this?*, 1:27) implies one reference (*touto, this*, is singular), signifying a seamless thought between "teaching" and the "casting." Also, the closest referent for their amazement (v. 27) is Jesus' rebuke and his casting out *the unclean spirit* (vv. 25–27).

The parallel between Mark 1:22 and 1:27 suggests that Jesus' authoritative teaching includes the authority he had to command *the unclean spirit* (vv. 23, 26). In both verses the onlookers were *amazed* at his *teaching*; both verses indicate that the *teaching* was with *authority*.

Mark 1:22	Mark 1:27
They were amazed[A] at His teaching; for He was teaching them as one having authority, and not as the scribes.	They were all amazed, so that they debated among themselves, saying, "What is this? A new teaching with authority! He commands even the unclean spirits, and they obey Him."

A. Mark uses a wide range of *awe*-related words to describe the various reactions to Jesus' ministry (1:22, 27; also note 6:2; 7:37; 10:24, 32; 10:26; 11:18).

While the content of Jesus' teaching is not indicated in the text (v. 22), the narrative implies that the *teaching with authority* (v. 27) includes (and possibly *is*) the authority to command (i.e., to rebuke and cast out) *the unclean spirit* (cf. vv. 22b, 27b)—the very activity Jesus commissions the created *twelve* to do (3:15; 6:7).

The absence of referenced content (i.e., what is taught) at the inaugural ministry-event focuses the attention of the readers/listeners on the activity of "casting" as the *teaching with authority* (v. 27b), particularly its programmatic link in the narrative to the arrival of the kingdom (1:15; note 4:11, 26, 30). First, this is suggested by the initial Jesus vs. Satan encounter in the desert (1:12–13). Second, the *unclean spirit* recognized the confrontation with Jesus as an eschatological battle, for the demon cites Jesus' name (*the Holy One of God*, 1:24c), which indicates an attempt to have "mastery over" him.[25] Third, the terminology used, "I know who you are" (v. 24; note 3:11), also suggests a battle context, for this was a common OT formula "within the context of combat or judgment."[26] The significance of the episode not only discloses Jesus' authority, the exorcism also indicates an eschatological event had occurred, affirming the appearance of God's rule as indicated in the mission summary (1:14–15) and, later, as portrayed by Jesus in the Beelzebul episode parables (3:23–27). The defeat of an unclean spirit is "the first of Jesus' actions to be reported" and, thus, it becomes programmatic for the whole of Mark's Gospel.[27]

The first ministry-event presents what the Mark 1:14–15 mission summary affirms, namely Jesus' public ministry focuses on the eschatological implications of the appearance of the kingdom. Perhaps this is the reason for the narrative juxtaposition of the Jesus vs. Satan encounter in 1:13 with the mission summary in 1:14–15. Later, immediately after the Mark 3 commission, Jesus refers to his activity as the Stronger Man who had arrived to overtake and destroy Satan-the strongman's kingdom (3:23–27). This is confirmed, first in the initial confrontation in the desert between Jesus-the Stronger Man and Satan-the strongman (1:7, 13) and, then, affirmed by multiple *casting*-events throughout the narrative (1:21–28, 32;

---

25. Edwards, *Gospel According to Mark*, 57; Marcus, *Mark 1–8*, 193.

26. Lane (*Mark*, 73) observes the use in the LXX: Judg 11:12; 2 Sam 16:10; 19:22; 1 Kgs 17:18; 2 Kgs 3:13; 2 Chr 35:21; Isa 3:15; 22:1; Jer 2:18; Hos 14:9; also Watts, *Isaiah's New Exodus*, 154.

27. Watts, *Isaiah's New Exodus*, 155; note Kee, *Miracle in the Early Christian World*, 161; also Iwe, *Jesus in the Synagogue of Capernaum*, 323.

Significance Before *Application (Mark 3:14–15)*

5:1–20; 7:26–30; 9:14–29, 38–41; cf. 6:7, 13; 8:33; cf. 16:9).[28] Mark 1:21–28 is the "mission" of Jesus, characterized by his confrontation with Satan's kingdom through casting out a demon. It seems apparent that the inaugural ministry-event offers a programmatic framework for both the following confrontations with Jewish leaders (2:1—3:6)[29] and, as well, the Mark 3 commission.

Mark presents a two-phase commission (3:13–15; 6:7–13). In Mark 3 the *twelve* are created to be *with him* and to be sent *to preach* and *to have authority to cast out the demons*. However, it is not until chapter 6 that Jesus actually gives the created *twelve* that *authority* for the casting component (*And He summoned the twelve and began to send them out in pairs, and gave them authority over the unclean spirits*, 6:7c). In fact, the *to preach* component is not repeated, suggesting that the Mark 6 re-commission affirms that the *authority to cast* is the content of the "preaching." This is further confirmed when Mark describes the ministry of the twice-commissioned *twelve*, then, with the *authority* to fulfill the casting component: *they were casting out many demons* (6:13a).[30]

"Preaching" and "casting" in the general gospel tradition

The other synoptic Gospels present similar commissioning paradigms and activities that suggest the content of "proclamation" in the general gospel tradition included the authority to confront the kingdom of Satan through the casting out of demons. Although the other synoptic writers did not use "create" (*poieō*) to describe the formation of the *twelve*, there is agreement regarding the relationship between "the preaching" and "the authority to cast." Matthew's account focuses on the authority that Jesus gave to the *twelve* for casting and healing:

> Jesus summoned His twelve disciples and gave them authority over unclean spirits, to cast them out, and to heal every kind of disease and every kind of sickness (Matt 10:1; note also vv. 7–8).

---

28. Watts, *Isaiah's New Exodus*, 146.

29. See chapter 4, "A Prelude to Judgment," for a fuller discussion on the conflict-thread between Jesus and Jewish leaders.

30. The addition of *healing* (6:13c) for the activities of the re-commissioned twelve (6:13b) mirrors the ministry of Jesus (i.e., *that they would be with him*, 3:14b), as does the casting; also, healing and demonic activity were clearly associated together in the NT world.

Luke, as well, offered a similar commission scene: *And He called the twelve together, and gave them power and authority over all the demons and to heal diseases* (Luke 9:1). Jesus is depicted granting the *twelve* the power and authority to overrule demons and disease, which corresponds with the Mark 3 commission and, as well, the chapter 6 re-commission.

Earlier in Luke, Jesus' own commission for ministry links proclamation of the Good News to actions (beyond mere verbal- and cognitive-based activities) that are the content of his preaching: *release for captives, recovery of sight to the blind*, and *freedom for the oppressed* (4:18–19). Later, after the seventy returned from their multi-city mission (10:1), Luke notes they rejoiced that *"even the demons are subject to us in Your* [Jesus'] *name"* (10:17). Jesus then declares, *"I saw Satan fall like lightening from heaven"* (v. 18). The "proclamation" of the kingdom directly affects Satan's position of authority. The advance of the kingdom of God constantly causes Satan to fall from heaven,[31] as seen repeatedly through the multiple *casting*-events throughout the Gospel narratives.

The narrative significance of the *to preach* component of the Mark 3 commission is directly linked to Jesus' activity of "casting out demons," indicating that *to have authority to cast* should be understood as the content of "the preaching" (that is, what is preached). At this point in the study, the interpretive summary (II) below gives this understanding of the Mark 3 commission:

> Interpretive Summary II
> As inaugurators of the kingdom, *fisher*-followers are created so they would be with Jesus and so that they would be sent forth to preach, that is, to have the authority to cast out demons.

THE NARRATIVE AND PROGRAMMATIC SIGNIFICANCE OF TO HAVE AUTHORITY TO CAST

Mark indicates that *Jesus came into Galilee, preaching the gospel of God* (1:14), then offers a summary of the content of that preaching—*The time is fulfilled, and the kingdom of God is at hand; repent and believe in the gospel* (1:15)—and thus, by implication, the assumed content of the Mark 3 commission *to preach* (3:14c). We will turn to the importance of the Mark

---

31. I want to thank my New England School of Theology colleague, Dr. Ray Pennoyer, for this observation.

Significance Before *Application (Mark 3:14–15)*

1:14–15 mission summary later in this section, however it should be noted here that the summary implies that "the gospel" preached (v. 14) is related more fully to the eschatological significance of the kingdom's arrival—that is, the content of the "preaching" is that God's reign and rule has invaded the realms of humankind—and not solely about the personal application of Jesus' sacrificial death on the cross. The kingdom as the content of the gospel to be preached is supported by Mark's narrative, particularly as the story and plot unfold to reveal Jesus' authority to cast out demons. The programmatic relationship that links "preaching the gospel of God" (1:14c), its inaugural-kingdom content (v. 15), and its narrative implications extends the significance of the mission summary (1:14–15) to the Mark 3 commission, which have a similar pattern. This section will concentrate on the narrative and programmatic significance of *to have authority to cast out the demons* (3:15) in order to decipher the significance of the Mark 3 commission to the Christian community on this side of the text.

The difficulty of applying the "casting" texts

The problem of application is plainly evident in our attempts to apply or "make practical" the biblical texts that reference miracles. How do we apply and demonstrate obedience to the creation story (Gen 1), Moses's rod turned into a snake (Exod 4:2–4), the parting of the sea at the Exodus (Exod 14), the stricken rock that gushed water (Exod 17:6), the talking donkey of Balaam (Numb 22:22–35), the fire called down from the sky by Elijah (1 Kgs 18), or the surviving of the fire-pit and the lion's den in the Book of Daniel (Dan 3, 6)? As evangelicals, we tend to treasure the miraculous in the Bible, but we are not sure what to do with it. Although most evangelicals believe miracles actually happened as described in the Bible, many are, nonetheless, skeptical how they are supposed to work today in application. Some affirm that miracles take place today and that is *how* they are applied. Some affirm the "potential" of miracles and/or simply spiritualize them for their personal meaning to the individual. Miraculous events and stories are often too easily "applied" without much consideration for why the stories were told in first place, that is, their literary role in the narrative plot.

On the other hand, rather than apply, many use the casting and other miracles in the gospels as apologetic "proof-texts" for Jesus' deity and/or to affirm that the disciples had authority from God. Miracles, to some, are used as evidence that the gospel is true—even if that evidence took place long ago in the days of Jesus and the early church. Utilized in this way, miracles are merely turned into cognitive-based instruction, apologetic proofs, or evangelistic tools, rather than for their literary or narrative significance.

The "casting" episodes in Mark's Gospel fall prey to the same approaches and are often reduced to mere information about the gospel or about Jesus, rather than deciphering the meaning implied by their emplotted use in the narrative. The reader/listener should ask, *What role does Mark intend the casting to play in his story?* In other words, how does casting out demons contribute to "the sequence of events emplotted"[32] in the narrative? What is the relationship between *to have authority* and *to cast out demons* in determining the significance of the Mark 3 commission for the church today? In order to apply more accurately the Mark 3 commission, the *emplotted* significance of *to have authority to cast out the demons* (v. 15) must be deciphered.

"To have authority to cast" is the mission

The centrality of casting out demons and unclean spirits in Mark cannot be overstated (1:23–27, 32–34, 39; 3:11; 5:2–8, 13; 6:13; 7:26–30; 9:14–29, 38–41; cf. cf. 3:22–27; 6:7, 13; 8:33; cf. 16:9). Jesus' authority over demons is "the single hallmark of his activity."[33] This fits the introductory and programmatic content of the Gospel, which is first initiated in the desert confrontation between Jesus and Satan (1:12–13) and, then, confirmed through multiple *casting*-events that reveal Jesus-the Stronger Man overtaking Satan-the strongman's dominion/house (cf. 3:23–27).[34] Jesus' authority to cast out demons reveals in deed (i.e., in action) the reality of what has been initiated through his appearance as God's Messiah-King (1:1): the rule and reign of God (his kingdom/house) has been inaugurated (cf. 1:14–15; 3:27). This sets the underlying framework for the narrative plot that explains and corresponds to the Mark 3 commission *to have authority to cast out the demons* (3:15; cf. 6:7, 13).

The commission in Mark 3, however, is not *to cast*, but *to have authority to cast* (v. 15). This is important, for applying "the casting" is not simply the replication or exhibition of exorcism, but is the dynamic association

---

32. Refer back to Kuruvilla, *Text to Praxis*, 72–75 (see p. 180n16).

33. Watts, *Isaiah's New Exodus*, 154, also note p. 145.

34. Ibid., 146; also Watts, referring to R. Leivestad, underscores that "each exorcism" was "an instance of binding and plundering" (*Christ the Conqueror*, 46ff.).

between Jesus' authority as God's premiere agent who has appeared to inaugurate his kingdom (1:9–10; 1:14–15) and his created *fisher*-followers who are to have the same task: as Jesus had authority to cast out demons, so, also, his *fisher*-followers were commissioned *to have authority to cast out the demons* (3:15).

Mark's Gospel associates Jesus' authority with his activity of "casting." This is seen first at Jesus' inaugural ministry-event in which it was observed that he had cast out an unclean spirit (1:25) with *authority (exousian*, v. 27c). The centrality of Jesus' authority is also in contrast to the religious/political leadership, first at the inaugural ministry-event (*He was teaching them as one having authority, and not as the scribes*, 1:22b) and, then, later when Jesus was challenged by the temple leadership who asked, *"By what authority [exousia] are You doing these things . . . ?"* (11:28b). This "authority" for *fisher*-followers, first commissioned in 3:15 and, then, granted in 6:7, was confirmed later in the parable that Jesus used to explain the role of his faithful followers as they persevere through the eschatological conclusion of history: Jesus, *like a man away on a journey, who upon leaving his house, gives his slaves authority, assigning to each one his task* (13:34, author's translation). So, as *fisher*-followers who are to be God's agents for inaugurating his kingdom (the meaning of the Mark 1:17 *fisher*-promise), Jesus gave them authority to cast out demons (6:7; cf. Matt 10:1; Luke 9:1) in order that they, too, would demonstrate the undoing of Satan's kingdom/house over the realms of humankind. This is, at least in part, the meaning behind Jesus creating his *fisher*-followers to be *with him* (3:14b), for the intimate relationship is also one of imitation—the mission of *fisher*-followers *is* the mission of Jesus.

Miracles as parables: evidential language of the in-breaking of God's reign

Miracles are obviously important to Mark, for they occupy a significant amount of space throughout his narrative. Twenty-seven percent of his Gospel is associated with miracles. If the passion segment is not included, forty percent of the verses reference miracles.[35] The emphasis on miracles in Mark's summaries also indicates their central role in his plot development

---

35. Note Mark 1:23–27, 32–34, 39; 3:11; 5:2–8, 13; 6:13; 7:26–30; 9:14–29, 38–41; cf. 3:22–27; 6:7, 13; 8:33.

(1:32–34, 39; 3:10–12; 6:5, 53–56).[36] The inclusion of multiple miracle stories in this Gospel means more than simply an apologetic for Jesus' deity. Instead, Mark leverages Jesus' miracles as an integral part of his Gospel narrative as he develops the plot and the story unfolds, particularly within the Galilean ministry that focuses on "casting" as a central miracle (1:23–27, 32–34, 39; 3:11, 22–27).

While most critics of the Gospels recognize that the parables and much of the teachings of Jesus were original, what is overlooked, however, is that the parables and the miracles attributed to Jesus are strikingly parallel in function.[37] Many recognize that miracles in the Gospel are deed-parables,[38] which not only have implications for the authenticity of Gospel miracle stories, but are also important for determining the significance of miracles for developing authoritative, analogous application. For Mark, miracles function as "another mode of language" to communicate the nature of *the gospel of God* (1:14). They, like the parables, are emplotted in the narrative as a means of teaching about "the mystery of God's action in the world."[39] As with Jesus' teaching and parables, the crowds reacted with awe at his miracles (1:22, 27; 2:12; 5:20, 42; 6:2, 51; 7:37; 9:15; 10:24, 26, 32; 11:18; 12:17).

This programmatic similarity between teaching/parable and miracle is made clear at Jesus' inaugural ministry-event in which the gathered crowd was "amazed" at Jesus' authority over an unclean spirit that is referred to as a "new teaching" (2:27). Also, miracles reveal and conceal the mysterious nature of Jesus and his ministry. The kingdom is veiled and disclosed through miracles, making them similar to the function of parables in revealing the nature and inaugural presence of God's kingdom.[40] Miracles in Mark's Gospel provide a "parabolic" key to his ministry and reveal "the in-breaking of the power of God's reign."[41] This is particularly noticeable

---

36. Watts, *Isaiah's New Exodus*, 139.

37. Blomberg, "Miracles as Parables," 327.

38. Blomberg, "The Miracles as Parables," 327; also note Achtemeier, "Origin and Function," 198–221; Achtemeier, "Toward the Isolation," 265–91; Beavis, *Mark's Audience*, 157ff.; Boucher, *Mysterious Parables*, 79–83; Donahue, "Jesus as the Parable of God," 369–86; Hawkin, "Symbolism and Structure," 98–110; Marshall, *Faith as a Theme*, 60ff.; Fuller, *Mission and Achievement of Jesus*, 73; Richardson, *Miracle Stories of the Gospels*, 48–49.

39. Blomberg, "The Miracles as Parables," 342.

40. Ibid., 341–42.

41. Ibid., 329.

Significance Before Application (Mark 3:14–15)

with regards to casting episodes, for they indicate his authority to destroy Satan-the strongman's house and to plunder his dominion—a visible and demonstrable action (with outcomes) indicating the presence of God's kingdom.

Additionally, the "transactions of the characters"[42] in the plot underscore the significance of the miracle-parables to the reader/listener on this side of the text. After Jesus presented the parable of the Sower who sowed (4:1–8), his followers began asking him about *the* parables (v. 10). Jesus replied, *To you has been given the mystery of the kingdom of God, but those who are outside get everything in parables* (4:11b). He then asks his followers, *Do you not understand this parable? How will you understand all the parables* [v. 13]? Later, the disciples dangerously showed lack of insight into Jesus miracles (Mark 6:52; 7:18; 8:14–21). Interestingly, the words that Jesus said to the disciples after the feeding miracle (Mark 8:18) were similar to those he used to explain the parables (4:12); both draw from the Isaiah 6 idolatry-taunt—*seeing but not perceiving . . . hearing but not understanding*. The miracles have the same outsider-insider effect as do parables, implying that they, too, reveal (i.e., proclaim) the mystery of the kingdom. As the parables reveal the presence of the kingdom, the miracles function in a similar manner. This challenges even *fisher*-followers to recognize that such deed-parables proclaim *and* demonstrate the arrival of God's dominion.

Finally, the Mark 3 sandwich and Beelzebul episode (3:20–35) also suggests the importance of recognizing the role of "casting" miracles in the narrative plot. When the Jerusalem leadership accused Jesus of being demon possessed and in league with Satan (3:22), Jesus defended his mission through parables that indicated the presence of the Stronger Man confirms the destruction of Satan-the strongman's reign over the affairs of humankind (vv. 23–27). The Mark 3 Beelzebul episode directs the attention of the reader/listener to the attributes of *outsiders* and *insiders* (as do the parables and other miracles). The activity of "casting" as a deed-parable gives evidence of the arrival of the kingdom of God, the purpose and meaning of the Mark 3 commission: *fisher*-followers are *insiders* who are true family and do the will of God (3:35) by revealing the inaugural presence of God's kingdom through the language of action/deed (3:15).

---

42. See Kuruvilla, *Text to Praxis*, 72–75.

The mission summary frames the Mark 3 commission

My syntactical conclusion developed above—the *authority to cast out the demons* (3:15) is the content of *to preach* (v. 14c)—is made more evident by the Mark 3 commission's link to the Mark 1:14-15 mission summary:

> Now after John had been taken into custody, Jesus came into Galilee, preaching the gospel of God, and saying, "The time has been fulfilled, and the kingdom of God has come near; repent and believe in the gospel."[43]

The geographic identifier—*Jesus came into Galilee* (1:14b)—indicates that these two verses form a summary for the Galilean ministry that runs from the *fisher*-promise—*And He was going along the Sea of Galilee . . . Jesus said to them, "Come follow (after) Me and I will create you to become fishers . . . "* (1:16-17, author's translation)—through 9:33-49, a teaching episode set in the Galilean town of Capernaum (9:33).[44] These geographic bookends focus the mission summary at a literary level on Jesus' Galilean ministry, forming an underlying relationship between "preaching the gospel of God" (1:14c) and Jesus' teaching *and* actions emplotted throughout the narrative. Furthermore, the central role of Jesus' *casting*-ministry is also clearly established by a *casting*-event bracket, first at the opening of the Galilean ministry (1:21-27) and, then, at the close (9:38-41) as Jesus begins turning his attention toward Jerusalem and the soon approaching passion. This bracketing affirms the importance of "casting" activities in the Galilean section of the Gospel narrative: the first time Jesus "came preaching the gospel of God" (1:14c) in Galilee involved an exorcism (1:21-28) and at the close of the Galilean ministry even those outside the inner-circle, who acted out the mission of Jesus, are associated with "casting" (9:38-41).

Mark 1:14-15 is clearly a summary and it functions as a programmatic and interpretative lens for his Gospel narrative and for the ministry of Jesus that was carried out through both teaching *and* miracle that reveal the nature and significance of the kingdom that *has come near* (1:15). The content of *the gospel of God* (v.14c) is epexegetically explained in 1:15.[45] The

---

43. The Mark 1:14-15 text here reflects my translation of the Greek, which will be used throughout the remainder of this section, unless otherwise noted.

44. Although most limit the Galilean ministry to Mark 1-6 (note for example Guelich, *Mark 1-8:26*, 41; Witherington, *Gospel of Mark*, 77), it appears that it continues through to Mark 9, which is indicated by the geographic bookends.

45. Guelich, *Mark 1-8:26*, 43.

Significance Before Application (Mark 3:14-15)

gospel that has come from God (1:14c)[46] is defined by each element in verse 15, clarifying God's decisive action in the appearance of his Son.[47] The mission summary is composed of two parts: first, an indication that Jesus had preached "the gospel of God" (v. 14); then, the content of that preaching (v. 15). The Mark 3 commission follows the same pattern set by Mark 1:14-15.

The gospel preached—1:14/3:14	Epexegetically defined—1:15/3:15
... Jesus came into Galilee, <u>preaching</u> the gospel of God ...	... and (*kai*) saying, "The time has been fulfilled, and the kingdom of God has come near; repent and believe in the gospel."
And he [Jesus] created twelve ... so that he would send them forth <u>to preach</u> ...	... namely, that is, (*kai*) to have authority to cast out the demons.[A]

A. Along with Mark 1:14-15, the Mark 3:14-15 reference here reflects the author's translation.

The *gospel of God* (1:14-15) and the Mark 3 commission both are announcement in which the content is the arrival of the kingdom of God and, as well, its implications.

The content of the *gospel of God* (1:14) that Jesus preached is summarized in declarations (v. 15) that Mark has carefully balanced, forming two pairs of statements "each constructed in synthetic parallelism."[48]

(1)	The time has been fulfilled	and	the kingdom of God has come near
(2)	Repent	and	believe in the gospel[A]

A. See Marcus, *Mark 1-8*, 175; this gird reflects the author's translation of Mark 1:15.

The first pair are declarative statements, each containing a perfect indicative verb that implies a completed action that continues in effect; the second are present imperatives—commands—that flow from the declarations. The first indicative is *the time has been fulfilled*, which corresponds to the first

46. Regarding the phrase *to euaggelion tou theou* (*the gospel of God*, Mark 1:14c), the genitive *tou theou* (*of God*, Mark 1:14c) is most likely used ambiguously by Mark to mean both the *Gospel about God* (objective genitive) and *the gospel from God* (subjective genitive). Nonetheless, here I indicate the phrase to mean "the gospel from God" emphasizing God's action in Christ Jesus, his appearance and ministry (e.g. see France, *Gospel of Mark*, 91).

47. Lane, *Gospel According to Mark*, 63-64; Witherington, *Gospel of Mark*, 77.

48. Guelich, *Mark 1-8:26*, 41; also Marcus, *Mark 1-8*, 175.

imperative "repent." The second indicative is *the kingdom of God has come near*, which corresponds to the second imperative "believe." The meaning is rather straightforward: the time of the old age has been completed (cf. this *present evil age*, Gal 1:4), that is, the time under Satan's dominion has come to its eschatological end; and, the time of God's kingdom has now been inaugurated, reorienting the realms of humankind to reflect his right to reign and rule.[49] The pattern established in 1:14–15 is exactly what happens throughout the Galilean ministry and is reflected in the Mark 3 commission.

Timing and the evangelistic task of fisher-followers

The question of timing is relevant, for the summary (Mark 1:14–15) informs us that both *the time has been fulfilled* and *the kingdom of God has come near* (author's translation). Discussions regarding the "time" fulfilled and the "nearness" of the kingdom typically focus on chronology: do these references indicate present or future events? Mark, however, uses the word *kairos* (*time*) to indicate a decisive moment (12:2; 13:33) or a span of current time (i.e., a season; 10:30; 11:13). Mark's use of *near* (*eggizō* centers on proximity (11:1; 14:42). These are significant observations, for at the literary level, Mark's narrative portrait of Jesus' "preaching of the Gospel of God" (1:14c) and its content (v. 15) parallel his immediate and proximate actions during the Galilean ministry: the end of Satan's dominion and the inaugural reign of God are demonstrated in Jesus' authority to cast out demons and through his other miracles as well.

A number of interrelated events follow the mission summary that stress arrival (i.e., *the kingdom has come near*). This is a function of the following miracle stories, particularly the casting, that demonstrate "God's rule had entered into history."[50] The weight of the narrative parts (i.e., the episodes, stories, and events throughout the narrative) indicates the timing is immediate in Jesus' ministry and, then, will continue through *the authority to cast* granted to the *fisher*-followers (3:15; 6:7), who are commissioned to imitate Jesus' mission. This fits the use of the perfect indicative verbal expressions in the mission summary (*peplērōtai*, *has been fulfilled*; *ēggiken*, *has come near*), the subsequent narrative (i.e., the Galilean ministry),

---

49. On this I follow Marcus, who has a good discussion on the meaning of the mission summary (*Mark 1–8*, 173–76).

50. Ibid., 46.

Significance Before *Application (Mark 3:14–15)*

and the Mark 3 commission. The kingdom of God is the substance of the created *fisher*-followers' evangelistic activities, not solely as proclamation, but primarily their actions (i.e., their deeds), which continuously reveal the kingdom's nearness. Like the word sowed by the Master Sower in the Mark 4 parables and Jesus' kingdom-deeds (i.e., deed-parables), this, too, is the evangelistic task of *fisher*-followers.

The significance of the Mark 3 commission

It is not coincidental that the *fisher*-promise (1:17) follows the mission summary (1:14–15), for the Mark 3 commission is the inaugural fulfillment of the *fisher*-promise and echoes the pattern set forth in the mission summary. The "casting" episodes act as indicators that *the time has been fulfilled* and *the kingdom has come near* (1:15), for Jesus is *already* invading Satan's territory. The role of *fisher*-followers is to imitate Jesus' activities: as Jesus was the premier inaugurator of the kingdom of God, thus ending Satan's dominion, which is demonstrated through *casting*, so, also, the *fisher*-followers (3:15). This is the significance of the Mark 3 commission: to be obedient to the commission, then, is to develop authoritative application through analogous deeds that demonstrate the defeat of Satan's kingdom and that reorient both people and the world toward God's dominion.

The final interpretive summary (III) below gives a sense of this fuller understanding of the Mark 3 commission and its significance for the reader/listener today:

> Interpretive Summary III
> *Fisher*-followers are created to imitate Jesus' mission, that is, they are commissioned to demonstrate the presence of God's kingdom through actions that evidence Satan's dominion has been destroyed and that reorient the realms of humankind under God's rule and reign.

SIGNIFICANCE: DETERMINE ANALOGOUS OBEDIENCE

The narrative and programmatic significance of both "preaching" and "casting" indicate that the content of the *to preach* (v. 14c) component of the Mark 3 commission is *the authority to cast out the demons* (v. 15). This is grammatically and syntactically allowable and is affirmed by how Mark crafted his narrative. Reading the commission in this way challenges a narrowly defined, verbal- and cognitive-based understanding of evangelistic activities. As *fisher*-followers, the church's paradigm for evangelism is found in the Mark 3 commission, which indicates that Christians and the Christian community should include evangelistic activities that confront Satan's dominion over the realms of humankind and that reorient those realms to reflect the inaugural presence of God's kingdom. Thus, the task of "casting" corresponds to any analogous obedience (i.e., application) that confronts what is contrary to God's design for living in the land[51] and that demonstrates how God's rule affects the realms of humankind.

In order to move appropriately from text to application, there should be a correspondence between the meaning of the text, its significance to the readers/listeners, and the action taken that indicates obedience to the text. For the church in front of the text, the significance of the Mark 3 commission is our alignment with and commitment to the mission of Jesus (1:14–15) and to exercise Jesus' authority through actions that demonstrate, concretely and evidentially, that God's rule and reign has entered time and space. Certainly, as the whole of the NT indicates, evangelism includes proclamation (i.e., verbal- and cognitive-based activities of communication) that presents *the information* of the Good News, announcing and explaining that the kingdom is near. Yet, such proclamation is not the end of evangelism. Mark's Gospel narrative as a whole and the Mark 3 commission specifically indicate there is also to be a resultant consequence of the "preaching," another viable mode of language, namely the doing of deed-parables. As parables revealed the mysteries of the kingdom, deed-parables evidence (i.e., have outcomes that indicate) the undoing of Satan's power over the affairs of humankind (Mark 3:27) and, as a result, seek to reorient people and the world back toward God's rightful dominion (an underlying significance of the Mark 4 parable of the mustard seed, vv. 30–32).[52]

---

51. The concept of "living in the land" is borrowed from Walter Brueggemann (*The Land*), who uses the terminology to refer how the Israelites were to live in the land of promise as neighbors, where everyone is to benefit from living in the land; the land-laws and covenant-stipulations governed how they were to live "in the land" together, specifically being mindful of the economically vulnerable and the poor. Although I am using it in a contemporary sense—Americans living in America—I am borrowing the idea that everyone, the rich, the poor, the middle class, all neighbors to some extent are "living in the land."

52. Note the final discussion on this parable (i.e., the mustard bush) in chapter 2, "Wasted Evangelism."

Significance Before *Application (Mark 3:14–15)*

Evangelism is the spread of the gospel, the seed sown (Mark 4), which according to Mark's narrative is dynamically linked to the end of Satan's dominion and the inauguration of God's rule and reign. This is what biblical evangelism looks like: as Jesus' "casting" action demonstrated the end of the strongman-Satan's kingdom and the arrival of God's kingdom—visible and evidential acts that indicate *the time has been fulfilled* and *the kingdom of God has come near* (1:15a, author's translation)—so, for the church seeking to obey this text, the significance of the "casting" component of the Mark 3 commission *is* the continuation of Jesus' mission to confront the powers that oppose God's dominion. Therefore, as indicated by the *fisher*-promise's association to OT contexts that include the issues of poverty and, as well, the implications of the Mark 12 poor widow episode (12:38–44), applications for "casting" should include advocating for those affected by poverty.[53]

Separating social action from evangelism is an unwarranted dualism

As I demonstrated in chapter 3 ("You Will Appear as *Fishers*"), the Mark 3 commission is the inaugural fulfillment and premiere application of the Mark 1:17 *fisher*-promise. The *fisher* role is related to God's judgment and action toward people and structures that distort God's creation from his design and reign over it, which includes advocacy for those affected by the issues of poverty and injustice. This allows evangelism, that is, the sowing of the word/gospel to also include the realm of social action, which demonstrates God's rule and dominion over the realms of society and people that impact the poor and economically vulnerable. This is supported by antecedent OT material related to the economically vulnerable that is associated with the judgment role of *fisher*-followers.[54] This implies that the Mark 3 commission (3:14–15), to some extent, should be associated at the application level with social action, which is legitimate obedience for following Jesus Christ and for being faithful to the gospel. Therefore, obedience to the Mark 3 commission includes "applications, activities, and outcomes of social action and justice" (p. 174) that should be an intentional

---

53. Refer back to chapter 1, "Widows in Our Courts," for a biblical illustration how both people and systems can cause others to live with the effects of poverty; additionally, review the OT texts that juxtapose idolatry with poverty in chapter 5 ("Idolatry and Poverty").

54. This is the argument of chapter 3, "You will Appear as *Fishers*."

component of a church's or Christian community's evangelistic activities, which is, at least in part, the *fisher*-follower's task.

The obedience (i.e., application) and the desired outcomes analogous to the purpose and intent of the commission *to have authority to cast* are those which demonstrate God's reign and rule. Separating social action from evangelism is an unwarranted dualism that is alien to the gospel as Mark presents it in his narrative and, as well, to the wider biblical record. As proclaiming the kingdom's arrival was demonstrated by Jesus' deed-parables (i.e., castings, healings, miracles), the evangelistic task of the church is to include analogous activities that indicate the presence of God's rule and reign. This also makes redemptive-historical sense of *the authority to cast out the demons* (Mark 3:15) as a display of the all-encompassing arrival of God's kingdom: God in Jesus Christ has *reconciled all things to Himself* (Col 1:20) and *with a view to an administration suitable to the fullness of the times, that is, the summing up of all things in Christ, things in the heavens and things on the earth* (Eph 1:10).

Social action that reflects God's design for living in the land—social action, that is, that demonstrates his reign and his righteousness that is to be expressed among people—is the responsibility of faithful *fisher*-followers of Jesus, God's Messiah-King. Consequently, evangelistic activities of the church ought to seek to ensure that the economically vulnerable and the poor (i.e., the land-less) are full participants in the benefits of living in the land. In other words, as Mark's narrative richly portrays *the gospel of Jesus Christ* (Mark 1:1), social action outcomes should be included as a component of a church's task of evangelism.

Bibliography

Abraham, William J. "A Theology of Evangelism: The Heart of the Matter." *Interpretation* 48, no. 2 (1994) 117–30.
Abraham, William J. *The Logic of Evangelism*. Grand Rapids: Eerdmans, 1989.
Achtemeier, P. J. "'He Taught Them Many Things': Reflections on Marcan Christology." *Catholic Biblical Quarterly* 42 (1980) 478–80.
———. "The Origin and Function of the Pre-Marcan Miracle Catenae." *Journal of Biblical Literature* 91(1972) 198–221.
———. "Toward the Isolation of Pre-Marcan Miracle Catenae." *Journal of Biblical Literature* 89 (1970) 265–91.
Acs, Gregory, and Seth Zimmerman. "U.S. Intragenerational Mobility From 1984–2004: Trends and Implications." Report. Washington, DC: The Pew Charitable Trusts, 2008.
Adeyemo, Tokunbon. "A Critical Evaluation of Contemporary Perspectives." In *In Word and Deed: Evangelism and Social Responsibility*, edited by Bruce Nicholls, 41–61. Grand Rapids: Eerdmans, 1985.
Anderson, Chip M. "A Prelude to Judgment: The Beelzebul Episode (Mk 3:22–28) and Its Significance for Evangelistic Social Action." *Africanus Journal* 6, no. 2 (forthcoming).
———. *Destroying Our Private Cities, Building Our Spiritual Life* (Maitland, FL: Xulon, 2003).
———. "Idolatry and Poverty: Social Action as Christian Apologetics." *Africanus Journal* 2, no. 2 (November 2010) 24–43.
———."Romans 1:1–5 and the Occasion of the Letter: The Solution to the Two-Congregation Problem in Rome." *Trinity Journal* 14, no.1 (1993) 25–40.
———."'Wasted Evangelism' (Mark 4): The Task of Evangelism and Social Action Outcomes." *Africanus Journal* 1, no. 2 (November 2009) 39–58.
———."'You Will Appear as Fishers' (Mark 1:17): Disciples as Agents of Judgment." *Africanus Journal* 5, no. 1 (April 2013) 21–36.
Arias, Mortimer. *Announcing the Reign of God: Evangelization and the Subversive Memory of Jesus*. Lima, OH: Academic Renewal, 1984.
Arndt, William F., and F. Wilbur Gingrich. *A Greek-English Lexicon of the New Testament and Other early Christian Literature*. Translated by Walter Bauer. 2nd ed. Chicago: University of Chicago Press, 1979.
Baggett, Jerome P. "Congregations and Civil Society: A Double-Edged Connection." *Journal of Church and State* 44, no. 3 (2002) 425–54.

Bibliography

Baldwin, J. G. "Idolatry." In *The New Bible Dictionary*, edited by J. D. Douglas, et al., 503–5. 2nd ed. Wheaton: Tyndale, 1982.

Beale, G. K. "Isaiah VI 9–13: A Retributive Taunt Against Idolatry." *Vestus Testamentum* 42 (1991) 257–78.

———. *The Temple and the Church's Mission: A Biblical Theology of the Dwelling Place of God*. Downers Grove: Intervarsity, 2004.

———. *We Become What We Worship: A Biblical Theology of Idolatry*. Downers Grove: IVP Academic, 2008.

Beauregard, Robert A. *When America Became Suburban*. Minneapolis: University of Minneapolis Press, 2006.

Beavis, Mary Ann. *Mark's Audience: The Literary and Social Setting of Mark 4.11–12*. Journal for the Study of the New Testament Supplement 33. Sheffield: JSOT, 1989.

Benson, Bruce Ellis, and Peter Goodwin Heltzel, editors. *Evangelicals and Empire: Christian Alternatives to the Political Status Quo*. Grand Rapids: Brazos, 2008.

Berger, Peter L., and Thomas Luckman. *The Social Construction of Reality: A Treatise in the Sociology of Knowledge*. New York: Anchor, 1966.

———, et al. *The Homeless Mind: Modernization and Consciousness*. New York: Vintage, 1974.

Blakley, J. Ted. "Incomprehension or Resistance? The Marken Disciples and the Narrative Logic of Mark 4:1—8:30." Ph.D. diss., University of St. Andrews, 2008.

Blomberg, Craig L. "The Miracles as Parables." In *Gospel Perspectives: The Miracles of Jesus* 6, editors David Wenham and Craig Blomberg, 327–359. Sheffield: JSOT, 1986.

———. *Neither Poverty nor Riches: A Biblical Theology of Possessions*. Downers Grove: InterVarsity, 1999.

Bock, Darrell. "Blasphemy and the Jewish Examination of Jesus." *Bulletin for Biblical Research* 17, no. 1 (2007) 53–114.

Boring, Eugene. "Mark 1.1–15 and the Beginning of the Gospel." *Semeia* 52 (1991) 43–82.

Boucher, Madeleine. *The Mysterious Parables*. CBQMS 6. Washington, DC: Catholic Biblical Association, 1977.

Brueggemann, Walter. *The Land: Place as Gift, Promise, and Challenge in Biblical Faith*. 2nd ed. Minneapolis: Fortress, 2002.

Brunner, Emil. *Man in Revolt: A Christian Anthropology*. Translated by O. Wyon. London: Lutterworth, 1947.

Budziszewski, J., editor. *Evangelicals in the Public Square: Four Formative Voices on Political Thought and Action*. Grand Rapids: Baker, 2006.

Caneday, A. B. "He Wrote in Parables and Riddles: Mark's Gospel as a Literary Reproduction of Jesus' Teaching Method." *Didaskalia* 10, no. 2 (1999) 35–67.

Cannon, Mae Ellis. *Social Justice Basic Handbook: Small Steps for a Better World*. Downers Grove: IVP, 2009.

Cassuto, Umberto Moshe David. *A Commentary on the Book of Exodus*. Translated by Israel Abrahams. Skokie, IL: Varda, 2005.

Chaney, Marvin L. "'Coveting Your Neighbor's House' in Social Context." In *The Ten Commandments: The Reciprocity of Faithfulness*, edited by William P. Brown, 302–317. Louisville: Westminster John Knox, 2004.

Childs, Brevard S. *The Book of Exodus*. Louisville: Westminster John Knox, 2004.

Christian, Jayakumar. *God of the Empty-Handed: Poverty, Power & the Kingdom of God*. Monrovia, CA: MARC, World Vision, 1999.

Bibliography

Cnaan, Ram A. *The Invisible Caring Hand: American Congregations and the Provision of Welfare*. New York: New York University Press, 2002.

———. *The Newer Deal: Social Work and Religion in Partnership*. New York: Columbia University Press, 1999.

Cole, Graham A. *Engaging with the Holy Spirit: Real Questions, Practical Answers*. Wheaton: Crossway, 2007.

Conchran, Clark E. "Sacramental Theology, Catholic Political Thought, and the Crisis of Institutions." Paper presented at the American Religious Seminar. University of Notre Dame, February 17, 1999.

Craigie, P. C. "Idolatry." In *Evangelical Dictionary of Theology*, edited by Walter Elwell, 542–43. Grand Rapids: Baker, 1984.

Crossan, John Dominic. *The Dark Interval: Towards a Theology of Story*. Chicago: Polebridge, 1988.

Curtis, Edward M. "Idol, Idolatry." In *ABD*, vol. 3. Edited by David Noel Freedman, 376–381. New York: Doubleday Image, 1992.

Danker, F. W. "Double-entendre in Mark XII 9." *Novum Testamentum* 10, no. 2 (1968) 162–63.

Davey, Andrew. *Urban Christianity and Global Order: Theological Resources for an Urban Future*. Peabody: Hendrickson, 2002.

Derrett, J. Duncan M. "'Eating Up the Houses of Widows': Jesus' Comments on Lawyers?" *Novum Testamentum* 14, no.1 (1972) 1–9.

Dey, Lala Kalyan Kumar. "Poverty: An Eschatological Perspective." *Drew Gateway* 52, no. 1 (1981) 1–8.

Donahue, John. "Jesus as the Parable of God in the Gospel of Mark." *Interpretation* 32 (1978) 369–86.

Douglas, J. D., editor. *Let the Earth Hear His Voice*. Minneapolis: World Wide Publications, 1975.

Duany, Andres, et al. *Suburban Nation: The Rise of Sprawl and the Decline of the American Dream*. New York: North Point, 2000.

Dunn, James D. G. *Jesus Remembered*. Vol. 1, *Christianity in the Making*. Grand Rapids: Eerdmans, 2003.

Durham, John I. *Exodus*. Word Biblical Commentary 3. Waco, TX: Word, 1987.

Edwards, James R. "Markan Sandwiches: The Significance of Interpolations in the Markan Narratives." *Novum Testamentum* 31, no. 3 (1989) 193–216.

———. *The Gospel According to Mark*. Grand Rapids: Eerdmans, 2002.

Elshtain, Jean Bethke. "Afterward." In *Evangelicals in the Public Square: Four Formative Voices on Political Thought and Action*, edited by J. Budziszewski, 195–210. Grand Rapids: Baker 2006.

Evans, Craig A. "Aspects of Exile and Restoration in the Proclamation of Jesus and the Gospels." In *Exile: Old Testament, Jewish, and Christian Conceptions*, edited by James M. Scott, 299–328. Leiden, Netherlands: Brill, 1997.

———. "Mark's Incipit and the Priene Calendar Inscription: From Jewish Gospel to Greco-Roman Gospel." *Journal of Greco-Roman Christianity and Judaism* 1 (2000) 67–81.

———. *Mark 8:27—16:20*. Word Biblical Commentary 34b. Columbia: Thomas Nelson, 2001.

Fee, Gordon, and Douglas Stuart. *How to Read the Bible for All Its Worth*. Grand Rapids: Zondervan, 2003.

Bibliography

Fensham, F. Charles. "Widow, Orphan, and the Poor in Ancient Near Eastern Legal and Wisdom Literature." *Journal of Near Eastern Studies* 21 (April, 1962) 129–39;

France, R. T. *The Gospel of Mark: New International Commentary on the Greek Testament.* Grand Rapids: Eerdmans, 2002.

Frug, Gerald E. *City Making: Building Communities without Building Walls.* Princeton: Princeton University Press, 2001.

Fuder, John, and Noel Castellanos, editors. *A Heart for the Community: New Models for Urban and Suburban Ministry.* Chicago: Moody, 2009.

Fuller, R. H. *The Mission and Achievement of Jesus.* Studies in Biblical Theology 12. London: SCM, 1954.

Funk, Robert W. "The Looking Glass Tree Is for the Birds." *Interpretation* 27 (1973) 3–9.

Gardella, Peter. *Domestic Religion: Work, Food, Sex and Other Commitments.* Cleveland: Pilgrim, 1998.

Gordon, Cyrus H. "A Note on the Tenth Commandment." *Journal of the American Academy of Religion* 31, no. 2 (1963) 208–9.

Greidanus, Sidney. *The Modern Preacher and the Ancient Text: Interpreting and Preaching Biblical Literature.* Grand Rapids: Eerdmans, 1989.

Guelich, Robert A. *Mark 1–8:26.* Word Biblical Commentary 34a. Dallas: Word, 1989.

Guinness, Os. "Evangelicals Among Thinking People" In *Let the Earth Hear His Voice*, edited by J. D. Douglas, 713–15. Minneapolis: World Wide Publications, 1975.

———. *The American Hour: A Time of Reckoning and the Once and Future Role of Faith.* New York: Free Press, 1992.

———. *The Last Christian on Earth: Uncover the Enemy's Plot to Undermine the Church.* Ventura, CA: Regal, 2010.

Gundry, Robert. *Mark: A Commentary on His Apology for the Cross.* Grand Rapids: Eerdmans, 1993.

Halpem, Baruch, et al. *Traditions in Transformation.* Winona Lake, IN: Eisenbrauns, 1981.

Halteman, James. "The Market System, the Poor, and Economic Theory." In *Toward a Just and Caring Society: Christian Responses to Poverty in America*, edited by David P. Gushee, 72–111. Grand Rapids: Baker, 1999.

Hamilton, Neill Q. "Temple Cleansing and the Temple Bank." *Journal of Biblical Literature* 83 (1964) 365–72.

Hawkin, David J. "The Symbolism and Structure of the Marcan Redaction." *Evangelical Quarterly* 49, no.2 (April-June 1977) 98–110.

Hayduk, Ronald. "Race and Suburban Sprawl: Regionalism and Structural Racism." In *Suburban Sprawl: Culture, Theory, and Politics*, edited by Matthew J. Lindstrom and Hugh Bartling, 137–70. New York: Rowman & Littlefield, 2003.

Henderson, Suzanne Watts. *Christology and Discipleship in the Gospel of Mark.* Cambridge: Cambridge University Press, 2006.

Henry, Carl F. H. *The Uneasy Conscience of Modern Fundamentalism.* Grand Rapids: Eerdmans, 2003.

Henry, Paul B. *Politics for Evangelicals.* Valley Forge: Judson, 1974.

Herzog, William R. *Parables as Subversive Speech: Jesus as Pedagogue of the Oppressed.* Louisville: Westminster John Knox, 1994.

Higle, Andrew Todd. "Seeds of Subversion: A Study of the Parables in Mark 4." Thesis, Emmanuel School of Religion, 2004. Johnson City, Tennessee. TREN Dissertations.

Hirsch, E. D. *Validity in Interpretation.* New Haven: Yale University Press, 1967.

Hooker, Morna. *Beginnings: Keys that Open the Gospels.* Harrisburg: Trinity, 1997.

Horsley, Richard A. *Hearing the Whole Story: The Politics of Plot in Mark's Gospel*. Louisville: Westminster John Knox, 2001.

———. *Jesus and Empire: The Kingdom of God and the New World Disorder*. Minneapolis: Fortress, 2003.

Horvath, Peter. "The Organization of Social Action." *Canadian Psychology* 40, no. 3 (August 1999) 221–31.

Isaacs, Julia B. "Economic Mobility of Families Across Generations." In "Getting Ahead or Losing Ground: Economic Mobility in America," edited by Julia Isaacs, et al. Washington DC: Brookings Institute, Economic Mobility Project, 2008. Online: http://www.brookings.edu/research/reports/2008/02/economic-mobility-sawhill.

Iwe, John Chijoke. *Jesus in the Synagogue of Capernaum: The Pericope and its Programmatic Character for the Gospel of Mark: An Exegetico-Theological Study of Mark 1:21–28*. Rome: Editrice Pontificia Universita Gregoriana, 1999.

Jeremias, Joachim. *The Parables of Jesus*. London: SCM, 1972.

Johnson, Luke T. *Faith's Freedom: A Classic Spirituality for Contemporary Christians*. Minneapolis: Fortress, 1990.

———. *Sharing Possessions: Mandate and Symbol of Faith*. Philadelphia: Fortress, 1981.

Juel, Donald H. *A Master of Surprise: Mark Interpreted*. Minneapolis: Fortress, 1994.

———. *The Gospel of Mark*. Nashville: Abingdon, 1999.

Kahl, Sigrun. "Christian Social Doctrines and the Welfare State: The case of poverty policy." Paper. New Haven: Yale, 2007.

———. "The Religious Roots of Modern Poverty Policy: Catholic, Lutheran, and Reformed Protestant Traditions Compared." Max Planck Institute for Study of Societies, 2004. Archives Europeennes de Sociologie. *European Journal of Sociology* 46, no. 1 (2005) 91–126.

Kaiser, Walter C. "Inner Biblical Exegesis as a Model for Bridging the "Then" and "Now" Gap: Hos 12:1–6." *Journal of the Evangelical Theological Society* 28, no. 1 (March 1985) 33–46.

———. *Toward an Exegetical Theology: Biblical Exegesis for Preaching and Teaching*. Grand Rapids: Baker, 1981.

Kee, Howard Clark. *Miracle in the Early Christian World: A Study in Sociohistorical Method*. New Haven: Yale University Press, 1983.

Keegan, Terence J. "The Parable of the Sower and Mark's Jewish Leaders." *Catholic Biblical Quarterly* 56, no.4 (1994) 501–18.

Kingsbury, J. D. *Conflict in Mark: Jesus, Authorities, Disciples*. Minneapolis: Fortress, 1989.

Kinnaman, David, and Gabe Lyons. *unChristian: What a New Generation Really Thinks about Christianity . . . and Why It Matters*. Grand Rapids: Baker, 2007.

Knighton, J. Raymond. "The Social Responsible of Evangelization Report." In *Let the Earth Hear His Voice*, edited by J. D. Douglas, 710–12. Minneapolis: World Wide Publications, 1975.

Kuruvilla, Abraham. *Text to Praxis: Hermeneutics and Homiletics in Dialogue*. London: T&T Clark, 2009.

Lane, William L. *The Gospel of Mark*. Grand Rapids: Eerdmans, 1974.

Leon-Guerrero, Anna. *Social Problems: Community, Policy, and Social Action*. Thousand Oaks. CA: Pine Forge, 2005.

Lindstrom, Matthew J., and Hugh Bartling, editors. *Suburban Sprawl: Culture, Theory, and Politics*. New York: Rowman & Littlefield, 2003.

Bibliography

Louw, Johannes P., and Eugene A. Nida, editors. *Greek-English Lexicon of the New Testament Based on Semantic Domains*. 2nd ed., 2 vols. New York: United Bible Societies, 1989.

Lupton, Robert D. *Toxic Charity: How Churches and Charities Hurt Those They Help (And How to Reverse It)*. New York: HarperOne, 2011.

Marcus, Joel. *Mark 1-8: A New Translation with Introduction and Commentary*. Anchor Bible 27. New York: Doubleday, 2000.

———. *The Mystery of the Kingdom of God*. Atlanta: Scholars, 1985.

Marsden, George. *Fundamentalism and American Culture*. 2nd ed. Oxford: Oxford University Press, 2006.

Marshall, Christopher D. *Faith as a Theme in Mark's Narrative*. Society for New Testament Studies Monograph Series 64; Cambridge: Cambridge University Press, 1989.

Mason, John D. "Biblical Teaching and Assisting the Poor." In *The Best in Theology*, vol. 2. Edited by J.I. Packer and Paul Fromer, 295–322. Carol Stream, IL: Christianity Today, 1987.

———. "Centralization and Decentralization in Social Arrangements: Explorations into Biblical Social Ethics." *Journal of the Association of Christian Economists* 13 (1992) 3–38.

May, David M. "Mark 3:20–35 from the Perspective of Shame/Honor." *Biblical Theology Bulletin* 17 (1987) 83–87.

McComiskey, Douglas S. "Exile and the Purpose of Jesus' Parables (Mark 4:10–12; Matt 13:10–17; Luke 8:9–10)." *Journal of the Evangelical Theological Society* 51, no. 1 (March 2008) 59–85.

McLaren, Brian. *Everything Must Change*. Nashville: Thomas Nelson, 2008.

Meadors, Edward P. *Idolatry and the Hardening of the Heart: A Study in Biblical Theology*. New York: T&T Clark, 2006.

Mendenhall, G. E. *Law and Covenant in Israel and the Ancient Near East*. Pittsburg: Presbyterian Board of Colportage of Western Pennsylvania, 1955.

Messia, Robert. "Lawns as Artifacts: The Evolution of Social and Environmental Implications of Suburban Residential Land Use." In *Suburban Sprawl: Culture, Theory, and Politics*, edited by Matthew J. Lindstrom and Hugh Bartling, 69–83. New York: Rowman & Littlefield, 2003.

Metzger, Paul Louis. *Consuming Jesus: Beyond Race and Class Divisions in a Consumer Church*. Grand Rapids: Eerdmans, 2007.

Miller, Patrick D. "Property and Possession in Light of Ten Commandments." In *Having: Property and Possession in Religious and Social Life*, edited by William Schweiker and Charles Mathewes, 17–50. Grand Rapids: Eerdmans, 2004.

Mills, C. W. *The Sociological Imagination*. New York: Oxford University Press, 1959.

Moberg, David O. *The Great Reversal: Evangelism and Social Concern*. Rev. ed. Philadelphia: Lippincott, 1977.

Monsma, Stephen V. "Poverty, Civil Society and the Public Policy Impasse." In *Toward a Just and Caring Society: Christian Responses to Poverty in America*, edited by David P. Gushee, 46–71. Grand Rapids: Baker, 1999.

Mott, Stephen. "Evangelism and Social Action." *Good News* (Summer 1974). No pages. Online: http://www.cscoweb.org/evmott.html.

Myers, Bryant L. *Walking with the Poor: Principles and Practices of Transformational Development*. Maryknoll, NY: Orbis, 2006.

Bibliography

Myers, Ched. *Binding the Strong Man: A Political Reading of Mark's Story of Jesus.* Maryknoll, NY: Orbis, 1989.
Neuhaus, Richard John. *The Naked Public Square: Religion and Democracy in America.* 2nd ed. Grand Rapids: Eerdmans, 1986.
Nicholls, Bruce, editor. *In Word and Deed: Evangelism and Social Responsibility.* Grand Rapids: Eerdmans, 1985.
Niebuhr, Reinhold, and Robin Lovin. *The Nature and Destiny of Man*, vol. 1. Louisville: Westminster John Knox, 1996.
Oakman, D. *Jesus and the Economic Questions of His Day.* Lewiston, NY: Mellen, 1986.
Olasky, Marvin. *The Tragedy of American Compassion.* Washington, DC: Regnery, 1992.
Osborne, Grant R. *The Hermeneutical Spiral: A Comprehensive Introduction to Bible Interpretation.* Downers Grove: InterVarsity, 1991.
Pahl, Jon. *Shopping Malls and Other Sacred Spaces: Putting God in Place.* Grand Rapids: Brazos, 2003.
Payne, P. B. "The Order of Sowing and Ploughing in the Parable of the Sower." *New Testament Studies* 25 (1978) 123–29.
Perkin, Richard. *Looking Both Ways: Exploring the Interface Between Christianity and Sociology.* Grand Rapids: Baker, 1987.
Rank, Mark. *One Nation Underprivileged.* New York: Oxford, 2005.
Resner, Andre, editor. *Just Preaching: Prophetic Voices for Economic Justice.* Atlanta: Chalice, 2006.
Richardson, A. *The Miracle Stories of the Gospels.* London: SCM, 1959.
Richardson, William J. *Social Action vs. Evangelism: An Essay on the Contemporary Crisis.* South Pasadena, CA: William Carey Library, 1977.
Ro, Bong Rin. "The Perspectives of Church History from New Testament Times to 1960." In *In Word and Deed: Evangelism and Social Responsibility*, edited by Bruce Nicholls, 11–40. Grand Rapids: Eerdmans, 1985.
Rodd, Cyril S. *Glimpses of a Strange Land: Studies in OT Ethics.* Edinburgh: T&T Clark, 2001.
Rosner, Brian S. "The Concept of Idolatry." *Themelios* 24, no. 3 (1999) 21–30.
———. *Greed as Idolatry: The Origin and Meaning of a Pauline Metaphor.* Grand Rapids: Eerdmans, 2007.
Rowland, Christopher. "Messiah." In *The Westminster Dictionary of Christian Theology*, edited by Alan Richardson and John Bowden, 358–59. Philadelphia: SCM Press, 1983.
Rudman, D. "The Significance of the Phrase 'Fishers of Men' in the Synoptic Gospels." *Irish Biblical Studies* 26, no. 3 (2005) 106–18.
Salamon, Lester M. *Partners in Public Service: Government-Nonprofit Relations in the Modern Welfare State.* Baltimore: Johns Hopkins University Press, 1995.
Samson, Will, and Lisa Samson. *Justice in the Burbs: Being the Hands of Jesus Wherever You Live.* Grand Rapids: Baker, 2007.
Savage, L., and M. Lapping. "Sprawl and Its Discontents: The Rural Dimension." In *Suburban Sprawl: Culture, Theory, and Politics*, edited by Matthew J. Lindstrom and Hugh Bartling, 5–17. New York: Rowman & Littlefield, 2003.
Schlossberg, Herbert, et al., editors. *Christianity and Economics in the Post-Cold War Era: The Oxford Declaration and Beyond.* Grand Rapids: Eerdmans, 1994.
Scobie, Charles H. H. *The Ways of Our God: An Approach to Biblical Theology.* Grand Rapids: Eerdmans, 2003.

Bibliography

Sider, Ronald J. *Just Generosity: A New Vision for Overcoming Poverty in America.* Grand Rapids: Baker, 1999.

———. *Rich Christians in an Age of Hunger: Moving from Affluence to Generosity.* Nashville: Thomas Nelson, 1997.

———. *The Scandal of Evangelical Politics: Why Are Christians Missing the Chance to Really Change the World?* Grand Rapids: Baker, 2008.

———. *The Scandal of the Evangelical Conscience: Why Are Christians Living Just Like the Rest of the World?* Grand Rapids: Baker, 2005.

Smith, Geoffrey. "A Closer Look at the Widow's Offering: Mark 12:41–44." *Journal of the Evangelical Theological Society* 40, no. 1 (March 1997) 27–36.

Smith-Christopher, Daniel L. *A Biblical Theology of Exile.* Minneapolis: Fortress, 2002.

Stearns, Richard. *The Hole in Our Gospel: The Answer that Changed My Life and Might Just Change the World.* Nashville: Thomas Nelson, 2009.

Stockwell, Clinton. "Cathedrals of Power: Engaging the Powers in Urban North America." In *Confident Witness—Changing World: Rediscovering the Gospel in North America*, edited by Craig Van Gelder, 80–93. Grand Rapids: Eerdmans, 1999.

Stott, John. *Christian Mission in the Modern World.* Downers Grove: Intervarsity, 1975.

Stuart, Douglas K. *Exodus: An Exegetical and Theological Exposition of Holy Scripture.* New American Commentary 2. Nashville: Broadman & Holman, 2006.

Sugirtharajah, R. S. "Widow's Mite Revisited." *Expository Times* 103, no. 2 (1991) 42–43.

———, editor. *Voices from the Margin: Interpreting the Bible in the Third World.* 2nd ed. Maryknoll, NY: Orbis, 1995.

Taylor, Vincent. *The Gospel According to St. Mark: the Greek Text with Introduction, Notes, and Indexes.* 2nd ed. New York: St. Martin's, 1966.

Theissen, Gerd. *The Miracles Stories of the Early Christian Tradition.* London: T&T Clark, 1983.

Thiselton, Anthony. *The Two Horizons. New Testament Hermeneutics and Philosophical Description.* Grand Rapids: Eerdmans, 1980.

Tolbert, Mary Ann. *Sowing the Gospel: Mark's World in Literary Historical Perspective.* Minneapolis: Fortress, 1989.

Townley, B., et al. "Performance Measures and the Rationalization of Organizations." *Organization Studies* 24, no. 7 (2003) 1045–72.

Trocmé, Etienne. *The Foundation of the Gospel According to Mark.* Translated by P. Gaughan. Philadelphia: Westminster, 1975.

Unruh, Heidi Rolland, and Ronald J. Sider. *Saving Souls, Serving Society: Understanding the Faith Factor in Church-Based Social Ministry.* New York: Oxford University Press, 2005.

Van Til, Kent. "A Biblical/Theological Case for Basic Sustenance for All." *Journal of Markets & Morality* 7, no. 2 (Fall, 2004) 441–66.

Virkler, Henry A. *Hermeneutics: Principles and Processes of Biblical Interpretation.* Grand Rapids: Baker, 1981.

Waetjen, Herman C. *A Reordering of Power: A Social-Political Reading of Mark's Gospel.* Minneapolis: Fortress, 1989.

Waldow, H. Eberhard von. "Social Responsibility and Social Structure in Early Israel." *Catholic Biblical Quarterly* 32 (1970) 182–204.

Watts, Rikki E. *Isaiah's New Exodus in Mark.* Grand Rapids: Baker, 1997.

Weber, Max. *Economy and Society: An Outline of Interpretive Sociology*, vol. 1. Edited by Guenther Roth and Claus Wittick. Berkeley: University of California Press, 1978.

———. *The Theory of Social and Economic Organization*. Translated by A. H. Henderson and Talcott Parsons. New York: Free Press, 1964.

Wilson, William Julius. *When Work Disappears: The World of the New Urban Poor*. New York: Vintage, 1996.

Witherington, Ben, *The Gospel of Mark: A Socio-Rhetorical Commentary*. Grand Rapids: Eerdmans, 2001.

Wright, Addison G. "The Widow's Mite: Praise or Lament?–A Matter of Context." *Catholic Biblical Quarterly* 44, no. 2 (1982) 256–65.

Wright, Christopher J. H. *An Eye for an Eye: The Place of OT Ethics Today*. Downers Grove: InterVarsity, 1982.

———. "Biblical Reflections on Land." *Evangelical Review of Theology* 17, no. 2 (1993) 153–67.

———. *God's People in God's Land: Family, Land, and Property in the OT*. Grand Rapids: Eerdmans, 1990.

———. "What Happened Every Seven Years in Israel: OT Sabbatical Institutions for Land, Debts, and Slaves, Part I." *Evangelical Quarterly* 56 (July, 1984): 129–38

Wright, N. T. "Continuing Exile: Paul and the Deuteronomy/Daniel Tradition." Paper presented at the Symposium on Exile, Trinity Western University, Langley, British Columbia, November 2010.

———. *Jesus and the Victory of God*. Minneapolis: Fortress, 1996.

———. *The New Testament and the People of God*. Minneapolis: Fortress, 1992.

Wuellner, Wilhelm H. *The Meaning of "Fishers of Men."* Philadelphia: Westminster, 1967.

Wytsma, Ken. *Pursuing Justice: The Call to Live & Die for Bigger Things*. Nashville: Thomas Nelson, 2013.

Scripture Index

OLD TESTAMENT

Genesis

1	189
1:26–27	149
5:1	149
5:7	149
7:11	92n
8:8–12	92n
9:6	149
18:18	149
22:2	93
24:7	58n
48:16	58n

Exodus

2–14	159n
3:2	56n, 131n
4:2–4	189
4:15	63n
4:22	93, 149, 149n
4:28	63n
13:21–22	131n
14	189
14:19	131n
14:24	131n
19:5	132
19:6	63n
19:7	63n
19:8	63n
20–23	57
20	144, 145, 164
20:1–23:33	151
20:1–17	151, 159n
20:1	63n
20:3–5b	56
20:3	151
20:4–5	151
20:16	153
20:17	151
20:18–22	152
20:23–24	152
20:23	148n, 151
21–23	7, 57, 67, 138, 160
21	144
22:18–20	152
22:18	57, 57n, 152, 153
22:19	57n, 152
22:20–25	57
22:20	56, 152
22–23	171
22	144
22:21–27	55
22:21–24	101, 155
22:21–22	152
22:21	55n, 137n
22:21a	137
22:22–24	29, 30, 31, 146, 152
22:22	57, 137
22:24	100, 155
22:25–27	152
22:25–26	137
22:28	121n, 129, 129n
23	54, 85, 131, 144, 159
23:1–9	153
23:1–3	153
23:3	55
23:6	55, 137

Scripture Index

Exodus (continued)

23:9	55, 101n, 152
23:9a	137
23:10–33	58–59
23:10–12	137n
23:11	55, 137
23:12	55n, 152
23:13	56, 152
23:19	152n
23:20–33	59, 152
23:20–23	130–131, 132, 151
23:20–21	131, 159
23:20	7, 12n, 52, 54, 58, 59, 99, 130, 131, 132, 133, 137, 151, 152
23:21–22	133, 133n
23:21	58, 58n, 131, 152, 159
23:22–23	132
23:23	131n
23:24	56, 151
23:27–30	132
23:30–31	159
23:32–33	56, 57, 131, 151, 152, 159
24:1–18	58
24:1–8	130
24:3	63n
31:14–15	125
32	102, 133
32:31	148n
32:34	131n
33:2	131n
33:9–10	131n
35:2	125
42:28	63n

Leviticus

1:14	31
5:7	31, 162n
5:11	27, 29, 31, 31n
9:11–17	153
12:6	31
12:8	29, 31, 31n
14:21–32	27
14:22	29, 31n
14:30	31
17:7	131n, 159n
19	144, 145, 162, 171
19:4	148n
19:9–10	29, 30, 137n
19:10	55n
19:18	149
19:33–34	101n
19:34	55n, 137n
20	144
23	144, 162
23:22	29, 30, 55n, 137n
24	171
24:15–16	129
25:35	101n
27:30	35

Numbers

9:15	131n
11:17	131
14:14	131n
15:32–36	125
22:22–35	189

Deuteronomy

1:16	101n
1:33	131n
4:1–8	164
4:5–8	149
4:8	54
5	144
7:25	151
9:10	63n
10:12–18	147
10:12	148
10:14	148
10:17	148
10:18–19	55n, 101n, 137n
10:18	146
14–15	162
14	144
14:28–29	29, 30
14:29	35, 55n, 137n
15	144, 145, 171
15:7–11	137n
15:9–11	55n
15:9	101n, 147
16:1	137n
16:14	55n, 137n

Scripture Index

24	144, 145, 161, 171
24:17–18	101n
24:17	137n, 55n
24:19–22	55n, 137n, 161
24:19–21	29, 30, 137n
24:19	55n
24:20	55n
24:21	55n
26:12–13	137n
26:12	34–35, 55n
26:13	55n
27:19	55n, 101n, 137n, 156n
28:14	101n, 156n
28:26–28	156
30	132, 133
30:15–20	132
30:30	132
32:4	54
32:17	131n, 159n
32:24	101n, 155n

Joshua

24:14	148n
24:19–24	133

Judges

2:1–4	131n, 133
2:20	133
3:10	91
6:11–14	58n
6:34	91
11:12	118n, 186n

1 Samuel

16:13	91

2 Samuel

16:10	118n, 186n
19:22	118n, 186n

1 Kings

17:18	118n, 186n
18	189
21:10–14	129

2 Kings

1:8	89
3:13	118n, 186n
17:29	148n
19:18	148n

1 Chronicles

29:11	150n

2 Chronicles

35:21	118n, 186n

Nehemiah

9:12	131n
9:20	131, 159

Job

34:28	101n, 147
35:9	101n

Psalms

2	93n
2:7	93
10:14	101n, 147
10:17–18	101n
10:18	147
24:1 1	50n
66:12 [LXX]	126n
68:5	101n, 146
68:18	129
77:3 [LXX]	92n
78:14	131n
89:11	150n
94:6	55n, 137n
95:4–5	150n
99:7	131n
105:39	131n
106:37	131n, 159n
109	100, 155
109:2–9	101n

Scripture Index

Psalms (continued)

115	146, 164
115:1–8	138n
115:1–4	65n
115:4	151
126:6	71n
135	146, 164
135:15–18	65n, 138n
146:9	147

Proverbs

2:13	106
23:10–11	101n
31:8–9	45

Isaiah

1–6	69, 144, 162
1–5	62, 63, 65, 66n, 67, 68, 71n, 127, 128, 135n, 138, 160, 162
1–4	69
1–3	68
1	144
1:3	63n, 65
1:4	66, 134
1:5	66n, 134n
1:7–8	67, 68n
1:9	53
1:10–15	67, 134n
1:10	53, 62, 66, 134
1:12–15	68
1:16–17	66, 68
1:17	55n, 66, 134, 137n, 138, 160
1:19	68n
1:21	66, 68, 138
1:23	55n, 66, 67, 134, 137n, 138, 160
1:26	66, 138
1:27	66, 138
1:28–31	68n
1:29–31	65, 67–68, 138, 160
1:29–30	68
1:29	151
1:31	68n
2	64n
2:1–4	64
2:1	62
2:12–15	68n
2:12–13	65, 138, 160
2:12	68
2:13	68
2:18	65, 138, 160
2:20	65, 68, 138, 151n, 160
2:3	62, 63, 149
2:4	68n
2:6–11	67
2:6–9	65, 138, 160
2:6–8	68
2:7	151n
2:9	66, 66n, 135
3:7	66, 66n, 135n
3:8	66, 134
3:10	66, 138
3:14–15	66, 67, 68, 134, 138
3:14	68n
3:15	118n, 186n
4:4	131n
5	61, 62, 68, 100n, 144, 162
5:1–7	69
5:1–2	68, 128, 162
5:1	92n
5:2	68
5:6	69
5:7–30	69
5:7–12	171
5:7–8	162
5:7	66, 69, 138
5:8ff.	69
5:8–10	68n
5:13	62, 66
5:16	66, 138
5:17	68n
5:20	66
5:24	66, 68n, 134
5:24a	63
5:24c	63
6	12n, 62, 66, 68n, 127, 128, 136, 138, 155n, 157–160, 158n, 160, 162
6:9ff.	69
6:9–13	65
6:9–10	64n, 65, 65n, 68, 127, 128, 12n, 131, 134, 138, 159, 160, 162
6:9	65

Scripture Index

6:10	66, 66n	40:24	164
6:13	68	40:25	153
9:3	71n	40:26	153
10	144, 145	41:17	154n
10:2	55n, 137n	41:21–29	54n
11:2	91	41:21–24	164, 164n
13:17	151n	42:1	53n, 91, 92, 93
16:9	71n	42:17	57n, 153n, 154n
17:5	71n	42:21	149
17:11	71n	43:25	121n
18:5–6	71n	44:3	53n, 90
18:6	92n	44:9–10	57n, 153n
22:1	186n	44:9	151
22:11	118n	44:10	164, 164n
24:13	71n	44:12–13	154n
24:18	92n	44:17–20	154n
27:11	63n	44:22	121n
29	144	45:16	57n, 153n
30	144	45:20	57n, 153n
30:22	151n	45:23–24	149
31:17	151n	46:1	57n, 153n
32:15	90	46:5–7	154
34:6–7	121n	46:6	151n
36–39	53	46:7	65n, 138n
37:29	99, 154	46:13	54, 54n
39:2	151n	48:5	57n, 153n, 154n
40	54, 54n, 55, 59n, 85, 89, 90, 153	48:16	53n
		49:13	53n
40:1	53, 53n	49:24–26	129
40:3	12n, 52, 52n, 53, 55, 59, 59n, 90, 99, 130, 151, 153	50:19–20	153
		51:3	53n
40:5	90, 153	51:4	149
40:9	55, 151n, 153	51:5	54n
40:9d	54n	51:12	53n
40:10–11	56	51:19	53n
40:10	53, 55, 90, 158	52:7–12	54n
40:1–11	54n	52:7	54n
40:11	55	52:9	53n
40:12	153	53	66n, 135n
40:13–14	153	53:12	129
40:13	53	55	64n
40:15	153	55:1–13	64
40:17	153	55:10–13	64n, 71n
40:18–26	164	56:1–7	162
40:18	164	56:1	31, 54, 54n
40:19–20	56–57	56:7	31
40:22	153	56:10–12	31
40:23	153	57:13	57n, 153n

Isaiah (continued)

57:18	53n
59:16–17	149
59:21	53n
60	54n
60:1–9	54n
60:1–7	54n
60:9	151n
60:21	71n, 149
61	54n
61:1–11	54n
61:1	53n, 91
61:2	53n
61:3	149
61:10	124n
61:11	149
62:1–2	149
63	159
63:1	149
63:9–11	131n, 133, 135, 159
63:10	53, 53n
63:12	159n
63:14	53n
63:16	149
63:19	92n
64:1	92
64:8	149
65:7	129
65:21–22	71n
66:3	57n, 153n
66:11	53n
66:13	53n
66:20	71n

Jeremiah

1:4	63n
1:11	63n
1:13	63n
2–5	144
2:3	71n
2:18	118n, 186n
3:19	149
4–8	171
5	71n
5:2	7, 153
5:4	153
5:17	71n
5:24	71n
7–8	29, 33, 144
7	30, 144, 145
7:4–11	161
7:4–8	29, 30–31, 31
7:6–7	101n
7:6	55n, 137n
7:8	31
7:9	7, 153
7:11	161
7:12–15	31
7:18	161n
8:8	33
8:13	161n
8:20	71n
10:4	151n
10:5	65n, 138n
10:9	151n
12:13	71n
15–19	100, 154
16–18	155
16–17	171
16	144, 154
16:4	101, 155
16:11–13	99, 154
16:16	94, 98, 99, 154
16:18–21	100
16:18–20	154
16:21	103, 155
17:2	100n, 154
17:23	100, 155
18:15	100
18:15a	155
18:21	101, 155
22	171
22:3	55n
22:13	137n
27	150n
31:27–2	71n 8
48:32	71n
50:16	71n
51:32–34	71n

Ezekiel

1:1	92n
7:19	151n

16:13	151n
16:17	151n
17–18	171
17	61, 144
17:23	72
18	144
19:4–5	94
20:49	61
21–24	61
22	171
28:4	151n
29	103, 155
29:4–5	94, 99, 154
29:6	155
31	61
31:6	72, 73, 73n
36:26–27	90
38:4	94, 99, 154
38:23	103, 155
39:39	90

Daniel

2	71n
3	189
4	73, 144
4:11–12	73
4:12	72
4:19–26	73
4:25	73
4:27	74
6	189
7:13	71n
8:17	71n

Hosea

2:8	151n
2:9	71n
2:14–20	124n
4:6	63n
6:11	71n
8:4	151n
11:1	149
14:3	55n, 137n
14:9	118n, 186n

Joel

1:11	71n
2:28–29	90
3:13	71n

Amos

2:6–7	102, 156
4	144, 154, 155
4:1–2	7, 99, 101, 101–102, 154, 156, 171
4:2	94
4:7	71n
5:10	102n
5:11–12	102, 157
8	144
8:4–6	103, 157

Micah

2:1–3	171
2:1–2	162n

Habakkuk

1	103, 155
1:14–15	99, 103, 154, 155
1:18	151n
2:18–19	146
2:19	151n

Haggai

2:5	131, 159
2:8	150n

Zechariah

6:11	151n
7	144, 145, 160, 171
7:4	138
7:8–14	138, 160
7:9–10	137n
7:10	55n, 101n
7:12	138
7:12a	138
7:14	159

Scripture Index

Zechariah *(continued)*

9:3	151n
13:4	89, 89n
14:4	92n

Malachi

1:7–12	57, 153
2:11	57, 153
3	30, 34, 36n, 55, 59n, 85, 144, 145, 152, 162
3:1–5	7, 29, 31, 36
3:1–2	137
3:1	7, 12n, 30, 32, 34, 36, 36n, 52, 54, 57, 58n, 59, 59n, 89, 90, 99, 130, 137, 151, 152, 153, 163n
3:2–4	57
3:5	29, 34, 35n, 36, 55, 55n, 57, 59, 137, 137n, 153, 163
3:7	34, 137
3:8–9	34
4:4	34
4:5–6	89

APOCRYPHA

2 Macc 3:10–11	24n

PSEUDEPIGRAPHA

Jub. 1:11	131n, 159n
Jub. 11:4–6	131n, 159n
Jub. 50:8	125
Jub. 50:13	125
Syr. Bar. 29:3	93n
Syr. Bar. 39:7	93n
Syr. Bar. 40:1	93n
Syr. Bar. 70:9	93n
Syr. Bar. 72:2	93n
T. Judah 21:1ff	93n
T. Judah 24:3	92n
T. Levi 7	93n
T. Levi 18:6–8	92n
1 En. 19:1	131n, 159n
1 En. 99:7	131n, 159n
2 Esd 12:32	93n

NEW TESTAMENT

Matthew

2:15	149
4:19	81, 84
5–7	143
5:46	122n
9:2–8	129n
10:1	187, 191
10:7–8	187

12:14	126n
12:31–32	129n
13:4	26
13:32	73n
18:17	122n
19:19	149
21:31–32	122n
23:14	26

Mark

1–6	194n
1	151, 157, 181, 188n, 196, 197
1:1–3	7, 12, 12n, 30, 61n, 85, 86, 131, 151–154, 154, 175
1:1–2	152
1:1–2a	51
1:1	2, 3, 4, 11, 13, 50n, 51, 51n, 52, 54, 85, 85n, 86, 90, 104n, 108, 130, 135, 174, 175, 177, 178, 190, 200
1:2–3	51, 52, 88, 89, 90, 91, 99, 129, 130, 130, 137, 137, 144, 175
1:2	36n, 59n
1:2a	52
1:2b–3	52
1:2b	52
1:3	52, 53, 153
1:4–19	86
1:4–17	87
1:4–15	154, 181
1:4–8	59, 86, 91, 152
1:4–7	85
1:4	86, 87–89, 89–91, 90, 97
1:5a	136
1:7–11	130
1:7–8	130
1:7	53, 89, 115
1:8	51n, 53, 89, 90, 91, 130, 158
1:9–10	86, 88, 191
1:9	86, 87–89, 87n, 90, 91–92, 97
1:10–11	130
1:10	53, 124, 158
1:11–13	86
1:11	50n, 86, 87–89, 90, 92–93, 97, 149n, 173
1:12–13	117, 130, 186, 190
1:12	92, 130
1:13–19	173n
1:13	52n, 186
1:14–15	4, 7, 11, 54n, 61, 62, 62n, 63, 93, 96, 104, 117, 117n, 136, 173, 174, 175, 178, 181, 182, 186, 189, 189–190, 190, 191, 194, 194n, 195, 196, 197, 198
1:14	2, 54, 96, 180, 188, 189, 192, 195
1:14b	194
1:14c	175, 180, 189, 194, 195, 196, 197
1:15	54, 85, 93–94, 95, 135, 136, 140, 175, 180, 186, 188, 189, 195, 196, 197
1:15a	199
1:16–45	63
1:16–28	85
1:16–20	105n, 184, 97
1:16–18	86
1:17	13, 81, 82–84, 83n, 86, 86, 87–89, 90, 94, 95, 96, 97, 98, 97n, 104, 140n, 144, 154, 154n, 173, 174, 175, 178, 180, 181, 182, 186, 191, 197, 199
1:17a–b	96, 180
1:17b	104
1:17c	96, 180
1:18	52n
1:19–20	97n
1:19	87n
1:20	52n
1:21–6:13	181
1:21–6:6	184n
1:21–3:12	104
1:21–3:6	182n
1:21–28	116–119, 118, 122, 126, 158, 185, 186, 187, 194
1:21–27	62, 115, 194
1:21–22	20, 24n, 122n, 125
1:21	52n, 61n, 126
1:22	18, 61n, 63, 117, 119, 121, 185, 186, 191, 192
1:23–27	116n, 117, 185, 190, 191n, 192
1:24	118, 186
1:24c	117–118, 186
1:25–27	185

219

Mark (continued)

1:25	117, 191
1:26	116n, 117, 185
1:27	61n, 64, 116n, 117, 121, 185, 186, 192
1:27b	117, 186
1:27c	191
1:28	118
1:29	119
1:32–34	185, 190, 191n, 192
1:32	115, 158n, 186
1:35	62n
1:37	118
1:38–39	61, 61–62
1:39	185, 190, 191n, 192
1:40–45	22
1:40–44	22
1:40	110n
2–3	112, 127, 128
2:1–3:6	12, 18, 20, 24n, 30, 38n, 111, 116, 117, 129, 134, 139, 187
2:1–12	66n, 116, 119, 119–122, 119, 120, 121, 122, 125, 126, 129n, 135n, 158
2:2	62, 64, 117n
2:2b	119
2:3–12	21
2:3–5	21
2:4	119
2:5–11	119
2:5	21
2:6–12	119
2:6–8	120
2:6	119
2:7	64, 120, 121
2:8	92
2:9	135n
2:10	120, 121, 124
2:12	75, 119, 119n, 192
2:13–17	116, 122–123, 158
2:13	62, 119n, 122
2:14–17	21
2:14	97n
2:14c	122
2:15	122
2:16	122, 123, 158n
2:16a	122
2:18–22	116, 123–125, 158
2:18	64, 158n
2:21–22	61, 134
2:21	11, 124
2:23–28	116, 125, 158
2:24	64, 158n
2:25a	125
2:27	192
2:28	124
3–4	69, 144
3	13, 58n, 95, 97, 98, 105, 118, 123, 128, 151, 174
3:1–6	22, 116, 124, 125, 125–127, 126, 158
3:1–2	126
3:1	119n
3:4c	126
3:5	64, 120, 126, 134
3:6	33, 64, 111, 111n, 116, 121, 124, 125, 126, 128, 129, 158n
3:7–10	64n
3:7–8a	64
3:7	64, 135n
3:8b	64
3:10–12	192
3:11	50n, 116n, 118, 185, 186, 190, 191n, 192
3:13–19	74, 96, 131
3:13–16	96
3:13–15	13, 104, 180, 181, 187
3:13	61n, 62n
3:13a	182
3:13b	96, 180, 182, 184
3:14–15	75, 117, 160, 175, 176, 178, 181, 182, 183, 183n, 195, 199
3:14	3, 97, 140n, 195
3:14a	96, 180, 181, 182
3:14b	181, 184, 187n, 191
3:14c–15	13, 180, 181, 184
3:14c	184, 185, 188, 194
3:15	121, 181, 184, 185, 186, 189, 190, 191, 193, 194, 195, 196, 197, 200
3:16	97
3:16a	96, 180
3:17–19	97
3:20–4:20	144

Scripture Index

3:20–35	12, 74, 107–108, 112, 112n, 116, 120, 157, 158, 193	4	11, 12, 60, 61, 68, 72, 131, 134, 151, 158n, 159n, 160, 197, 198, 199
3:20–25	175	4:1–5:43	181
3:20–21	114	4:1–34	74
3:20–12	112	4:1–20	112n, 139
3:20	114, 119, 119n	4:1–10	117n
3:20a	114	4:1–8	12, 69, 110, 115n, 134, 135, 193
3:21	110, 113, 114, 115, 118, 119, 120, 140, 158n	4:1	61n, 119n
3:21a	113n	4:2	61, 61n
3:21b	114, 118	4:3–32	115n
3:22–30	53, 53n, 64, 66, 69, 112, 112n, 116, 121, 134,	4:3–8	48, 48n, 61
3:22–27	64n, 129, 185, 190, 191n, 192	4:3	48n, 61, 65n
3:22–25	134, 135	4:3b	48n
3:22	110, 115, 116, 117, 128, 135, 159, 193	4:4	26, 71
		4:5–6	71
3:23–29	135	4:7	71
3:23–27	119, 128, 136, 158, 158, 160, 186, 190, 193	4:8	59n, 71
3:23	159	4:9	65n
3:24–36	115n	4:10–13	69
3:24	130, 158, 158n	4:10–12	61, 116, 120, 123, 127, 128, 134, 135, 136
3:25	140	4:10–11	158n, 184
3:27	53, 68n, 115, 130, 158, 190, 198	4:10	64, 193
		4:11–12	70, 12, 115, 126, 144, 160
3:28–29	119, 129n, 136	4:11	65, 127, 158n, 186
3:28	110n	4:11a	128
3:29–30	121	4:11b–12	65
3:29	58, 58n, 66, 92, 121, 123, 127, 129, 131, 135, 158, 158n	4:11b	193
		4:12	12n, 58, 58n, 64n, 65, 65n, 66, 66n, 127, 131, 134, 135, 135n, 136, 138, 159, 193
3:29a	111		
3:30–21	116	4:12a	65
3:30	116n	4:12c	158n
3:31–35	112, 114, 116, 158n	4:13–30	69
3:31–32	140	4:13–20	61, 115n, 117n
3:31	110, 113, 114, 118	4:13	66, 193
3:32	114, 115, 118	4:14–20	12, 48n, 110
3:33–35	182	4:14	11, 12, 48, 60, 62, 62n, 71
3:33–27	115	4:16–17	71
3:34–35	113, 128, 136	4:18–19	71
3:34	114	4:20	71
3:34a	114	4:21–25	61
3:35	13, 36, 111, 114, 132, 134, 135n, 136, 139, 176, 184, 193	4:23	62n, 65n
		4:24	65n
3:39	127	4:26–29	61, 67n, 70, 71n
4–8	94	4:26	186

221

Scripture Index

Mark (continued)

4:28a	71n	6:7	75, 115, 116n, 121, 184, 186, 187, 190, 191, 191n, 196
4:28b	71n	6:7c	187
4:29	71n	6:12	62n, 75
4:30	186	6:13	115, 185, 187, 190, 191n
4:30–32	61, 67n, 72, 144, 198	6:13a	187
4:32	144	6:13b	187n
4:33–34	61	6:14–29	110n
4:33	11, 48, 62, 62n	6:34	61n, 122n
4:35–41	74, 158n, 184	6:45	97n
4:38	61n	6:51–52	36n, 112, 136n
4:41	65n	6:51	119n, 192
5	74–76, 75, 115n	6:52	127, 193
5:1–6:6	184	6:53–56	192
5:1–53	74	7	151
5:1–43	74	7:1–13	20
5:1–20	115, 187	7:1–5	128n
5:1–19	22	7:1	158n
5:2–13	185	7:4–8	30
5:2–8	190, 191n	7:5	158n
5:2	116n	7:6–7	144
5:3	76	7:6	134
5:8	116n	7:7	61n, 122n
5:10–13	115n	7:9–13	110n
5:13	116n, 190, 191n	7:11	30
5:20	134–135, 192	7:14	66
5:21–43	112n	7:18	66, 193
5:21–24	21, 22	7:24–30	21, 22, 22n, 64n
5:21	119n	7:25–30	185
5:22	110n	7:25	116n
5:25–34	21	7:26–30	115, 187, 190, 191n
5:34–42	22	7:29	21
5:34	21	7:31	119n
5:35–46	21	7:37	75, 117n, 185, 192
5:35	61n	8:1	119n
5:36	21	8:12	92, 110n
5:42	119n, 192	8:13	33
6	95, 97, 187	8:14–21	36n, 193
6:1–6	74, 140	8:15b	22
6:1	61n	8:16–21	112, 136n, 140
6:2	117n, 122n, 185, 192	8:16–18	120
6:4	110n	8:17	66, 66n, 120, 127
6:5	192	8:18	193
6:6	61n	8:22–26	21, 22
6:7–30	112n	8:23	21
6:7–13	74, 97n, 181, 187	8:31	24, 61n, 122n, 128n
6:7–12	117	8:33–38	140
		8:33	115, 187, 190, 191n

8:33b	140	11–12	30
8:34–38	112, 136n	11	151, 161n
8:34	140, 140n	11:1–13:36	36n
8:38	50n, 140	11:1–12:37	18, 20, 24
8:39	158n	11:1–11	30
9	194n	11:1	196
9:1	110n	11:11–12:2	28
9:7	50n	11:11	29, 32, 162
9:11–13	89	11:12–21	29, 112n, 144
9:11	128n, 158n	11:12–14	29, 32, 59n, 124n
9:14–29	115, 187, 190, 191n	11:13	196
9:14	128n, 158n	11:15–17	24, 30, 29, 32, 59n, 161
9:15	192	11:15	24, 31, 162n
9:17–27	21	11:15b	162
9:17	61n	11:17	30, 31, 61n, 122n, 161
9:23	21	11:18	61n, 75, 111, 117n, 121, 124, 125, 128n, 158n, 185, 192
9:25–29	185		
9:25	116n	11:18a	33
9:31	122n, 61n	11:18b	33
9:32	66, 75	11:19–20	29
9:33–49	194	11:20–21	59n, 124n
9:33–34	120, 136n, 140	11:20	32, 33
9:33	194	11:20b	33
9:35	120	11:23	110n
9:38–41	115, 187, 190, 191n, 194	11:27	119n, 128n, 158n, 162
9:38	61n, 185	11:28b	191
9:41	110n	11:30–32	36n
9:52	21	11:31	120, 136n
10–12	144	11:33	66, 126n
10	151	12	34, 35, 59n, 11, 151, 162, 171n, 199
10:1–2	122n		
10:1	119n	12:1–9	61
10:2–9	161	12:1	144
10:4	144	12:2	196
10:5	110n, 134	12:6	50n
10:9	144	12:10–12	134
10:10	119n	12:12	33
10:17	61n, 110n	12:13–44	30
10:20	61n	12:13	128n, 158n
10:24	117n, 185, 192	12:14	61n, 122n
10:26	117n, 185, 192	12:17	192
10:29	110n	12:19	61n
10:30	196	12:24	66
10:32	117n, 119n, 185, 192	12:28–31	149
10:33	33, 128n, 158n	12:28	128n, 158n
10:35–45	110n	12:31	144
10:35	61n	12:32	61n, 128n, 158n
11–13	28, 29, 30, 34, 35, 36, 37	12:33	66

Mark (continued)

12:34	32, 126n
12:35–38	128n, 158n
12:35	122n
12:36	92
12:38–44	11, 12, 17–18, 22, 23, 29, 32, 37, 38, 39, 42, 110n, 139, 145, 161, 162, 199
12:38–40	23, 24, 33, 37
12:38	37, 61n
12:38b	22, 23. 25
12:40	26, 35, 44
12:40a	24
12:40c	20, 28
12:41–44	24, 30, 34, 37, 144
12:42	27, 35
12:42a	26
12:43	110n
12:44	39
12:44c	19, 28
13–19	182
13–15	173
13	37, 59, 124n, 145, 151, 161
13:1–2	32, 33, 29, 124, 134, 138, 144
13:1	36, 39, 61n, 162
13:2	18, 20, 28, 30, 31, 33, 34, 35, 36, 37, 44, 144
13:2c	30
13:3–37	36
13:5	37
13:9	37
13:11	92
13:14	66
13:14b	36
13:23	37
13:24–27	134
13:28–29	61
13:30	110n
13:32	50n
13:33–37	37
13:33	37, 196
13:34–37	61
13:34	191
13:35–37	36
13:35	36, 37
13:37	36
14–15	111n
14:1–11	112n
14:1	128n, 158n
14:14	61n
14:17–31	112n
14:18	110n
14:25	110n
14:30	110n
14:42	196
14:43	128n, 158n
14:49	61n, 122n
14:53–72	112n
14:53–65	20, 110n, 121, 128n, 129, 129n
14:61	50n
14:62–64	121
14:62	134
14:63–64	125
14:64	121, 129
14:66–72	110n
14:7	37, 144
14:9	110n
15:1	128n, 158n
15:10	109, 111
15:19	110n
15:31	128n, 158n
15:33	144
15:38	124
15:39	50n
15:40–16:8	112n
16:9	115, 187, 190
16:14	112, 127, 136n, 140

Luke

3:38	149
4:18–19	188
5:10	88
5:18–26	129n
6	143
6:7	126n
6:11	126n
7:47–50	129n
8:5	26
9:1	188, 191
10:1	188
10:17	188
10:18	188
10:27	149

Scripture Index

12:10	129n
13:19	73n
14:1	126n
15:30	26
16:16	62n
16:19–31	149
20:47	26
20:20	126n

John

10:20	119
12:31	129
12:40	126

Acts

2–4	143
6:7	72
9:24	126n
12:24	72
14:15	164
19:20	72
20:33	151n
26:24	119

Romans

2:28–29	132n
8	149n
9–11	127n
9:4	149
10:6–8	132n
11:7	126
11:25	126
13:9	149
13:11–14	127n
14:1–12	122n
16:20	127n

1 Corinthians

3:6–7	72
8:4–6	164n
8:4	164
10:1	131n
10:19	164
10:20	131n, 159n

2 Corinthians

3:14	126
5:13–15	119n

Galatians

1:4	196
4:8	164
5	149n
5:14	149

Ephesians

1:10	200
2:2	129
2:21	72
4:15	72
4:18	126, 127
6:12	129

Colossians

1:5b–6	72n
1:10	72
1:13	129
1:19	72
1:20	200
3	149n

Philippians

2:3–4	44

James

1–2	143, 149n
2:8	149

1 Peter

2:22	72n
3	149n
3:20–21	92n

2 Peter

3:18	72n

Scripture Index

Revelation

11:5	26
11:15	129
12:4	26–27
12:10–12	129
20:9	27

DEAD SEA SCROLLS

1QH 7–8	95
1QS 5:17	52n
1QS 9:11	93n

RABBINIC WRITINGS

b. Ber. 53b	92n
b. Š49a	92n
Ct. Rab. 1:15, 2	92n
Ct. Rab. 2:14, 1	92n
Ct. Rab. 4:1, 2	92n
Ex. Rab. 32:6	58n
Ex. Rab. 32:9	58n
Lev. Rab. 3:5	27
m. Seqal. 1:3	31
m. Seqal. 3:47–48	31
m. Seqal. 5:3–5	31
Midr. Ps 90:9	58n

EARLY CHRISTIAN WRITINGS

Dial. Trypho 125:1–2	70n

www.ingramcontent.com/pod-product-compliance
Lightning Source LLC
Chambersburg PA
CBHW070248230426
43664CB00014B/2448